HORSES

DORLING KINDERSLEY
—**HANDBOOKS**—

HORSES

ELWYN HARTLEY EDWARDS

Photography by
BOB LANGRISH

A Dorling Kindersley Book

Dorling Kindersley

LONDON, NEW YORK, MUNICH,
MELBOURNE AND DELHI

Project Editor Jo Weeks
Project Art Editor Amanda Lunn
Designer Deborah Myatt
Editor Helen Townsend
Production Caroline Webber

First published in Great Britain in 1993
Reprinted with corrections in 2000
by Dorling Kindersley Limited,
80 Strand, London WC2R 0RL

See our complete product line at
www.dk.com

A CIP catalogue record for this book is available from the British Library

ISBN 0-7513-2736-0

Computer page make-up by
The Cooling Brown Partnership,
Great Britain

Text film output by The Right Type,
Great Britain

Reproduced by
Colourscan, Singapore

Printed and bound by South China Printing Company in China

CONTENTS

TYPES • *238*

PONIES • *48*

HORSES • *104*

HEAVY HORSES • *214*

AUTHOR'S INTRODUCTION

It is difficult to categorize horse and pony breeds in the same way, and with the same accuracy, as cat and dog breeds. Horses have not been subject to such intensive selective breeding of pure-bred stock, and the horse's gestation period is longer than that of cats and dogs, so that it takes far longer for distinctive and easily recognizable breeds to be developed. Despite this, it is still possible to trace a pattern in the jigsaw of equine evolution.

A CLEAR DISTINCTION can be made between the heavy, "coldblood" horses originating in northern Europe, and the swift, light-limbed desert horses that we term "hotblood". There are also differences in size which result, not from differences in origin, but from the influence of environment. These size differences are perhaps best exemplified by the ponies, whose natural habitats were the in-hospitable mountains and moorlands of Europe. The lack of sustaining food, combined with a harsh climate, governed their size, and the demands made by the rough terrain produced a distinctive and sure-footed action.

MUSTANGS IN THE NEVADA DESERT
These feral mustangs are descendants of Spanish horses, which were much influenced by the "hot" Barb blood of North Africa.

For ease of reference, these distinctions – of hot and cold blood, and of size – have been recognized and employed in this book. Thus ponies, "light horses" (both for riding and driving), and heavy horses are placed in separate sections, and are further sub-divided by geographical origin. A final section is devoted to equines that fall into the category of "types", rather than recognized "breeds".

DEFINITIONS

If full use is to be made of this book, it is necessary to provide some basic defin-itions: for example, what is meant by "hot-" and "cold-blood" (see box), what con-stitutes a "breed", and how breeds differ from "types".

CONNEMARA PONY
The sure-footed, incredibly hardy Connemara derives its special qualities from the inhospitable conditions of its natural habitat.

Hot, Warm, and Coldblood

The Arab (and, to a lesser extent, the Barb) represents the fountainhead of the light horse breeds, its influence extending even into the heavy draught breeds. It is termed "hotblood" (indicating a unique purity of line) – a title that is also given to its direct derivative, the Thoroughbred. The "third man" (after the Arab and the Barb) in the development of many breeds in Europe and the Americas was the Spanish Horse. Although not a hotblood in the same way as the Arab, Barb, or Thoroughbred, it comes closer to that title than any other horse. At the other end of the spectrum are the heavy horses of Europe, the "coldbloods". In between are horses that might combine both hot and cold blood in varying percentages, the "warmbloods".

ARAB

BARB

SPANISH

THOROUGHBRED

What is a Breed?

Before the "improving" hand of man, a breed was a group, or groups, of equines inhabiting a particular area. Influenced by environment and the relationship between members of the group, they exhibited similarities of conformation, coat colour, height, action, and general character. These breeds, such as the Arab and Barb, and to a lesser degree the early pony breeds, may be considered as "natural" breeds.

In the modern context, a breed relies on the existence of a stud book. This records and registers pedigree. Horses so registered have been bred selectively over a sufficient period of time to ensure the consistent production of stock sharing common and clearly defined characteristics in respect of size, conformation, action, and, perhaps, colour. Breeds that conform to these requirements are a relatively recent innovation, and few stud books are more than 100 years old.

What is a Type?

Horse "types", like the cob, the hunter, the hack, and the polo pony, are equines that do not qualify for breed status because they lack fixed character. For example, a hunter can properly be defined as any horse that is used for the purpose of hunting. This definition takes no account of conformation, character, size, or colour.

COB AND RIDING PONY
The heavy bodied cob is built for strength; the lighter riding pony is bred for elegance.

STUD BOOKS

There are two kinds of stud book – a "closed" book and an "open" one. In the closed type, stock can only be registered if both parents are already entered in that particular book. Conversely, the open book allows the admission of horses of a different breed, provided they are the progeny of pedigree parents. Many Warmblood societies have open stud books. This enables breeders to tailor breeds to market requirements, but it can result in the loss of the fixed type that is ensured by a closed stud book. The Arab is the prime example of pure, closed stud-book breeding. Totally unmistakable in appearance, it transmits its character in a way that is not possible with breeds that are derived from a variety of blood strains.

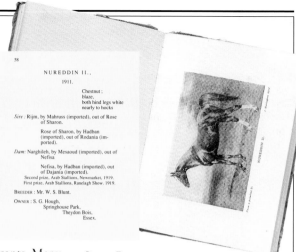

58

NUREDDIN II.,
1911.

Chestnut;
blaze,
both hind legs white
nearly to hocks

Sire : Rijm, by Mahruss (imported), out of Rose of Sharon.

Rose of Sharon, by Hadban (imported), out of Rodania (imported).

Dam: Narghileh, by Mesaoud (imported), out of Nefisa.

Nefisa, by Hadban (imported), out of Dajania (imported).
Second prize, Arab Stallions, Newmarket, 1919.
First prize, Arab Stallions, Ranelagh Show, 1919.

BREEDER : Mr. W. S. Blunt.

OWNER : S. G. Hough,
Springhouse Park,
Theydon Bois,
Essex.

STUD BOOK

A page from the British Arab Horse Society Stud Book. Wilfrid Scawen Blunt, breeder of Nureddin, was the first President of the AHS.

EVOLUTION

This book features the pre-eminent horse breeds. It also traces the equine progression from *Eohippus*, the Dawn Horse of the Eocene period, to "primitive" horses – Przewalski's Horse (the Asian Wild Horse), the Tarpan, and the heavy Forest or Diluvial Horse. These primitive horses were the source of all equine breeds and types.

THE AIM OF THE BOOK

It would be impossible to identify the exact antecedents of the numerous cross-bred "mongrels" of the equine world, and therefore this book cannot guarantee immediate recognition of every horse in the world. Neverthe-

PRZEWALSKI'S HORSE (ASIAN WILD HORSE)

less, it gives a broad insight into the remarkable range of *established* horse and pony breeds, provides an explanation of the way they evolved, and describes their chief characteristics. In fact, it forms an illuminating overall picture of the fascinating world of horses and ponies.

EOHIPPUS

HOW THIS BOOK WORKS

THIS BOOK is arranged according to the four major divisions of horses: ponies, light horses, heavy horses, and types. Within these four divisions, the entries are arranged by country of origin, beginning with Scandinavia, then northern and southern Europe, northern Eurasia, Australasia, India, and, finally, the Americas. Each entry gives detailed information, in words and pictures, on the history, breeding, and characteristics of the particular equine. This annotated example shows how a typical entry is organized.

environment that has had most influence on breed

approximate date of breed's origin

hot-, warm- or coldblood, depending on history of breed

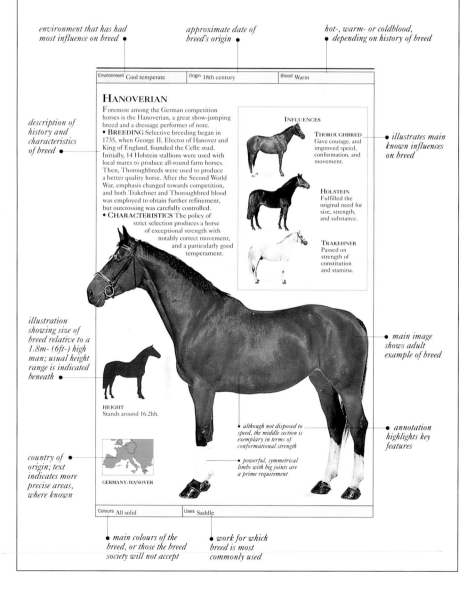

| Environment Cool temperate | Origin 18th century | Blood Warm |

HANOVERIAN

Foremost among the German competition horses is the Hanoverian, a great show-jumping breed and a dressage performer of note.
• **BREEDING** Selective breeding began in 1735, when George II, Elector of Hanover and King of England, founded the Celle stud. Initially, 14 Holstein stallions were used with local mares to produce all-round farm horses. Then, Thoroughbreds were used to produce a better quality horse. After the Second World War, emphasis changed towards competition, and both Trakehner and Thoroughbred blood was employed to obtain further refinement, but outcrossing was carefully controlled.
• **CHARACTERISTICS** The policy of strict selection produces a horse of exceptional strength with notably correct movement, and a particularly good temperament.

description of history and characteristics of breed

INFLUENCES

THOROUGHBRED Gave courage, and improved speed, conformation, and movement.

HOLSTEIN Fulfilled the original need for size, strength, and substance.

TRAKEHNER Passed on strength of constitution and stamina.

illustrates main known influences on breed

illustration showing size of breed relative to a 1.8m- (6ft-) high man; usual height range is indicated beneath

HEIGHT
Stands around 16.2hh.

main image shows adult example of breed

GERMANY: HANOVER

country of origin; text indicates more precise areas, where known

although not disposed to speed, the middle section is exemplary in terms of conformational strength

powerful, symmetrical limbs with big joints are a prime requirement

annotation highlights key features

| Colours All solid | Uses Saddle |

main colours of the breed, or those the breed society will not accept

work for which breed is most commonly used

THE HORSE FAMILY

In 1867, A SKELETON was found in Eocene rock in the southern USA. This was *Eohippus*, and equine development can be traced from it, over a period of 60 million years, to the emergence, about one million years ago, of *Equus caballus*, the forebear of the horse. *Eohippus* was about the size of a fox, with four toes on the front feet and three toes on the back feet. Its coat was probably blotched or striped to blend in with its environment. As marshy lands gave way to treeless plains, the descendants of *Eohippus* adapted. From America, they spread across the world, via the land bridges that existed before the Ice Ages. Then, 8–10,000 years ago, the horse became extinct in America, until its reintroduction by the Spanish *conquistadores* in the 16th century.

DEVELOPMENT OF THE HOOF

Eohippus   *Miohippus*   *Pliohippus*

Mesohippus   *Merychippus*   *Equus*

The multi-toed feet of *Eohippus*, suitable for marshy ground, adapted as conditions changed. *Mesohippus* had three toes while *Merychippus*, which had longer legs, made use of only the central toe. *Pliohippus*, emerging some six million years ago, was the first single-hoof equine, and was equipped for survival in the savanna-type conditions of the Miocene period.

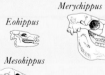

EPIHIPPUS

ASINUS

EOHIPPUS   MESOHIPPUS   MIOHIPPUS   MERYCHIPPUS   PLIOHIPPUS

EQUUS

OROHIPPUS

SKULLS

Early horses had short-crowned teeth, suitable for browsing. As their food changed, their teeth adapted to enable grazing on abrasive grasses. The neck lengthened so that the head could be raised higher and the animal could graze at ground level. In addition, the position of the eyes altered, allowing all-round vision.

Eohippus

Mesohippus

Miohippus

Merychippus

Pliohippus

Asinus

Equus

ZEBRA

After the land bridges disappeared, the striped species of *Equus (Equus zebra)*, were distributed throughout southern Africa. Three subgeneric forms remain: Grevy's, Mountain, and Burchell's Zebras.

ZEBRA

ASS

Equus hemionus hemionus, the wild ass, and the related subspecies, are found in western Asia and the Middle East, the swift Onager occurring particularly in Iran.

ASS

DONKEY

The domestic ass, the donkey *Equus asinus*, was originally distributed throughout North Africa, from where it has spread to many countries and is common throughout Europe.

DONKEY

MULE

The mule is a hybrid, a cross between a jackass (male donkey) and a horse mare. The less usual cross between a horse and a female donkey (jenny) is a hinny, regarded as inferior in strength to the mule.

MULE

PRZEWALSKI'S
HORSE

TARPAN

TUNDRA

FOREST HORSE

PONY TYPE 1
PONY TYPE 2
HORSE TYPE 3
HORSE TYPE 4
(SEE P.14)

MODERN

MODERN BREEDS

Man has developed the modern horse, by means of selective breeding, to produce stock that will be well-equipped to meet the purposes for which it is required.

PRIMITIVE HORSES

FOR MOST of the Ice Ages, *Equus* moved into Europe and Asia from the Americas. The process stopped about 10,000 years ago when the horse became extinct in the Americas. Four primitive horses evolved in Europe and Asia, according to their environment. In Asia, there was the steppe horse, *Equus przewalskii przewalskii poliakov*, now known as the Asian Wild Horse or Przewalski's Horse; further west the light-limbed plateau horse, *Equus przewalskii gmelini antonius*, the Tarpan, developed; and in northern Europe, the heavy, slow horse, *Equus przewalskii silvaticus*, the Forest or Diluvial Horse, evolved. In north-east Siberia there is evidence of another primitive, the Tundra Horse.

PRZEWALSKI'S HORSE

The Asian Wild Horse is found in zoos, but there are moves to reintroduce it to its wild habitat. Its heavy, convex-profiled head and upright mane are distinctive. Its chromosome count differs from the domestic horse's – 66 as opposed to 64.

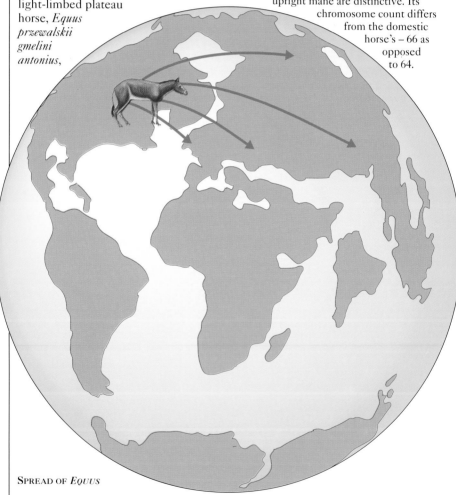

SPREAD OF *EQUUS*

TARPAN

The swift-moving Tarpan was slim and lightly built. Its dun coat resembled a deer's, and turned white in winter. There may be a link between the Tarpan and Arab root stock. Technically extinct, the Tarpan survives in a maintained herd in Poland.

FOREST HORSE

The extinct Forest Horse appears to have been a massive, thick-legged, browsing animal. It was large-footed, enabling it to live in the swamps, and had thick, coarse hair, which was probably dappled for camouflage. It is thought to be the ancestor of the European heavy horse breeds.

TUNDRA HORSE

The remains of what may have been the Tundra Horse, along with those of mammoths, have been found in the Yana valley in north-east Siberia. The local Yakut ponies, with their thick, white coats, are held to be its descendants. Otherwise, this fourth primitive does not seem to have had any direct influence on equine development.

KEY

TUNDRA

FOREST

TARPAN

PRZEWALSKI

DISTRIBUTION OF THE FOUR PRIMITIVES

POSTULATED HORSE TYPES

URING THIS CENTURY, Professors J.G. Speed of Edinburgh, Edward Skorkowski of Cracow, and Hermann Ebhardt of Stuttgart made detailed analyses of early equine bone structure, dentition, and other evidence. They concluded that a further four sub-species of *Equus* existed prior to the domestication of horses in Eurasia some 5–6,000 years ago. These were called Pony Type 1, Pony Type 2, Horse Type 3, and Horse Type 4. The nearest modern equivalents of each are: Pony Type 1 – the Exmoor; Pony Type 2 – the Highland; Horse Type 3 – the Akhal-Teke; and Horse Type 4 – the Caspian.

PONY TYPE 1
From north-west Europe, this pony stood between 12 and 12.2hh and had a straight profile, broad forehead, and small ears. It was highly resistant to wet and able to thrive in harsh conditions. Remains in Alaska show a jaw formation similar to the Exmoor's.

PONY TYPE 2
From northern Eurasia, this type was between 14 and 14.2hh. Heavily built and coarse in appearance, this animal had a heavy head and convex profile, and resembled Przewalski's Horse most closely. It was resistant to cold and vigorously prepotent.

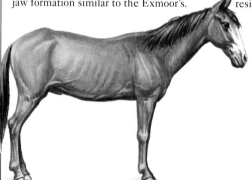

HORSE TYPE 3
From central Asia, this animal was about 14.3hh, was lean and thin-skinned, with a thin neck and fine ears, a long and narrow body, and a goose-rump. It was resistant to extremes of heat and was capable of surviving in desert conditions.

HORSE TYPE 4
From western Asia and put forward as a prototype Arab, this horse stood between 10 and 11hh, and was very refined and slimly built, with a small head and concave profile. The tail was noticeably high-set. A desert or steppe horse, it was resistant to heat.

Modern Equivalents

The four postulated types are obvious derivatives of the early primitive horses (see pp.12–13), bringing us a step closer to the modern breeds. Pony Type 1, for example, has its present-day equivalent in the Exmoor (p.72), which still retains the peculiar jaw formation. The Highland (pp.66–67) clearly owes something to Pony Type 2, although it is the Asiatic Wild Horse that is most similar. The Akhal-Teke (pp.176–77) has all the characteristics of Horse Type 3, while the Caspian (pp.88–89) is closest to Horse Type 4.

Key to Map

The four horse and pony types occurred principally in those areas (shaded on the map) in which the early horse-cultures evolved, particularly the Middle East and Asia, spreading outwards from those regions.

PONY
TYPE 1

HORSE
TYPE 4

PONY
TYPE 2

HORSE
TYPE 3

PONY TYPE
2 & HORSE
TYPE 4

PONY
TYPE 2 &
HORSE
TYPE 3

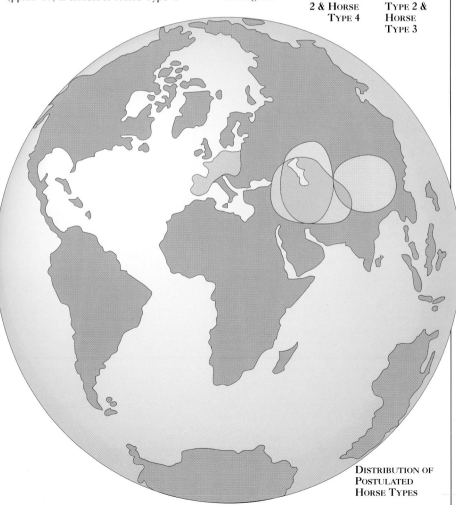

**DISTRIBUTION OF
POSTULATED
HORSE TYPES**

ARAB, BARB, AND SPANISH INFLUENCE

THE GREATEST IMPACT on the development of the world's breeds was made by the hugely prepotent Arab horse. It was supported by the genetically powerful Barb of North Africa, which in turn was responsible for the equine race's "third man", the Spanish Horse. This latter breed dominated Europe between the 16th and 18th centuries, and laid the foundations for the American breeds. The evolution of the Thoroughbred in England in the 17th and 18th centuries is credited to the import of "eastern" or

"Arab" sires. However, Barbs, Spanish Horses, and swift native stock provided the basis for the English "running horses", which made possible the development of the Thoroughbred.

ARAB

The Islamic *Jihad* of the 7th century was as much a watershed in equine as in human history, as it ensured the spread of the Arab horse into the Iberian Peninsula and eventually Europe. Within 120 years of the death of the Prophet Mohammed, the Muslim empire extended from China to Europe. The steppe horses, spreading outwards from Asia

Minor, were all influenced by Arab blood, and by that of other "oriental"-type hot-bloods, such as the ancient Akhal-Teke and Turkmene. These horses are closely linked with those of the Arabian Peninsula.

BARB

In the 7th century, the Berber horsemen pushed into Spain from North Africa, there-after thrusting upwards to Gaul. The Moorish invasion of Europe was halted by Charles Martel and his Frankish knights at Poitiers in AD732, but by then the presence of eastern blood was sufficiently well-established to become a principal influence in Europe and the foundation for many of the present-day breeds.

SPANISH

The Spanish Horse was the premier horse of Europe for over two centuries, and the favoured mount of kings and captains. Its influence was pervasive and remarkable. In the early 16th century, Spanish Horses were taken to the Americas by the *conquistadores*, and they founded breeds that remain with us, the indelible imprint of Spanish blood still being apparent. Few of the European breeds are without the Spanish influence, which extends into the Lipizzaners of the Spanish School and underpins breeds such as the Friesian and Welsh Cob. Although the Spanish Horse was not noted for its speed, it combined great strength with exceptional courage and fire.

KEY TO MAP

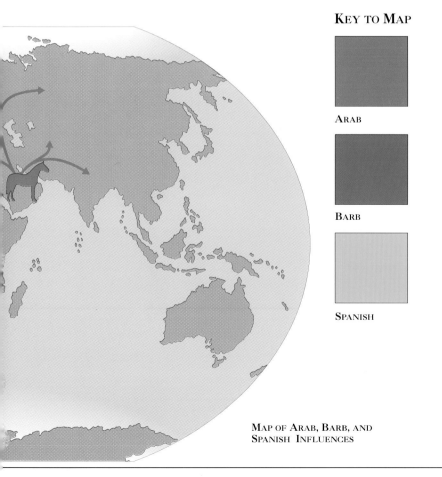

ARAB

BARB

SPANISH

MAP OF ARAB, BARB, AND SPANISH INFLUENCES

CONFORMATION

GENERALLY, "CONFORMATION" is used to describe the shape or form of a horse. More specifically, conformation is concerned with the structure of the skeletal frame. Conformation is the perfection of component parts and their relationship, which contributes to the overall perfection of an animal.

In well-made horses, no single feature is exaggerated or so deficient as to disturb the general symmetry. What constitutes "correct" conformation is governed by the work the horse is bred to do. Well-made, proportionate horses, of whatever type, are able to perform work more efficiently and over a greater period of time. There is less risk of strain because no single part of the structure receives excessive or disabling wear as a result of being asymmetrical, or out of proportion. The balance and athletic qualities are greater, and potential performance is higher, because the limbs function to their full capacity.

HORSE SKELETON

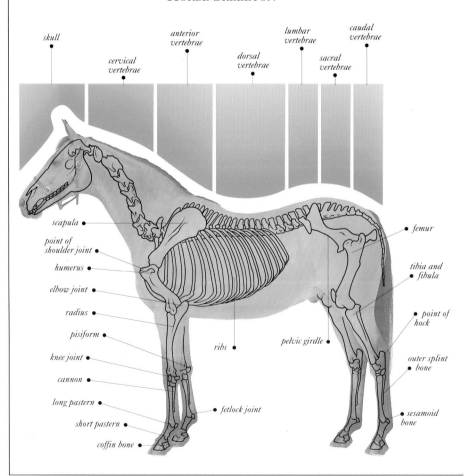

skull

cervical vertebrae

anterior vertebrae

dorsal vertebrae

lumbar vertebrae

sacral vertebrae

caudal vertebrae

scapula

point of shoulder joint

humerus

elbow joint

radius

pisiform

knee joint

cannon

long pastern

short pastern

coffin bone

ribs

fetlock joint

pelvic girdle

femur

tibia and fibula

point of hock

outer splint bone

sesamoid bone

POOR CONFORMATION

Where the conformation is unsuited to the work demanded, and thus creates physical difficulties for the animal, temperamental problems are likely to occur. The specific conformational failings exhibited in this example are: the inclination to a "ewe neck", causing bitting and carriage difficulties (a); a long, weak back structure (b); slackness through the loin (c); insufficient depth of girth (d); and weak quarters (e). All these deficiencies contribute to an inefficient mechanical structure and increase the likelihood of strain and disease in the component parts.

POINTS OF THE HORSE

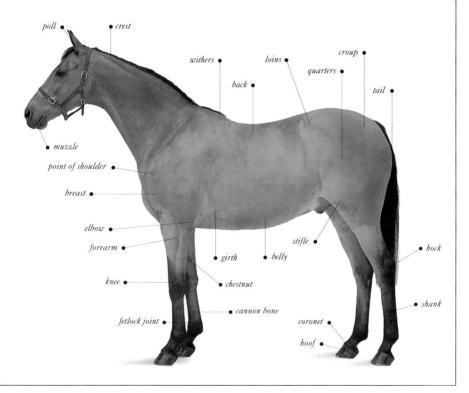

poll
crest
withers
loins
croup
quarters
back
tail
muzzle
point of shoulder
breast
elbow
forearm
stifle
hock
girth
belly
knee
chestnut
shank
fetlock joint
cannon bone
coronet
hoof

LIFE-CYCLE OF THE HORSE

THE AVERAGE equine gestation period is 11 months and a few days. Within half an hour of being born, the foal will be on its feet and nuzzling the mare for its first feed. Once on its feet, the foal, although unsteady, is able to follow its dam (mother). Mares reach puberty at between 15 and 24 months. They can breed from two to three years old, although four is more acceptable. Males are often sexually capable as yearlings, but in domestic conditions they are not used as stallions before three to four years. Mature at five to six years, the horse can live for 20 to 30 years or more.

FIRST 12 MONTHS

The young foal has long legs in proportion to the body, a natural defence against predators in the feral state. Foals are able to eat at about six weeks. At two months, the foal loses the furry, milk hairs, and in domestic conditions will be weaned from its dam when between four-and-a-half and six months old.

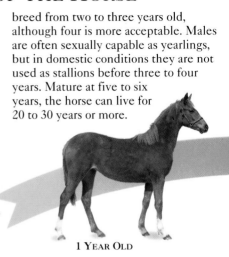

1 YEAR OLD

FOAL

AGEING BY TEETH

At birth a foal has no teeth; the central two incisors cut through the gums at ten days old. By the time it is six to nine months, the foal has a full set of milk teeth. A full set of permanent teeth are in place by five to six years. A horse can be aged accurately by the teeth up to the age of ten, but after this it becomes more difficult.

ADULT JAW
Each jaw has 12 molars and six incisors. Males have additional "tushes" between the molar, and incisor teeth on each jaw.

LATE YEARS

The joints may become puffy as the circulation becomes less effective, and the effects of work become evident in the limbs. Old horses often stand "over at the knee". Hollows sometimes develop over the eyes, and the back may dip more than usual (a "sway" back). The teeth become worn with age and mastication becomes difficult. The digestive process is also less effective and it may become difficult to keep the horse in a good and healthy condition.

OVER 20 YEARS OLD

YEARLING

A Thoroughbred horse, bred to mature quickly, becomes a yearling on the first day of the January following its birth. The age of non-Thoroughbred horses is usually accepted as being taken from May 1. At 12 months, the young horse is still leggy, and somewhat uncoordinated in its movements, but the frame is beginning to fill out, a process that continues up to maturity, when the highest point of the croup will be in line with the withers. Up to that time, the croup is noticeably higher, the horse "coming up in front" by gradual stages as it gets older. The last points of growth in the horse are the epiphyses, the "growth plates" on the long bones of the legs.

Until these are closed, the leg is not capable of sustaining the effects of work, particularly under weight, without the risk of the limb being damaged or becoming misshapen. The epiphysis at the end of the cannon bone, above the fetlock joint, is usually closed at between 9 and 12 months. However, that at the end of the radius, immediately above the knee, does not close until the horse is between two and two-and-a-half years old.

2 YEARS OLD

 flat, oval tables; long, small cups

JAW AT 5 YEARS
Central, lateral, and corner incisors are permanent. "Cup" marks appear.

 round tables; oval cups

JAW AT 12 YEARS
Teeth slope more; the groove is about halfway down upper corner incisors.

 triangular tables; rounded cups

JAW IN OLD AGE
Teeth are long and the groove on the corner teeth is hardly apparent.

3 YEARS OLD

MIDDLE YEARS

In the middle years (from 5 to 10 years of age), the body is fully formed, and the distance between wither and elbow is close to that of the elbow to the ground. All the internal organs are, of course, fully developed and the physical proportions are established. In a well-made horse the length of neck will be about one-and-a-half times the measurement from poll to lower lip, taken down the front of the face. At this stage in its development, the horse should be at the peak of its powers, provided the early training has been directed at the formation of the correct musculature.

10 YEARS OLD

COAT COLOURS

THE ORIGINS of the varied equine coat colours lie in the individual genes, of which there are 39. They result in thousands of possible combinations of colour. For some breeds, colour is a prime consideration, although all breed societies insist on points such as correct conformation and movement taking precedence. Palominos, Appaloosas, and other spotted breeds, like the Knabstrup, as well as the American Pintos, Paints, and Albinos, are often considered "colour breeds", despite the fact that they are essentially practical, working horses. It is interesting to note that the spectacular colourings of these breeds all derive from strains that were once relatively common in the Spanish Horse, but which no longer exist in the modern Spanish horses. Thoroughbred, Arab, and Barb horses do not have part-coloured, spotted, or palomino coats.

GREY
Black skin with white and black hairs. Coat lightens with age.

FLEA-BITTEN
Grey coat, developing small dark specks with age.

PALOMINO
Gold coat, the colour of a newly-minted coin; white mane and tail.

CHESTNUT
Gold/yellow shades. "True" has lighter or darker mane and tail.

RED CHESTNUT
A variation on chestnut. Sometimes includes black hairs.

LIVER/DARK CHESTNUT
Dark, liver-coloured hairs, almost the colour of a bloodstone.

BLUE ROAN
Black or black-brown body, with white hairs giving a bluish tinge.

RED ROAN
Bay or bay-brown body, with white hairs giving a red tinge.

BLACK
Black pigment throughout the coat, limbs, mane, and tail.

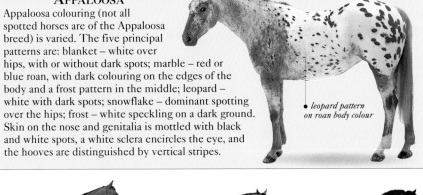

APPALOOSA

Appaloosa colouring (not all spotted horses are of the Appaloosa breed) is varied. The five principal patterns are: blanket – white over hips, with or without dark spots; marble – red or blue roan, with dark colouring on the edges of the body and a frost pattern in the middle; leopard – white with dark spots; snowflake – dominant spotting over the hips; frost – white speckling on a dark ground. Skin on the nose and genitalia is mottled with black and white spots, a white sclera encircles the eye, and the hooves are distinguished by vertical stripes.

• *leopard pattern on roan body colour*

BAY
Red-brown to dark gold, with black mane, tail, and limbs.

LIGHT BAY
A variation on bay caused by yellow or chestnut hairs.

BRIGHT BAY
Predominating red hairs give the bright bay colouring.

YELLOW-DUN
Yellow hair on black skin. Blue dun has greyish or black hair.

BAY BROWN
Mainly brown, with black muzzle, limbs, mane, and tail.

BROWN
Mixture of black and brown, with black limbs, mane, and tail.

DAPPLE GREY
Rings of dark hair on a grey coat. These disappear with age.

SKEWBALD
Large irregular patches of white and any other colour but black.

PART-COLOURED
Skewbald refers to a coat having patches of white and any other defined colour except black (see left). A black-and-white coat is called piebald. The part-coloured coat of the American Pinto is described as either ovaro or tobiano (see pp.204–205).

MARKINGS

THE WHITE MARKINGS that occur on the face, muzzle, and legs are a means of positive identification and are carefully recorded in the documentation required by breed societies. In addition to the common markings, flesh marks or patches of white occur on the underside of the belly and the flank area. Flesh marks occur more frequently on the Clydesdale than on other breeds.

IDENTIFICATION MARKS

White hairs caused by saddle or girth galls are "acquired markings", as are brands and freeze marks, both of which are a means of identification – a precaution against theft. Freeze marking results in a set of identifying letters and figures made up of white hairs (or, in grey horses, black hairs). Identification marks can also be im-printed on the hoof with a heated iron. Whorls, or "cowlicks", are an irregular setting of coat hairs, also used for identification. They are permanent. Chestnuts, the horny prominences on the inside of all four legs, are like an equine fingerprint. They are individual and permanent, but are not used in identification.

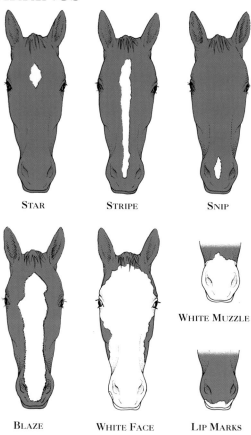

STAR **STRIPE** **SNIP**

BLAZE **WHITE FACE** **LIP MARKS**

WHITE MUZZLE

BRAND MARKINGS

On horses, a brand can be used to denote ownership or identify a specific breed. The mark is made with a hot iron on the actual hide, and is perma-nent. Brand marks are made in prominent positions, like the thigh or shoulder. Normally, only one mark is made, but occasionally several brands are used, each having a different meaning. Lipizzaners, for example, have four: the stud brand, the ancestral brand, the foal brand, and the traditional brand, a simple L.

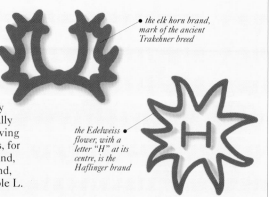

• the elk horn brand, mark of the ancient Trakehner breed

the Edelweiss flower, with a letter "H" at its centre, is the Haflinger brand

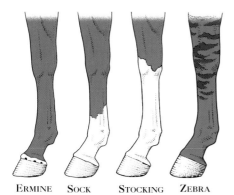

ERMINE   SOCK   STOCKING   ZEBRA

LEG MARKINGS

Leg markings are usually white. They are: ermine marks, when the marks are around the coronet; socks, when the white extends from the foot to the knee but does not encompass that joint; and stockings, when it extends over the knee. Zebra markings, rings of dark hair on the lower limbs, are of primitive origin and were for camouflage. They are seen on breeds of great antiquity, like the Highland and the Fjord. The horses depicted on the cave walls at Lascaux, France, have these markings, and are extraordinarily similar to the Highland.

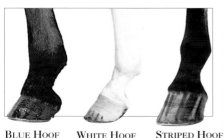

BLUE HOOF   WHITE HOOF   STRIPED HOOF

HOOF MARKINGS

Hooves of slate-blue horn (blue hoof) are preferred. Blue horn is considered to be dense in texture and very hard-wearing. Conversely, a hoof of white horn (white hoof) is thought to be soft and not able to stand up to wear well. There is no proof to support these contentions. White feet accompany legs with white socks or stockings. The Appaloosa and other spotted horses have hooves with black and white in vertical stripes (striped hoof).

DORSAL OR EEL-STRIPE

The dorsal or eel-stripe extends from the tail, and is often accompanied by a band across the withers. It is almost always found with a dun coat, either yellow, blue, or mouse dun, and there will sometimes be zebra markings on the legs.

The dorsal stripe and dun colouring are characteristic of primitive stock existing before and after the Ice Ages. The Tarpan and Przewalski's Horse have these colourings, which are also reproduced in stock having strong connections with them. The Spanish Horse included a spectacular yellow-dun strain, with black mane and a prominent dorsal stripe.

the dorsal or eel-stripe extends back from the withers, sometimes continuing down the tail

the dark hairs of the dorsal or eel-stripe are evident throughout the length of the tail, in this instance

PACES

T HE FOUR PACES that are natural to
the horse are the walk, the trot, the
canter, and the gallop. The first three
of these may be sub-divided in
accordance with modern dressage
requirements. The walk, for instance,
is divided into medium, collected,
extended, and free. The sub-divisions
for trot and canter are medium,
working, collected, and extended. In
addition to the four natural paces, there
are the specialized gaits based loosely
on the amble and the pace, in which
the legs move in lateral pairs. The pace,
employed by modern harness-racing
horses, is a faster version of the amble.

THE WALK

The walk is a pace of four beats marked
by the successive placing of each lateral pair
of feet. When the walk begins with the left
hindleg, the sequence of footfalls is: left hind;
left fore; right hind; right fore. Medium walk
is the hindfeet touching the ground in front of
the prints made by the forefeet. In collected
walk, steps are shorter and more elevated,
with the hindfeet touching the ground behind
the prints of the forefeet. In extended walk,
the hindfeet touch down in advance of the
prints of the forefeet. In free walk, the whole
outline is extended .

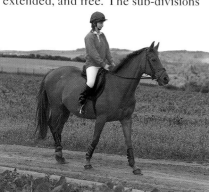

THE TROT

The trot is a two-beat pace in which one
diagonal pair of legs is placed down simultaneously and then, following a moment
of suspension, the horse springs on to the
other diagonal pair. For instance, the first
beat is as the left fore and right hind touch
the ground (the left diagonal). The second
is made on the touch down of the right fore
and left hind (the right diagonal). At the
trot, the knee is never advanced beyond a
line drawn from the poll to the ground.
The extremes of collection in the trot pace
are the movements of *piaffe* and *passage*.

THE CANTER

The canter is a three-beat pace, the horse leading with the right foreleg when circling to the right and vice-versa. When the horse attempts to lead with the outside foreleg, i.e. right foreleg on a circle to the left, it is a "false" lead, termed cantering on the "wrong leg". The sequence of footfalls that give the three rhythmic beats are, on the right lead: left hind, left diagonal, in which the left foreleg and right hindleg touch the ground simultaneously, and then the right foreleg – called the leading leg.

THE GALLOP

The gallop is the fastest of the four natural paces. It is usually understood to be a four-beat pace, but there are variations in the sequence according to the speed. With the right fore leading, the sequence of footfalls is: left hind, right hind, left fore, right fore, followed by a period of full suspension with all feet off the ground. A Thoroughbred gallops at 48km/h (30mph) or more. The leading foot touches the ground in line with the nose, even though at full stretch the foot will be in the air in advance of that line.

SPECIALIZED GAITS

The pacing gait has two beats, the legs moving in lateral pairs (left fore and left hind, followed by right fore and right hind). The fastest exponents of the pacing gait are the American Standardbred harness racers. With the exception of the Icelandic Horse, which employs the specialized and very fast *tölt*, a four-beat running walk, the more "artificial" gaits are confined to the Americas, although a number of Asian breeds also pace naturally.

A UNIQUE GAIT
The gait of the Peruvian Paso evolved over 400 years.

SPORT AND LEISURE

SINCE MAN has always enjoyed competition, horses were probably raced against each other very early in the history of equine domestication. The first recorded races, however, are those between chariots, and they preceded ridden races by many centuries.

DRIVING

Chariot racing was popular in Ancient Greece and was part of the Roman circus. The modern equivalent is harness racing. Pleasure driving, often involving the use of elegant vehicles, is more leisurely. Competitive driving trials also require a degree of elegance; they include a "Presentation" phase and a dressage test, but this is then followed by a tough and demanding cross-country marathon over 27km (17miles).

RACING

Racing, the "Sport of Kings", has been part of the sporting scene for centuries, but owes its modern form to the evolution of the

FLAT RACING
Flat-racing takes place in almost every country in the world. Newmarket is the centre of British racing and Kentucky is America's "horse state".

Thoroughbred horse in 17th- and 18th-century England. Many of the famous British courses were laid out in the 18th century and the British pattern of Classic Races, such as the Derby and the Oaks, are followed in most of the countries that have a racing industry (for example, the Kentucky Derby in the USA and the New Zealand Classic Races). In Britain and Ireland, particularly, racing

HARNESS RACING
Harness racing has a huge following in the United States, where most horses are pacers, and is carried on extensively in Europe where the conventional trotter predominates.

continues during the winter in the form of steeplechasing over fences, the most famous British races being the Grand National at Aintree and the Cheltenham Gold Cup. Point-to-point events for amateurs are held in both countries.

DRESSAGE, JUMPING, AND EVENTING

Most modern horse-sports originated in the practices of war. Even the formal and highly skilful dressage test, the 20th-century version of the classical art of the Renaissance, derives from cavalry horse tests carried out by the armies of Europe in the 19th century. However, it was the Greek general and historian, Xenophon (c.430–355BC), who first described a progression of training and defined specific movements.

Showjumping, an enormously popular sport, also has its military connections, the system of "forward riding" over obstacles being introduced into cavalry training by the Italian Captain Federico Caprilli (1868–1907).

Eventing derives from the old "Military", a complete test for officers and their horses. It involves three phases: a dressage phase, a steeplechase and cross-country course, and a final show-jumping phase.

ENDURANCE AND PLEASURE

Endurance riding over long distances also has a military precedent in cavalry practice, and in its modern form is a highly sophisticated, specialist sport. Usually, the best long-distance

SHOW JUMPING
Show-jumping competitions were first included as part of the Olympic Games in Paris in 1900.

horses are Arabs or Arab part-breds. Otherwise, horses are used for the sheer pleasure of riding in the country, whether riding "Western" or "English" seat, while enthusiasts in England and Ireland devote the winter to the chase, following a pack of hounds across country, taking their fences as they come. Hunting also occurs elsewhere, particularly in France and North America.

SIDE-SADDLE
Up to the 1920s, the majority of ladies rode side-saddle. Today, there is a revival of this graceful art, particularly in Britain, where there is a flourishing Ladies' Side-saddle Association, which organises an annual show and holds numerous clinics.

DRESSAGE
Dressage is a major discipline in Europe and America.

WORKING HORSES

For 4,000 YEARS, the horse was primarily used for the purposes of war, but there were also many peaceful uses to which it could be put. Horses were used to draw loads in harness and to pull travelling chariots. Later, in the 18th and 19th centuries, horses were also used to pull light coaches and elegant vehicles, the development of which was encouraged in Europe by increasingly sophisticated road systems.

MILL HORSE
A horse-operated grist mill, commonplace up to the beginning of the 20th century.

INDUSTRY

The coming of the railways in the first half of the 19th century may have sounded the death knell for the magnificent era of the road and mail coach but, in fact, it created greater employment for horsepower. Thousands of light horses were used for delivery work of all kinds, and drew buses and cabs in the heavily populated towns and cities. Heavy horses moved raw materials to and from the railheads. They were used in goods yards and for shunting rolling stock, so that for over a century the railway companies were the biggest owners and employers of horses. The huge British canal network was serviced by barge horses, the "boaters" who drew loads of 60 to 70 tonnes. Mining companies used great numbers of ponies underground, and horses were needed at the pit heads to turn the windlass of the hoist, as well as draw coal wagons. (The power of the steam engine, invented by James Watt in 1769, was measured in horsepower).

In England, well into the 19th century, Dales and Fell ponies and Cleveland Bays were still used in the pack trains that carted lead ore from the hill mines to the Tyneside docks, while pack ponies were still commonplace all over Europe.

AGRICULTURE

Horses were also essential to agriculture through both the 18th and l9th centuries, taking the place of the slower oxen teams that had worked the land from medieval times. The agricultural cycle, from the preparation of the land, through sowing and cultivating, to the harvesting of the crop and its subsequent delivery to the consumer, was dependent upon horsepower. In the United States, the huge combine harvesters were drawn by 40-horse teams. Between 1900 and 1910, there were over 5,000 breeders of Percheron horses alone in the United States, and the number of registrations had reached a massive 31,900.

PLOUGHING
Up to the Second World War, horses played a large part in the rural economy.

MILITARY AND POLICE

Up to the First World War, millions of horses were employed in the armies of the world; even in the Second World War large numbers were still in use. The German Army had thousands of horses on the Eastern Front, the Poles in 1939 had 86,000 horses, and the Russians a staggering 1.2 million.

Today, many nations still employ cavalry for ceremonial purposes, and no state occasion is thought to be complete without the pageantry of mounted horsemen. Police forces, too, appreciate the psychological power of the horse, and make use of

DRUM HORSE
The Drum horse of the British Household Cavalry, Blues and Royals.

MOUNTED POLICE IN NEW YORK
New York, as well as other American cities, employs a mounted police branch to carry out regular patrol duties in the city.

mounted branches for controlling crowds, and for patrolling the busy city streets, as well as park areas.

HOLIDAY AND LEISURE

A worldwide industry has been built on trekking, trail riding, and other holidays involving horses. Riding schools form a significant part of the leisure industry and there is a constant demand for qualified instructors. All in all, there is still a place in society for the working horse.

DRIVING WAGON
The gypsy wagon is almost as old as the history of wheeled vehicles.

SADDLES

THE FIRST SADDLES built on a wooden frame were developed in the early Christian era by the Sarmatians, a tribe of nomads from the steppes bordering the Black Sea. They formed the basis for saddle construction up to modern times. Many saddles still use a wooden tree, now usually made from strips of laminated wood reinforced with metal plates through the frame. Some trees are moulded from plastic.

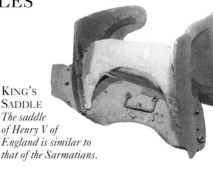

KING'S SADDLE
The saddle of Henry V of England is similar to that of the Sarmatians.

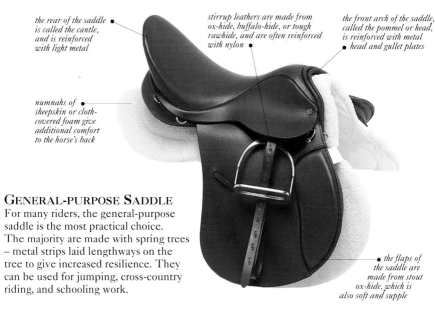

the rear of the saddle is called the cantle, and is reinforced with light metal

stirrup leathers are made from ox-hide, buffalo-hide, or tough rawhide, and are often reinforced with nylon

the front arch of the saddle, called the pommel or head, is reinforced with metal head and gullet plates

numnahs of sheepskin or cloth-covered foam give additional comfort to the horse's back

the flaps of the saddle are made from stout ox-hide, which is also soft and supple

GENERAL-PURPOSE SADDLE

For many riders, the general-purpose saddle is the most practical choice. The majority are made with spring trees – metal strips laid lengthways on the tree to give increased resilience. They can be used for jumping, cross-country riding, and schooling work.

SPECIAL SADDLES

Different types of saddle are designed specifically for particular pursuits. There are dressage saddles, which are cut straight in the flap to allow the rider to sit with a long stirrup leather. The forward-cut, lightweight saddle is used for show jumping. There are also saddles for show-ring classes, and long-distance riding, and very light race saddles, weighing 450g (1lb) or less.

RACING SADDLE
Flat-race saddles can weigh as little as 220g (8oz).

JUMPING SADDLE
This is cut so that the rider is positioned well forward in the saddle.

WESTERN SADDLE

The Western saddle derives from saddles brought to America by Spanish settlers, which were adapted to the requirements of the cowboy. They are comfortable for long journeys, they can be fitted to almost any horse without risk of damaging the back, and all of the cowboy's gear can be fastened to them.

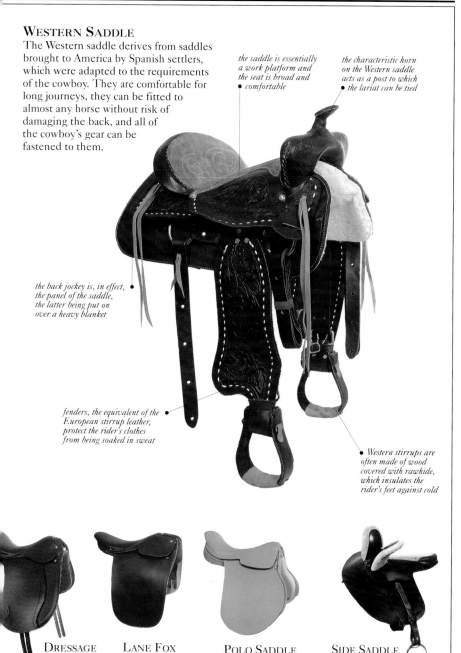

the saddle is essentially a work platform and the seat is broad and comfortable

the characteristic horn on the Western saddle acts as a post to which the lariat can be tied

the back jockey is, in effect, the panel of the saddle, the latter being put on over a heavy blanket

fenders, the equivalent of the European stirrup leather, protect the rider's clothes from being soaked in sweat

Western stirrups are often made of wood covered with rawhide, which insulates the rider's feet against cold

DRESSAGE
Fitted with long girth straps.

LANE FOX
Favoured in the American gaited show classes.

POLO SADDLE
Built on an extra strong tree to allow for hard usage.

SIDE SADDLE
Originated in Europe in the 14th century.

BRIDLES AND BITS

A BRIDLE COMPRISES a head piece and reins attached to a bit, and provides a means of control. In general terms, bridles fall into one of five categories: the snaffle, the simplest control; the double bridle, the most sophisticated; the pelham, a compromise between snaffle and double; the gag, with an upward sliding motion; and the bitless bridle, also known as the hackamore.

SNAFFLE BRIDLE

This bridle applies pressure upwards against the mouth's corners and also across the jaw, when the head is a little in advance of the vertical. The bit lies on the gum, the "bars" of the mouth, between the molar and incisor teeth. The construction of the mouthpiece can be varied to produce specific actions.

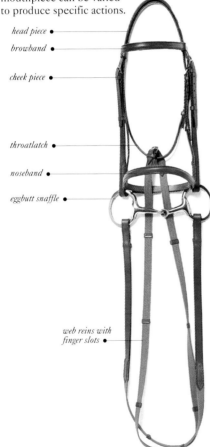

- head piece
- browband
- cheek piece
- throatlatch
- noseband
- eggbutt snaffle
- web reins with finger slots

DOUBLE BRIDLE

This bridle applies complex pressures, allowing the rider to keep a balanced head carriage. It is suitable for the schooled horse and rider, allowing a degree of finesse not found in other bridles. The bridoon acts to raise the head, whereas the curb lowers it causing the nose to be retracted.

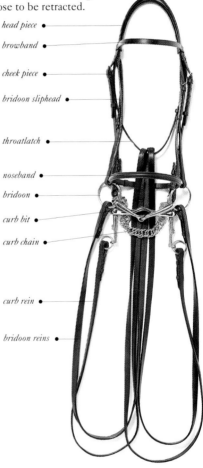

- head piece
- browband
- cheek piece
- bridoon sliphead
- throatlatch
- noseband
- bridoon
- curb bit
- curb chain
- curb rein
- bridoon reins

WESTERN BRIDLE

This bridle is dependent solely on curb action. The differences in construction (the open-end reins, for instance) are just variations in detail. The Western bridle is the culmination of a system of training involving the progressive use of carefully balanced nosebands *(bosal)*, prior to control being transferred to the bit. The method derived from the horsemanship of the Iberian Peninsula, and was brought to America by the *conquistadores*. Although the bit is potentially severe, control on the schooled horse can be exercised by minimal indications made by the rider's hand.

BITS

The majority of bits are made from metal – stainless steel being the preferred material. Otherwise, mouthpieces may be of vulcanite, nylon, flexible plastics, or india-rubber, all of which are softer in their effect. The mildest form of snaffle, for instance, has a rubber mullen, or half-moon mouth-piece. A joint in the mouthpiece produces a "nutcracker" action, which is more severe.

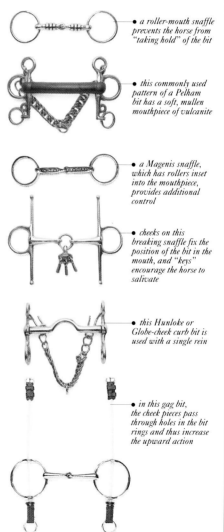

- head piece
- browband
- cheeks
- throatlatch
- curb strap
- open-end reins

- *a roller-mouth snaffle prevents the horse from "taking hold" of the bit*
- *this commonly used pattern of a Pelham bit has a soft, mullen mouthpiece of vulcanite*
- *a Magenis snaffle, which has rollers inset into the mouthpiece, provides additional control*
- *cheeks on this breaking snaffle fix the position of the bit in the mouth, and "keys" encourage the horse to salivate*
- *this Hunloke or Globe-cheek curb bit is used with a single rein*
- *in this gag bit, the cheek pieces pass through holes in the bit rings and thus increase the upward action*

CARRIAGES

THE FIRST CARRIAGES were chariots. These were light vehicles drawn by a pair of horses or a team of four horses abreast. The small size of the horses made riding impractical, hence the use of swift-moving, spoke-wheeled chariot formations on flat and open terrain.

The sophisticated Egyptian war chariot was established by 1600BC and the Chinese developed a similar vehicle 300 years later. The Chinese contributed some of the most important advances in horse driving, inventing the breast harness, the horse collar, the breeching strap, and lateral shafts for single-horse vehicles.

HUNGARY

In the middle ages the Hungarians were in the forefront of carriage and coach design, their forebears having swept into Europe with Attila and his armies, all supported by a sophisticated

wagon-train. Hungarian craftsmen, of the Komorne area, made the first road coaches in the late 15th century. The trade was centred on the village of Kocs in the Kormone, and the coach *(koksi)* takes its name from there.

The most important feature of the Hungarian coach was that, for almost the first time in the history of vehicle

GOVERNESS CART
A member of the gig group, entrance was by the rear door.

the collar is essential for efficient traction •

the pole, on either side of which are hitched the • *"wheel horses"*

the traces attach the horse to the load •

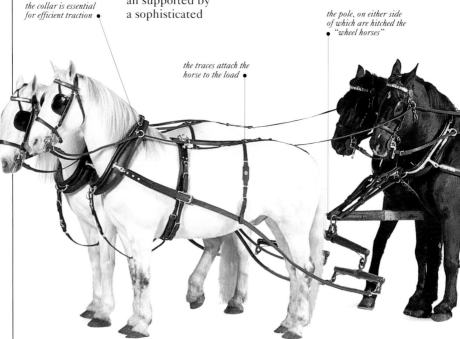

building, the front wheels were smaller than the rear ones, allowing the fore-carriage to turn on a very tight lock. Hungarian vehicles also had a lower centre of gravity than their predecessors, and so could be driven very much faster. The light body, supported in leather slings like a hammock, proved to be far more comfortable for the passengers. The multi-leaved elliptical spring, another Hungarian invention, led to the coach's improved performance, increased comfort for passengers, and enabled the vehicle to be drawn safely at higher speeds.

FRENCH DEMI-MAIL PHAETON
The largest and heaviest of the phaeton family.

WESTERN COACH
The rounded body was suspended on leather "thorough-braces" to counteract the effects of rough ground.

BRITAIN AND EUROPE

The final improvements to coach design were made in Britain, largely as a result of the hard roadways established in the early 19th century, and because of the availability of Thoroughbred horses developed in the previous century. Although it lasted only until the mid-19th century, the English "coaching era" marked the culmination of a great driving tradition, and inspired "private driving", which resulted in the establishment of the huge carriage-building industry. In other parts of Europe, where roads were less advanced, the breeding of heavy, coach-type horses, deriving from the draught breeds, was encouraged.

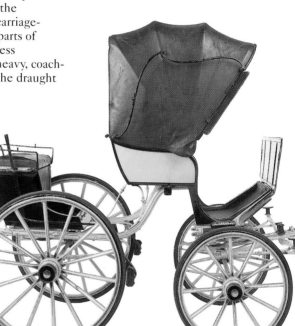

IRISH JAUNTING C.
The passengers sat facin outwards on seats set each side of the body.

AMERICA AND AUSTRALIA

The American equivalent of the British mail coach was produced in 1825. The best models were made by Abbot-Downing Co. at Concord, New Hampshire – and were known as "Concords". In 1853 they were introduced to Australia and were successfully adapted to the local conditions.

SPIDER PHAETON
The vehicle originated in America. Drawn by a pair, it was the fashionable turnout for park or town driving in the 19th century.

CARRIAGE GROUPS

There were four groups of carriages and carts: phaetons, gigs, sporting dog-carts, and breaks. The phaetons were a large family, of which the "spider" was the

COCKING CART
Used to carry fighting birds, it was usually drawn by two horses harnessed in tandem.

children for drives without fear of them falling out. The fourth group, the breaks, were four-wheeled sporting vehicles which carried up to six passengers, as well as the dogs and game. A Skeleton Break was used for breaking young horses to harness, and there were other variations, such as Wagonettes for passengers and luggage. These could be drawn by a single horse, a pair, "unicorn" (a pair hitched behind a leader), or a team. Finally, there were the char-a-bancs (cars with benches) and omnibuses.

FOUR WHEEL RALLI CAR
An off-shoot of the dog-cart, it seated four people with room under the seat for luggage.

most elegant. Gigs were vehicles that were drawn by a single horse. They were the equivalent of family cars and were much used by doctors, businessmen, and commercial travellers. From the sporting dog-carts emerged Ralli cars, market and country carts, the traditional Irish Jaunting Car, the Governess Cart, and the Cocking Cart, so called because of its association with cock-fighting. The Governess Cart, entered by a rear door, enabled governesses to take

HOODED WELL GIG
A most practical vehicle for doctors, businessmen, etc., it also provided protection against the weather.

BAROUCHE
This was the most fashionable of the larger carriages and was drawn by a pair of quality horses.

IDENTIFICATION KEY

T HE BREED SECTION of this book has been divided into three main parts: ponies, light horses, and heavy horses, with a final section on types (horses and ponies that do not qualify for breed status). This identification key follows the same structure, the main groups being described in Stage 1 (below), with the breeds then grouped by geographical location in Stage 2 (pp.44–47).

pp.44–47

STAGE 1

THE THREE GROUPS

The main differences between ponies, light horses, and heavy horses are in weight, body build (which extends to differences in proportion), surface area, gaits (arising as a result of the conformational proportions), and, to a lesser degree, height.

Weight varies considerably between groups and also within a group: an Arab, for instance, may weigh on average 418kg (920lb) and a Thoroughbred 484kg (1,066lb). A riding or carriage horse can be as tall as a draught breed. Ponies are

held, perhaps too arbitrarily, to be those breeds and types below 15hh.

But the real difference between the pony and the horse is one of proportion. In Thoroughbreds, the distance from wither to ground exceeds the length of the body, the legs being longer than the girth measurement. The opposite is true of the pony.

HEAVY HORSE

LIGHT HORSE

PONY

Horses and ponies are measured from the highest point of the withers to the ground. The hand measurement (hh) is medieval in origin and a hand is accepted as being 4 inches (10cm), the approximate breadth of a man's hand. Measuring in hands is largely a British and American convention, but is the traditional form. In Europe and indeed elsewhere, however, measurement is more commonly made in centimetres – a practice likely to become universally acknowledged.

WHAT IS A PONY?

Ponies differ from horses by virtue of their unique character and size. They are deeper through the body in relation to their height, while the length of the head is usually equal to the wither-to-point-of-shoulder measurement, and that of the back from wither to croup. There is also a difference in the action, stemming from the early environment. Horses are rarely as sure-footed, and they do not have such a developed sense of self-preservation, as ponies.

HEIGHT
Ponies stand between 10 and 15hh.

withers are inclined to roundness

short, strong back

thick tails and manes provide protection against cold and wet

neat head, broad between eyes, with tapered muzzle

depth through girth is characteristic

cannons are short, with more than adequate bone for the body build

feet are small, hard, and often of blue horn

ACTION
There is noticeable knee action with strong flexion of the hocks. The fore limb then extends before the foot touches down to give length to the stride.

head is short with very mobile, sharp, and small, pointed ears

WHAT IS A LIGHT HORSE?

The light horse exhibits conformational features that make it suitable to be ridden. The form of the back allows for a saddle to be fitted easily. The "true" ribs, the first eight, are flat, so that the saddle lies behind the trapezius muscle. The ten "false" ribs are rounded and "well-sprung". The withers are clearly defined, and the slope of the shoulders, from their junction with neck and withers to their point, is about 60°.

HEIGHT
Horses usually stand between 15 and 17.2hh.

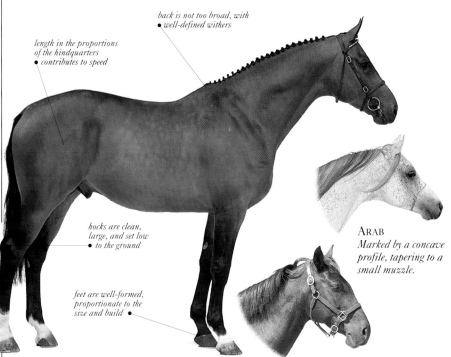

*back is not too broad, with
• well-defined withers*

*length in the proportions
of the hindquarters
• contributes to speed*

*hocks are clean,
large, and set low
• to the ground*

*feet are well-formed,
proportionate to the
size and build •*

ARAB
*Marked by a concave
profile, tapering to a
small muzzle.*

BARB
*Less quality than the
Arab, with thickness
through the jowl.*

ACTION
The long, low, economical action, with little bend or lift in the knee, covers a lot of ground. The slope of the shoulders is critical for producing a smooth, effective riding movement.

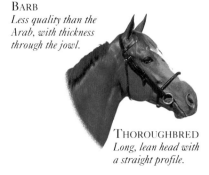

THOROUGHBRED
*Long, lean head with
a straight profile.*

WHAT IS A HEAVY HORSE?

The heavy draught horse gives an impression of weight combined with strength. The body is wide and the back is broad, often accompanied by rounded withers, which in some breeds, in the interest of increased pulling power, may be higher than the croup. The body is heavily muscled, particularly over the loin and quarters. The shoulders are relatively upright to accommodate the collar, and the limbs are thick and short.

HEIGHT
Heavy horses usually stand between 16 and 18hh.

back is broad and fairly short; withers are round
• and inclined to be flat

hindquarters are short, very wide, and
• heavily muscled

• chest is very broad, with forelegs set well apart

FEATHER
Pronounced feathering, typical of the heavy breeds, can cause an irritative skin condition, by retaining wet soil. Clean-legged breeds are better equipped to work in deep, heavy ground.

ACTION
A short action gives maximum traction. The straight angle of the shoulders causes the forelegs to be bent at the knees, which are lifted high before the feet are brought down.

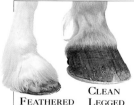

FEATHERED   CLEAN LEGGED

STAGE 2

The following pages show all the breeds featured in this book grouped by their geographical origin, with the page reference given directly beside the breed name. Coloured tint bands indicate which of the three main groups (ponies, light horses, or heavy horses) the breed belongs to. Many of the more popular breeds are to be found distributed throughout the world and, therefore, cannot be identified purely by geographical location. However, a pony at a trekking centre in Iceland will most certainly be of the Icelandic Horse breed and,

ICELAND

Icelandic Horse **48**

FINLAND

Finnish Horse **106**

DENMARK

Danish Warmblood **114**

OTHERS
Frederiksborg **110**,
Knabstrup **112**

Jutland **216**

BELGIUM

Belgian Warmblood **124**

Brabant **218**

GERMANY

Oldenburg **134**

Holstein **132**

AUSTRIA

Haflinger **58**

Noriker **220**

FRANCE

Ariègeois **60**

OTHERS
Landais **62**,
Pottock **63**

Selle Français **146**

OTHERS
French Trotter **147**,
Camargue **148**,
Anglo-Arab **150**

at a similar establishment in Scotland, it will probably be a Highland pony. Similarly, a heavy horse in Italy is more likely to be an Italian Heavy Draught than a Clydesdale. Of course, many horses are crossbreds, but in western countries, and others where breeding

is practised selectively, the stallions used are registered in a stud book and stamp their progeny with their own dominant characteristics. This is particularly true of Arabs, Thoroughbreds, Cleveland Bays, and many of the native ponies registered in closed stud books.

NORWAY

Fjord 50

Døle Gudbrandsdal 104

SWEDEN

Swedish Warmblood 108
OTHERS
Gotland 52

North Swedish Horse 214

NETHERLANDS

Friesian 116

OTHERS
Gelderlander 118,
Groningen 120,
Dutch Warmblood 122

POLAND

Huçul 54

Konik 56

Wielkopolski 128
OTHER
Trakehner 126

Württemburg 136
OTHERS
Bavarian Warmblood 130,
Hanoverian 131,
Rhinelander 138

HUNGARY

Nonius 140

Furioso 141
OTHERS
Shagya Arab 142,
Lippizaner 144

Boulonnais 223
OTHERS
Ardennais 222,
Breton 224,
Percheron 226,
Norman Cob 228

UK & IRELAND

Shetland 64

OTHERS
Highland 66,
Dales 68, *Fell*
69, *Hackney
Pony* 70

Connemara 76

OTHERS
Exmoor 72, *Dartmoor* 73, *New Forest Pony*
74, *Welsh Mountain Pony* 78, *Welsh Pony* 79,
Welsh Pony of Cob Type 80, *Riding Pony* 241

ITALY

Maremmana 164

OTHERS
Bardigiano 82, *Salerno*
160, *Sardinian* 162,
Murgese 165

Italian Heavy Draught
236

PORTUGAL

Sorraia 84

Lusitano 168

OTHER
Alter-Real 170

GREECE

Skyrian Horse 86

Pindos Pony 87

N. EURASIA

Bashkir 90

Akhal-Teke 176

OTHERS
Budenny 178, *Kabardi*
180, *Karabakh* 181,
Orlov Trotter 182,
Don 184

INDIA

Indianbred 190

Kathiawari 188

NORTH AMERICA

Rocky Mountain Pony 96

OTHERS
American Shetland 94,
Chincoteague/Assateague 98,
Sable Island 99

Pinto 204

OTHERS
Saddlebred 194,
*Missouri Fox
Trotter* 198

MEXICO

Galiceno 100

Thoroughbred 152

OTHERS
Hackney Horse 154, *Cleveland Bay* 156,
Irish Draught 157, *Welsh Cob* 158,
Hunter 238, *Hack* 240, *Cob* 242

Clydesdale 230

OTHERS
Suffolk Punch 232,
Shire 234

AIN

Andalucian 166

OROCCO

Barb 172

IDDLE EAST

Caspian 88

Arab 174

ONGOLIA

Przewalski's Horse 186

USTRALIA

Australian Pony 92

*Australian Stock
Horse* 192

Mustang 202

OTHERS
Morgan 200,
Standardbred 209

Palomino 203

OTHERS
Quarter Horse 206,
*Tennessee Walking
Horse* 208

Appaloosa 196

OTHERS
Colorado Ranger
210

UTH AMERICA

Falabella 102

Criollo 212

OTHERS
Paso 213,
Polo Pony 244

PONIES

Environment Tundra	Origin Pre-Ice Age	Blood Warm

ICELANDIC HORSE

Despite its small stature, the Icelandic Horse is referred to as
a horse rather than a pony, and it occupies a special place in
the lives of the Icelanders. Horses were brought to Iceland in
the longboats of the Norsemen between AD860 and AD935.

• **BREEDING** Few breeds can boast such purity of blood as
the Icelandic Horse. There has been no outcross to other
breeds for almost 1,000 years. Selective breeding has been
practised from the earliest times, but practical breeding
programmes were first introduced in the principal breeding
area of Skagafjördur in 1879. The quality of the five gaits
that are peculiar to the breed is given particular consideration
and many studs also breed to the 15 accepted colour types.

• **CHARACTERISTICS** The horses are often kept in a
semi-feral state and can to winter-out in severe conditions.
They are used for all sorts of work, they provide meat,
and they are integral to the traditional sporting activities
of the island. As well as the basic paces of walk, trot,
and gallop, Icelandic Horses may pace (*skeid*) or move
at the famous *tölt*, a fast running walk.

ICELAND

HEIGHT
Stands between 12.3 and 13.2hh.

*inherently sound
and noted for sure-
footedness in
• difficult country*

INFLUENCES

TARPAN
Gave the breed
constitutional
hardiness and
increased speed.

FJORD
Combined prim-
itive qualities
with some added
refinement.

Colours All	Uses Saddle, Harness

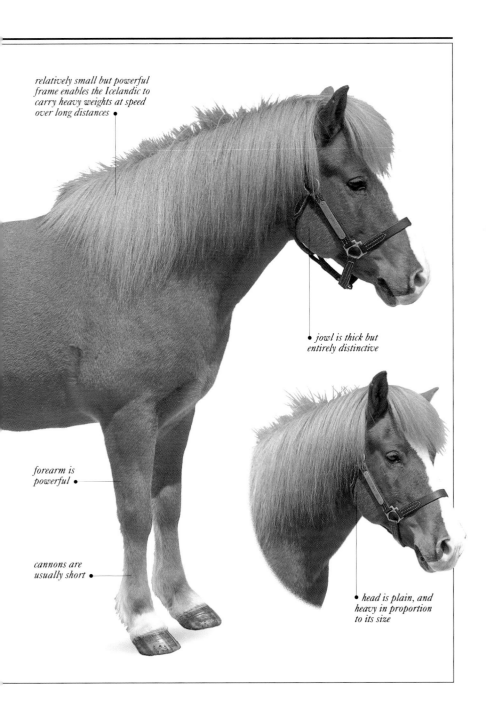

relatively small but powerful
frame enables the Icelandic to
carry heavy weights at speed
over long distances •

• jowl is thick but
entirely distinctive

forearm is
powerful •

cannons are
usually short •

• head is plain, and
heavy in proportion
to its size

Environment Taiga	Origin Pre-Ice Age	Blood Warm

FJORD

The attractive Fjord of Norway, with its pronounced dorsal
stripe and zebra-barred legs, is closest in appearance to the
primitive Mongolian or Asian Wild Horse (Przewalski's Horse,
see pp.186–187) from which it descends. Since Viking times, it
has been traditional to cut the coarse mane so that it is erect,
the central black hair standing above the rest.

NORWAY

• **BREEDING** Descended from Przewalski's Horse, the Fjord
also has more than a suggestion of Tarpan influence. This horse
of the Vikings was taken in longboats to Scotland's Western
Isles and to Iceland. Bred throughout Scandinavia, but
principally in Norway, the Fjord is exported to Germany,
Denmark, and central European countries where its
qualities of endurance and hardiness are highly valued.

• **CHARACTERISTICS** The powerful, compact
Fjord is a versatile animal. It takes the place of the
tractor on mountain farms, it will plough and carry
pack-loads over steep tracks, and it is as good
under saddle as in harness. It is economical to
keep, courageous, and has a will of its own.

*dun colouring is accompanied
by dorsal stripe running from
forelock to tail tip •*

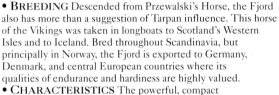

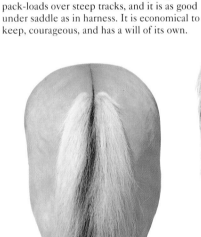

*• hock joints
are particularly
strong*

*• tail is thick
and full, often
silver, and
sometimes
low set*

Colours Dun	Uses Pack, Harness, Saddle

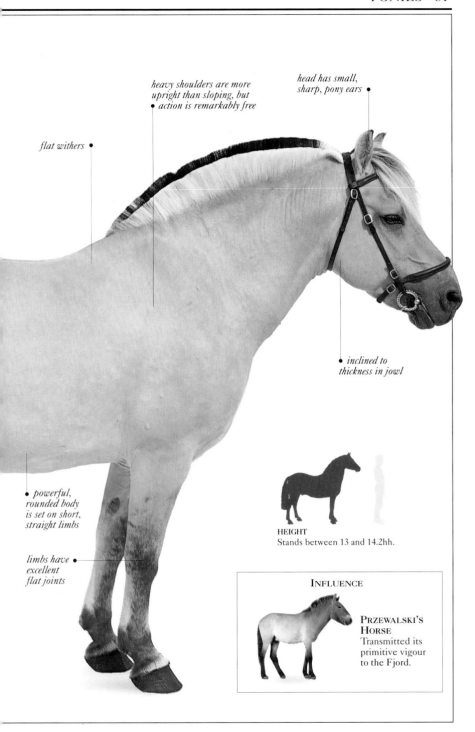

heavy shoulders are more
upright than sloping, but
• action is remarkably free

head has small,
sharp, pony ears •

flat withers •

• inclined to
thickness in jowl

• powerful,
rounded body
is set on short,
straight limbs

limbs have •
excellent
flat joints

HEIGHT
Stands between 13 and 14.2hh.

INFLUENCE

**PRZEWALSKI'S
HORSE**
Transmitted its
primitive vigour
to the Fjord.

Environment Temperate, Controlled	Origin Pre-Ice Age	Blood Warm

GOTLAND

The Swedish Gotland or Skogruss pony is probably the oldest
of the Scandinavian breeds and it retains much of its primitive
character. It once lived in a semi-wild state on the island of
Gotland in the Baltic Sea and in the Löjsta forest in Sweden.
• **BREEDING** The ponies originated on Gotland, where they
have probably lived since the Stone Age. They are considered
to be descendants of the Tarpan, but Arab blood seems
to have been introduced in the last century and selective
breeding is now practised. Today, Gotland ponies are also
bred on the Swedish mainland.
• **CHARACTERISTICS** The Gotland was once employed
as a general-purpose farm pony, but the modern ponies are
now used for riding and are said to excel at jumping and
in trotting races. The action at walk and trot is quick
and active, but the gallop is not a favoured gait.

SWEDEN: GOTLAND

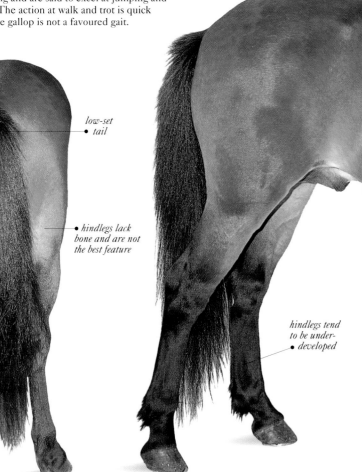

*low-set
• tail*

*• hindlegs lack
bone and are not
the best feature*

*hindlegs tend
to be under-
• developed*

Colours Brown to Palomino	Uses Saddle, Harness

shoulders, though strong, are relatively upright •

• *short neck*

frame is narrow and lightly built, but the Gotland has great endurance •

hard feet •

HEIGHT
Stands between 12 and 12.2hh.

INFLUENCES

TARPAN
Transmitted a primitive vigour, great hardiness, and endurance.

ARAB
The refining, upgrading influence improved action.

Environment Cool temperate	Origin Pre-Ice Age	Blood Warm

HUCUL

The Polish Huçul is a prime example of a working horse. It is the standard workhorse in the farming communities of southern Poland and the Carpathian Mountains. Principally a harness animal used in light agricultural work, the Huçul is also used as a pack pony to transport loads over difficult mountain tracks.

• **BREEDING** The breed can be regarded as a descendant of the Tarpan, the "primitive" horse which survived in Poland until relatively recently. The Huçul originated in the Carpathian Mountains where similar ponies have existed for many thousands of years. At some stage, there was possibly an oriental influence, and the modern pony, which is bred selectively, is more refined than previously.

• **CHARACTERISTICS** The Huçul is strong, hardy, sensible, and docile.

POLAND: CARPATHIAN
MOUNTAINS

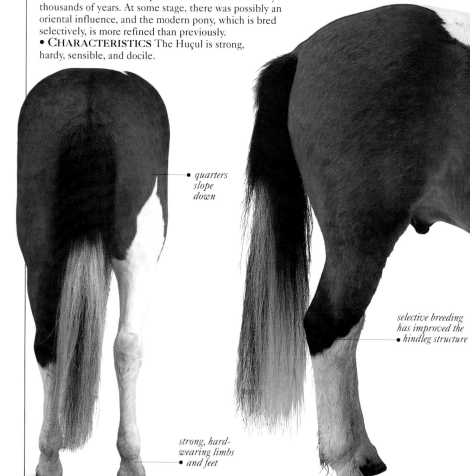

*quarters
slope
down*

*selective breeding
has improved the
• hindleg structure*

*strong, hard-
wearing limbs
• and feet*

Colours Dun, Bay, Piebald	Uses Harness, Pack

round, flat withers •

shoulders are inclined to be upright •

head is medium-sized, "primitive" in most respects, but not without some quality •

• *short, compact body*

feet are uniformly sound and the pony is sure-footed •

HEIGHT
Stands between 12.1 and 13.1hh.

INFLUENCE

TARPAN
Provided the essential base stock for the modern Huçul.

Environment Cool temperate	Origin Pre-Ice Age	Blood Warm

KONIK

The Konik can be described as one of Poland's base breeds. The word means "little horse" and the Konik is, indeed, more horse than pony, even though it rarely exceeds 13hh.

• **BREEDING** The Konik is one of the few direct derivatives of the vigorous, primitive Tarpan and, as such, is of particular interest. The breed, which has inhabited Poland from ancient times, has been "improved" by infusions of oriental blood. It is officially recognized and is bred at some of the Polish state studs, as well as by numerous farmers. A uniform type has existed for many years.

• **CHARACTERISTICS** The Konik retains all the hardiness and robust constitution of its ancestor, the Tarpan, but is very quiet in temperament, easily managed, and capable of working hard on minimum rations. It is used in all forms of light agriculture, for haulage, and in harness.

POLAND: SOUTH AND EAST

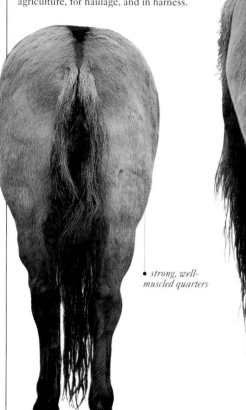

• *strong, well-muscled quarters*

strong, well-made • hindlegs

some feathering occurs at • the heels

Colours Dun	Uses Harness, Light Draught

back is compact
• and fairly wide

• strong, short
neck

• forehand, with
relatively upright
shoulders, is well-
suited to harness

HEIGHT
Stands around 13hh.

body is notably •
strong and there
is depth through
the girth

INFLUENCES

TARPAN
Passed its
constitutional
strength to
base stock.

ARAB
Provided the
refining and
upgrading
influence.

Environment Mountain	Origin 18th–19th century	Blood Cold

HAFLINGER

The Haflinger of the Austrian Tyrol is distinguished by its striking chestnut or palomino colouring, accompanied by a flaxen mane or tail. All Austrian Haflingers bear the Edelweiss brand mark with the letter "H" at its centre, and they are sometimes referred to as the Edelweiss Ponies.

• **BREEDING** The centre of Haflinger breeding is the village of Hafling in the Etschlander Mountains in Austria, the principal stud being at Jenesien. The pony is technically a coldblood but has an Arab foundation sire, El Bedavi XXII. The base stock was the now extinct Alpine Heavy Horse. Huçul, Konik, and related Bosnian ponies are all genetically related to the Haflinger.

• **CHARACTERISTICS** A mountain pony, reared on the high alpine pastures, the Haflinger works easily on the steep slopes. It is ridden, used in forestry work, and will draw a sleigh or wheeled vehicle. The breed is strong and hardy and is very long-lived. Haflingers are not worked until they are four years old, but may continue to be active and healthy at 40 years of age.

AUSTRIA: TYROL

strong loins

head has lively and kindly expression, with large eyes, wide nostrils, and small, mobile ears

Colours Chestnut, Palomino	Uses Pack, Saddle, Light Draught

neck is invariably
well-formed, giving
overall impression of
muscular development •

HEIGHT
Stands around 13.3hh.

body is relatively long, •
but deep through the girth

naturally sure-
footed, with the very
best of limbs and feet •

INFLUENCES

FOREST HORSE
Ancient stock
provided base for
many of the cold-
blood breeds.

NORIKER
Transmitted its
improved action
and much better
conformation.

ARAB
Gave quality and
sound physique;
produced lighter,
faster stock.

Environment Mountain	Origin Prehistoric	Blood Cold

ARIEGEOIS

The black Ariègeois, sometimes called *cheval de Mérens*, is a true mountain pony, at home in conditions of snow and ice and impervious to the coldest weather. It is not, however, resistant to heat. In appearance, it resembles the British Fell, and is an almost exact replica of the Dales pony.

• **BREEDING** It takes its name from the Ariège river and its home is the eastern Pyrenees, which divide France from Spain, particularly in the high valleys towards Andorra. It may be the descendant of the horses depicted in the wall pictures of Ariège some 30,000 years ago, subsequently being influenced by Roman mares and then by oriental blood.

• **CHARACTERISTICS** Primarily a pack pony, the breed can work unshod on the steep and icy mountain paths. For this reason, it was much in demand by smugglers operating along the Spanish border. It works, too, on the steep slopes of the upland farms where tractors are impractical. The breed is versatile, hardy, and able to work hard on minimal rations. White markings on the solid black coat are exceptional.

FRANCE: EASTERN PYRENEES

• *tail is low set and, like the mane, thick and harsh*

• *hindlimbs are often cow-hocked*

Colours Black	Uses Pack, Light Draught

upright shoulders •

• flat withers

facial hair is • thick and coarse as protection against cold

• body has depth but quarters often slope from croup

feet are so hard that they rarely require shoes, the density of horn being exceptional •

HEIGHT
Stands between 13.1 and 14.3hh.

INFLUENCES

ROMAN PACK HORSE
Base stock, added size and substance.

BARB
Gave spirit, constitution, stamina, and endurance.

Environment Cool temperate	Origin Pre-Ice Age	Blood Warm

LANDAIS

The Landais, originally semi-wild, is now bred selectively to fulfil the demand for children's ponies generated by the formation of pony clubs in France. It also provides the base stock for the French Riding Pony (*Poney Français de Selle*), a pony of greater quality following the pattern set by the British Riding Pony.

• **BREEDING** The original habitat of the Landais was the heavily wooded Landes region, south of Bordeaux. There was also a bigger strain, often termed Barthais, which inhabited the Chalosse plain where the grazing was better. Both are probable descendants of the Tarpan. After the Second World War, Welsh Section B stallions and Arabs were introduced.

• **CHARACTERISTICS** The modern Landais is lightly built, but hardy and easy to keep. It is said to be docile and intelligent.

INFLUENCES

ARAB
Gave physique along with quality and temperament.

WELSH B
Contributed its substance and action, adding to Arab qualities.

straight
• shoulders

back is
• usually long

quarters often
look weak, even
if they are not •

short neck •

a tendency •
towards
cow-hocks

HEIGHT
Stands between 11.3 and 13.1hh.

• limbs are rarely
well-made but stand
up to hard work

FRANCE: LANDES

Colours Bay, Brown, Chestnut	Uses Saddle

Environment Mountain	Origin Post-Ice Age	Blood Warm

POTTOCK

The Pottock is one of the few indigenous ponies remaining in France and is still semi-wild. On the whole, it is unprepossessing in appearance, but it is tough and very hardy. There are three recognized types: the Standard and the Piebald (between 11 and 13hh), and the bigger Double Pottock (12.2 to 14.2hh).
• **BREEDING** The Pottock is another Tarpan descendant and its habitat is the mountainous Basque region where, for generations, it was used as a pack pony. Attempts have been made, with some success, to upgrade the ponies using Welsh and Arab blood.
• **CHARACTERISTICS** The Pottock is hardy and resourceful and is said to be of a tractable disposition, but has a number of conformational defects. Interestingly, there is a slight concavity between the eyes on the otherwise unremarkable head.

INFLUENCES

ARAB
Added quality, temperament, and the usual sound physique.

WELSH B
The source of bone, substance, and definite pony character.

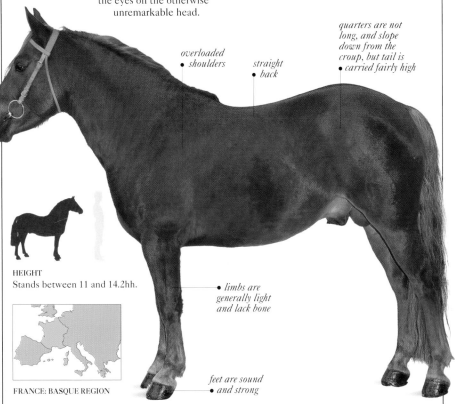

overloaded • shoulders

straight • back

quarters are not long, and slope down from the croup, but tail is • carried fairly high

HEIGHT
Stands between 11 and 14.2hh.

• limbs are generally light and lack bone

FRANCE: BASQUE REGION

feet are sound • and strong

Colours Bay, Brown, Part	Uses Pack, Saddle, Harness

Environment Cool temperate	Origin Pre-Ice Age	Blood Warm

SHETLAND

In comparison to its size, the diminutive pony of the
Shetland Islands is one of the world's most powerful
equines. It is capable of carrying a man over rough country
and is able to work on the crofts under heavy loads. It is now
popular and bred extensively all over Europe and in the
Americas and Australasia. It can be ridden by small children,
is excellent in harness, and is still in demand for circus work.

UK: SHETLAND ISLANDS,
SCOTLAND

• **BREEDING** Its original habitat is the bleak Shetland
Islands, north-east of Scotland, and this inhospitable
environment has governed its character and size. The
ponies arrived in Shetland, probably from Scandinavia,
as long as 10,000 years ago, and may have been
related to primitive Tundra stock. In the 19th
century, Shetlands were used extensively in the
coal mines and a heavier type developed which
has now been largely eradicated. The first
export of 75 ponies was made to Eli Elliot in
America in 1885. Since then, American and
Canadian breeders have produced a new
"Shetland" pony (see pp.94–95), which
bears little resemblance to the original.
• **CHARACTERISTICS** The Shetland
is naturally hardy and able to thrive in the
harshest environment. It is long-lived,
robust, and sound. The action is quick,
free, and straight, with a characteristic
lift in the knee and hock joints.

*limbs have sharply
defined joints and
• strong, flat bone*

*sensible, intelligent •
head with a neat
and sometimes
square muzzle*

Colours All	Uses Saddle, Harness

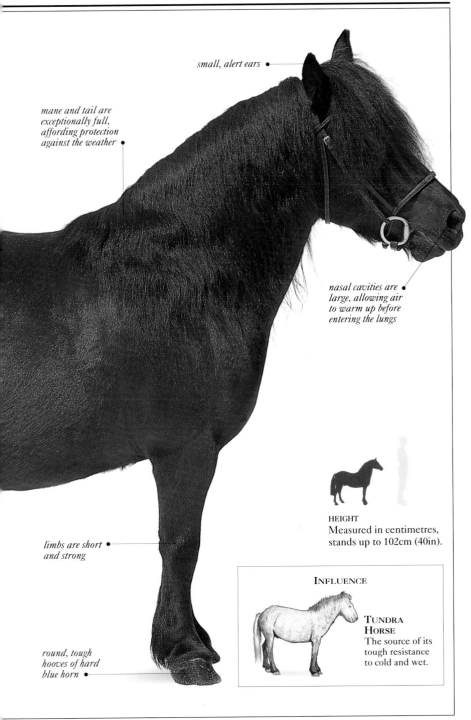

small, alert ears •

*mane and tail are
exceptionally full,
affording protection
against the weather* •

*nasal cavities are
large, allowing air
to warm up before
entering the lungs* •

HEIGHT
Measured in centimetres,
stands up to 102cm (40in).

*limbs are short
and strong* •

*round, tough
hooves of hard
blue horn* •

INFLUENCE

**TUNDRA
HORSE**
The source of its
tough resistance
to cold and wet.

Environment Cool temperate	Origin Pre-Ice Age	Blood Warm

HIGHLAND

The Highland is a breed of great antiquity. There were ponies inhabiting northern Scotland and the Scottish islands following the Ice Age, and some of the horses depicted in cave drawings at Lascaux, France (15–20,000 years ago) strongly resemble the modern Highland.

• BREEDING In the early 16th century, French horses, probably predecessors of the Percheron, were crossed with native stock. Spanish horses were introduced over the following 200 years. The Dukes of Atholl, foremost among Highland breeders, used oriental blood, and, in the 19th century, a Syrian Arab established the Calgary strain on the Island of Mull. There was also a strong Clydesdale influence.

• CHARACTERISTICS The Highland has exceptional strength and a docile temperament. It is used in forestry, in harness, and to carry deer carcasses (weighing 114kg/251lb) off the hills when herds are culled. The Highland is also an active riding pony, much used for trekking. The breed is sure-footed, easily kept, free from hereditary disease, and long-lived.

UK: HIGHLANDS AND ISLANDS, SCOTLAND

back is very strong and usually marked by a dorsal eel stripe •

good hooves, free • from disease

INFLUENCES

PONY TYPE 2
Provided the primitive base; governed the initial type.

PERCHERON
Increased size, combined with free movement and refinement.

ARAB
Improved quality and movement; contributed to riding action.

CLYDESDALE
Gave more size and weight, but also introduced coarseness.

Colours All, including Dun	Uses Saddle, Pack, Harness

HEIGHT
Stands around 14.2hh.

*neck is strong,
but does not
lack length* •

*withers are
inclined to be low* •

*head, which has an alert, kindly
expression, is short between eyes
and muzzle, with a wide forehead
• and wide nostrils*

conformation is compact, •
*with depth through the big
body and well-sprung ribs*

soft, silky •
*feathering
on legs*

Environment Moorland	Origin 1st–2nd century AD	Blood Warm

DALES

The powerful Dales pony is a close relation of the Fell pony, both geographically and genetically. However, it is a more heavily built animal and taller than the Fell.

• **BREEDING** The Dales comes from the eastern Pennine area of North Yorkshire, Durham, and Northumberland. It was developed as a pack pony in the 18th and 19th centuries to take lead ore from the moorland mines to the Tyne seaports. It was also used in coal mines and for farm work. Outcrosses were made to Welsh Cobs and to the Clydesdale.

• **CHARACTERISTICS** The modern, more refined Dales pony is a brilliant performer in harness, and its calm temperament, sure-footedness, and weight-carrying ability make it a valuable riding pony.

INFLUENCES

FRIESIAN Appearance (including colour) and good action were transmitted.

HEIGHT
Stands around 14.2hh.

great propulsive power of hocks is made possible by strong quarters •

• *head is sensible and now shows no trace of Clydesdale influence*

strong shoulders are of harness type and contribute to the raised knee action •

limbs are short and powerful with • *silky feathering*

breed is famous for the excellence of its hard feet •

UK: EASTERN PENNINES, ENGLAND

Colours Black	Uses Harness, Saddle

Environment Moorland	Origin 1st–2nd century AD	Blood Warm

FELL

The Fell is the modern equivalent of the now extinct Scottish Galloway, a swift, enduring horse which probably formed part of the stock of English "running horses" from which the Thoroughbred racehorse evolved.

• **BREEDING** The native heath of the Fell lies in the western Pennines, in Cumbria, England. As with the Dales, it was influenced by the coldblood Friesian horses, used by the Roman legions. The most famous of the Fell lines is Lingcropper, a stallion found on the fells during the Jacobite uprisings of 1745.

• **CHARACTERISTICS** Acknowledged as a harness pony of competition standard and a riding pony of particular ability, the Fell provided a base for the Hackney Pony (see pp.70–71) and is an excellent cross to produce competition horses in the ridden disciplines.

INFLUENCES

FRIESIAN Provided sound base stock with excellent bone and substance.

GALLOWAY Added speed, spirit, and sure-footedness to the Fell pony.

neck is longer than that of the Dales

sloped riding shoulders

deep, compact body

HEIGHT
Stands around 14hh.

UK: WESTERN PENNINES, ENGLAND

hard feet of blue horn stand up to work on the rough uplands

Colours Black, Brown	Uses Saddle, Harness

Environment Moorland, Stud	Origin 19th century	Blood Warm

HACKNEY PONY

The Hackney Pony shares the stud book with the bigger Hackney Horse (see pp.154–155) and to a large degree has a common ancestry in the Norfolk and Yorkshire Trotters of the 18th and 19th centuries. The Hackney Pony is a real pony with pony character, not simply a little horse. The modern Hackney Pony is confined largely to the show ring, where its spectacular action is an exciting sight.

• **BREEDING** Essentially the breed was the creation of Christopher Wilson of Kirkby Lonsdale in Cumbria. By the 1880s, he had created a distinctive type, based on the local Fell pony with occasional Welsh outcrosses. Wilson's champion pony stallion, Sir George, was by a Yorkshire Trotter and traced his descent through the great Norfolk Phenomenon to the first notable racehorse, Flying Childers. Sir George's female progeny were mated back to their sire to produce elegant ponies with brilliant harness action. Their height was limited by being wintered on the fells, where they were left to fend for themselves, a practice that ensured a remarkable hardiness of constitution.

• **CHARACTERISTICS** The Hackney Pony has a naturally brilliant, high-stepping action in harness. Full of courage, it has great stamina and is hardy and constitutionally sound. A very elegant pony, it shows notable quality in the head, and the coat is particularly fine and silky.

UK: CUMBRIA, ENGLAND

broad, strong loins •

big, clearly defined joints allow maximum • *flexion*

INFLUENCES

FELL
The hardy base stock descended from the swift Galloways.

NORFOLK TROTTER
Gave fast trotting action and endless stamina.

WELSH A
Contributed pony character, along with quality, spirit, and movement.

Colours All solid	Uses Harness

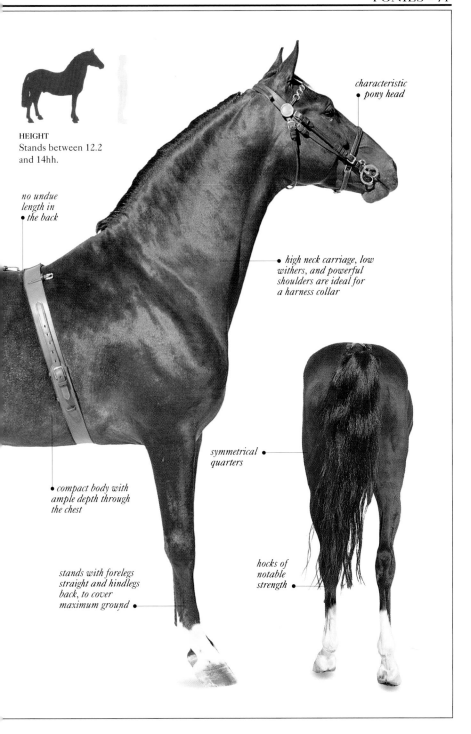

HEIGHT
Stands between 12.2
and 14hh.

no undue
length in
• the back

• characteristic
pony head

• high neck carriage, low
withers, and powerful
shoulders are ideal for
a harness collar

symmetrical •
quarters

• compact body with
ample depth through
the chest

stands with forelegs
straight and hindlegs
back, to cover
maximum ground •

hocks of
notable
strength •

| Environment Moorland | Origin Pre-Ice Age | Blood Warm |

EXMOOR

The Exmoor, the oldest of the British mountain and moorland breeds, is probably as old as any equine. It has a number of unique features found in its ancestor, Pony Type 1 (see pp.10–11). These include, for example, a particular jaw formation, with a seventh molar, not present in other equines.

• **BREEDING** This breed belongs on Exmoor in south-west England. Efforts to "improve" the breed have usually had no success, the ponies retaining the character brought about by the isolation and harshness of their home. When they are bred away from Exmoor they soon lose type, and it is necessary to return to moor stock to keep character.

• **CHARACTERISTICS** Exmoors are strong enough to carry a grown man. Although they have an independent nature, they make magnificent children's ponies and are exceptional jumpers. They are hardy, robust, and sound. Crossed with the Thoroughbred, they produce tough perfomance horses.

INFLUENCE

PONY TYPE 1
Gave a strong constitution and resistance to the cold and wet.

HEIGHT
Stands between 12.2 and 12.3hh.

"ice" tail has a thick, fan-like growth at the top as weather protection

"toad" eye is hooded

long nasal passages, which allow air to be warmed before inhalation

limbs are short and uniformly correct, with good bone

feet are hard and neat

UK: EXMOOR, SOMERSET, ENGLAND

| Colours Bay, Brown, no White | Uses Saddle |

Environment Moorland	Origin 12th century	Blood Warm

DARTMOOR

The Dartmoor is the neighbour to the Exmoor. It has been subject to a far greater degree of outside influence than the Exmoor because of the geographical position of its habitat, affording access from the sea and from the route existing between Plymouth and Exeter from early times. Few pure-bred Dartmoors are found on the moor today, the modern Dartmoor, now a most elegant riding pony, being bred at private studs all over Britain, as well as some on the European mainland.

• **BREEDING** The breed originated on the rough moorland of the Dartmoor Forest in Devon, which has had an equine population since ancient times. Oriental blood was introduced as early as the 12th century, and there is a Welsh and Thoroughbred influence. The greatest modern influence was The Leat, a stallion foaled in 1918, by the Arab, Dwarka.

• **CHARACTERISTICS** The modern Dartmoor is a brilliant riding pony with great jumping ability, and is notable for its long, low action.

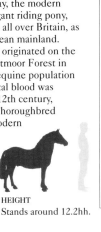

HEIGHT
Stands around 12.2hh.

INFLUENCES

ARAB
The upgrading and refining influence on the base stock.

WELSH A
Acted to retain pony character with good bone and substance.

THOROUGHBRED
Gave the breed better scope and much improved the riding action.

• *fine, sloped riding shoulders ensure a brilliant movement*

excellent limbs and good feet are the hallmark of the • Dartmoor

UK: DARTMOOR, DEVON, ENGLAND

Colours Bay, Brown	Uses Saddle

Environment Moorland	Origin Prehistoric	Blood Warm

NEW FOREST PONY

The New Forest Pony is one of the larger of the native British breeds and one of the most commercially viable because of its versatility. The best of the modern "Foresters" are usually stud-bred, although the New Forest itself still supports a large number of feral ponies. The latter are owned by the Commoners, who hold traditional grazing rights.

UK: NEW FOREST, ENGLAND

• **BREEDING** Due to the accessibility of the New Forest, through which ran the western routes to Winchester (once England's capital city), the New Forest Pony has very mixed origins. Welsh ponies were used to upgrade stock as early as 1208. Marske, the sire of Eclipse, arguably the greatest racehorse ever, was used briefly around 1765. An Arab and a Barb stallion were loaned by Queen Victoria in the following century, and Lord Cecil and Lord Lucas brought in Highlands, Fells, Dales, Dartmoors, Exmoors, and more Welsh stock. Despite this broad mix of blood, the New Forest Pony is stamped as a product of its environment.

• **CHARACTERISTICS** The New Forest Pony is an excellent all-rounder. Big enough to carry adults, it has exceptional riding shoulders and a long, low action that is particularly marked at the canter. The ponies are easy to handle and friendly.

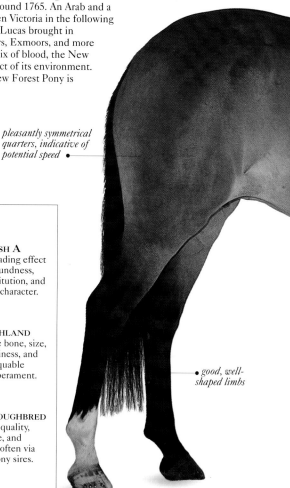

pleasantly symmetrical quarters, indicative of potential speed •

• *good, well-shaped limbs*

INFLUENCES

WELSH A
Upgrading effect on soundness, constitution, and pony character.

HIGHLAND
Gave bone, size, hardiness, and an equable temperament.

THOROUGHBRED
Added quality, courage, and action, often via polo pony sires.

Colours All solid	Uses Saddle, Harness

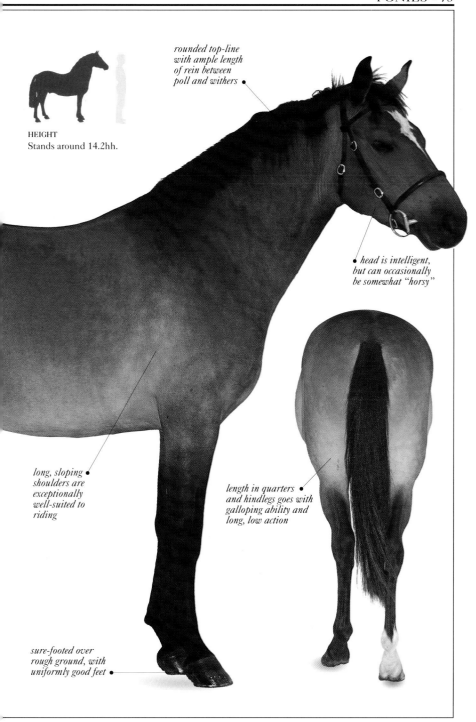

rounded top-line
with ample length
of rein between
poll and withers •

HEIGHT
Stands around 14.2hh.

• head is intelligent,
but can occasionally
be somewhat "horsy"

long, sloping •
shoulders are
exceptionally
well-suited to
riding

length in quarters •
and hindlegs goes with
galloping ability and
long, low action

sure-footed over
rough ground, with
uniformly good feet •

Environment Moorland	Origin 15th–16th century	Blood Warm

CONNEMARA

The Connemara, which originated on Ireland's western seaboard, is that country's sole indigenous pony. It is now bred throughout Europe, as well as further afield. Of all the mountain and moorland breeds, it is probably the most commercially viable for it is fast, a brilliant performance pony, and a superb jumper, while being big enough to be ridden by older children and lightweight adults.

IRELAND: CONNEMARA

• **BREEDING** Barb and Spanish horses were introduced to the indigenous stock early. The result was the renowned fast, agile, and hardy Irish Hobby of the 16th and 17th centuries. In the 19th century, government schemes, aimed at checking degeneration in the native stock, used Arabs, Welsh Cobs, Roadsters, and Thoroughbreds. Later, Irish Draughts were also used. The first stallion in the stud book was Cannon Ball, grandson of the Welsh Cob, Prince Llewellyn. More recent lines are Carna Dun by the Thoroughbred, Little Heaven, and Clonkeehan Auratum by the Arab, Naseel.

• **CHARACTERISTICS** The Connemara has emerged as a fixed type, retaining the hardiness inherited from its environment. Crosses to the Thoroughbred produce excellent competition horses with much pony hardiness and sense.

• *length from hips to hocks contributes to speed and jumping ability*

• *distinctive head is invariably fine and neat, never becoming heavy, and reveals Arab and Thoroughbred blood*

Colours All solid, including Dun	Uses Saddle

HEIGHT
Stands between 13 and 14.2hh.

length of rein is exceptional

excellent sloping shoulders of a pronounced riding type

bone measurement is often a surprising 18–20cm (7–8in)

INFLUENCES

SPANISH
Passed on Barb qualities as well as Sorraia vigour and hardiness.

WELSH D
The source of the breed's robust constitution and marked strength.

THOROUGHBRED
Transmitted its scope, courage, speed, and improved action.

Environment Mountain, Moor	Origin Prehistoric	Blood Warm

Welsh Mountain Pony

The Welsh Mountain Pony (Section A in the Welsh Pony and Cob Society Stud Book, opened in 1902) is probably the most numerous of the British mountain and moorland breeds. It is the base from which the Welsh Pony (Section B) and the two divisions of Welsh Cobs (Sections C and D) evolved.

• **BREEDING** Indigenous ponies populated the Welsh hills long before the Roman occupation of Britain. The Romans introduced eastern blood, and eastern influence continued until the birth of the breed's patriarch, Dyoll Starlight, in 1894.

• **CHARACTERISTICS** The Welsh Mountain Pony is recognized as being the most beautiful of the pony breeds. As well as this beauty, it retains all the hardiness and hereditary soundness derived from its early environment on the wild Welsh uplands.

INFLUENCES

ARAB
Gave quality, kind temperament, and sound physique and constitution.

BARB
Transmitted fire, toughness, powers of endurance, and marked stamina.

THOROUGHBRED
Noted for its speed and courage, its presence improved scope and action.

• *beautiful head clearly reveals powerful eastern influence*

HEIGHT
Stands around 12hh.

• *body is notably compact, with great depth through the girth*

UK: WALES

Colours All solid	Uses Saddle, Harness

Environment Mountain, Moor	Origin Prehistoric	Blood Warm

WELSH PONY

The Welsh Pony (Section B) is described as a riding pony that retains the character and temperament of the Welsh Mountain Pony.

• **BREEDING** Early Section B ponies were often the result of crossings between small Welsh Cobs and Welsh Mountain Ponies. The foundation of the modern pony is attributed to Tan-y-Bwlch Berwyn, foaled in 1924, by the Arab (or Barb) stallion Sahara. Berwyn's son, Berwynfa, founded the Coed Coch Section B herd. Other notable lines have descended from the Arab sires, Skowronek and Raseem.

• **CHARACTERISTICS** The Section B pony is an elegant, quality pony. More versatile than the Mountain Pony because of its larger size, it excels in the competitive disciplines and jumps well. Its action is longer and lower than that of the Mountain Pony.

INFLUENCES

ARAB
Gave quality, kind temperament, and sound physique and constitution.

BARB
Transmitted fire, toughness, powers of endurance, and marked stamina.

THOROUGHBRED
Noted for its speed and courage, its presence improved scope and action.

HEIGHT
Stands around 13.2hh.

UK: WALES

• *excellent depth of girth, sometimes called "Welsh bread basket"*

noticeably longer • *proportions than those of the Welsh Mountain Pony*

Colours All solid	Uses Saddle, Harness

Environment Mountain, Moor	Origin 12th century	Blood Warm

WELSH PONY OF COB TYPE

The smaller of the two Welsh Cobs is that belonging to
Section C in the stud book, where it is referred to as "the
Welsh Pony of Cob Type". These small cobs were often
called "farm ponies". They were used for every sort of
work on the Welsh hill farms, as well as being employed
extensively in the North Wales slate mines during the 19th
century. After the Second World War, when the type seemed
in danger of disappearing, a new section (Section C) was
opened in the stud book to preserve this essentially Welsh
working pony. Today, the Section C ponies are still used
very successfully in harness, as they were in the past. They
are also an excellent choice for trekking and trail riding.
Naturally courageous and good jumpers, they make
wonderful hunting ponies for young people and light adults.
• **BREEDING** In the early days, the cob-type pony was
usually the progeny of a Welsh Mountain mare and a small
cob stallion. The stallions were, in effect, slightly larger,
heavier, and more thick-set versions of the Welsh
Mountain Pony. In recent years, the most significant
Section C stallions have had a strong background
of Mountain Pony, their sires being Section A
stallions, like the prolific and very successful Coed
Coch Madog, the sire of both Lyn Cwmcoed and
Synod William. Increasingly, however, the
Welsh Pony of Cob Type is being produced
by the mating of parents, both of whom are
registered in Section C of the stud book.
• **CHARACTERISTICS** The Section C Cob
has all the attributes of the Welsh Mountain
Pony. It is tough, hardy, constitutionally
sound, and has wonderfully made limbs and
feet. Able to live out all the year round, it
is easy to manage and economical to keep.

UK: WALES

*overall outline
is compact and
indicative of strength* •

INFLUENCES

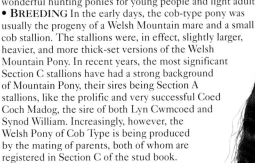

WELSH A
Imparted the
essential Welsh
character to the
Welsh Section C.

WELSH COB
Responsible for
the increase in
size required in
the "farm pony".

Colours All solid	Uses Saddle, Harness

HEIGHT
Stands around 13.2hh.

thick-set neck,
carried high
and arched

arresting head
reflects the Welsh
Mountain Pony

despite low withers,
shoulders are long
and action is strong
and vigorous

strong limbs may
have fine, silky
feathering at heels

feet are strong
with hard horn

| Environment Cool temperate | Origin Pre-Ice Age | Blood Warm |

BARDIGIANO

Outside of Britain, there are few European pony breeds of note in the modern context. Italy's Bardigiano, although little known and not enjoying the benefit of the "closed" stud books, is a possible exception, along with the obscure Asturçon pony, which exists in very small numbers in the mountainous regions of northern Spain.

• **BREEDING** The Bardigiano is a mountain breed from the northern Appenine region of Italy. Like the Asturçon, it resembles to a degree the oldest of the British native ponies, the Exmoor, and there is probably some common Celtic pony root stock. It is generally accepted, however, that the Bardigiano, while owing something to the heavier Italian mountain strains, has a pronounced connection with the Avelignese, an Italian breed that is related to the Haflinger. Indeed, the Avelignese has the same ancestors as the latter, and both descend from the extinct Avellinum-Haflinger. The Arab El Bedavi was the recognized founding stallion of the Haflinger and had considerable influence on the Avelignese. The oriental influence is apparent in the Bardigiano.

• **CHARACTERISTICS** This is a strong, well-made pony of considerable character. It is hardy, quick-moving, sure-footed, and ideally suited to any kind of mountain work.

ITALY: NORTHERN
APPENINE REGION

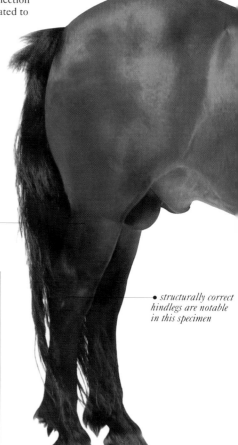

prominent
second thigh •

• *structurally correct
hindlegs are notable
in this specimen*

INFLUENCES

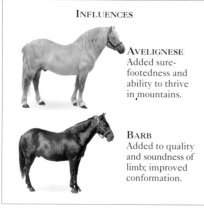

AVELIGNESE
Added sure-
footedness and
ability to thrive
in mountains.

BARB
Added to quality
and soundness of
limb; improved
conformation.

| Colours All solid | Uses Pack, Light Draught |

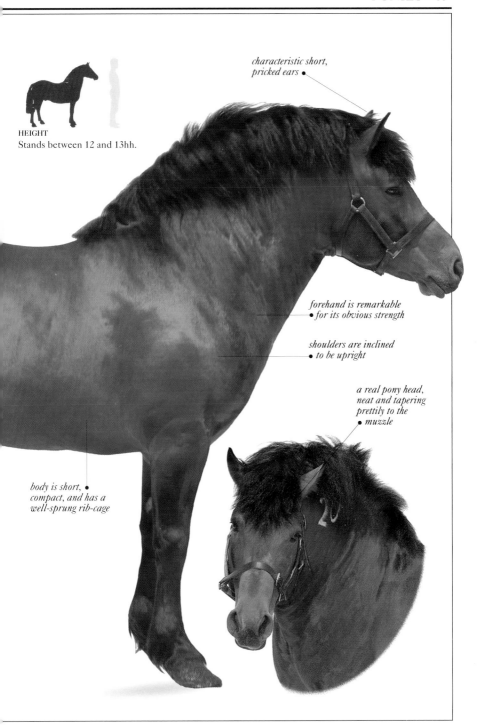

HEIGHT
Stands between 12 and 13hh.

characteristic short, pricked ears

forehand is remarkable for its obvious strength

shoulders are inclined to be upright

a real pony head, neat and tapering prettily to the muzzle

body is short, compact, and has a well-sprung rib-cage

Environment Hot temperate	Origin Pre-Ice Age	Blood Warm

SORRAIA

The first horses to be domesticated in Europe are thought to be those of the Iberian Peninsula. Today, descendants of those early equines, the "primitive" founding races, are still found in both Spain and Portugal. Among these are the Sorraia, in some specimens still bearing a remarkable resemblance in colour and conformation to the Tarpan, and the more refined Garrano or Minho, of the same root stock, with a habitat further to the north in the mountain valleys of Garrano do Minho and Traz dos Montes.

• **BREEDING** The Sorraia lived in the plains between the rivers Sor and Raia, and for some years the famous d'Andrade family kept a small herd in its natural state. It has to be assumed that this native base stock, once it had been subjected to the powerful North African Barb influence, contributed to the renowned Spanish horse, and via that pervasive blood to a variety of different breeds.

• **CHARACTERISTICS** For centuries, the Sorraia was used by local cowboys and for light agricultural work and, in times past, it could hardly have been considered a prepossessing specimen. Nonetheless, for all its heavy head and low-set tail, it retained all the primitive vigour of its wild ancestors.

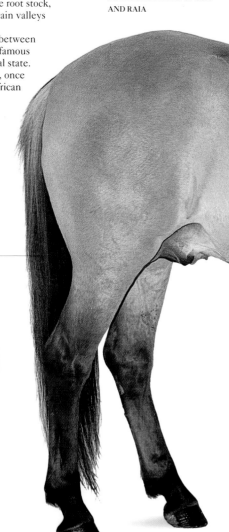

PORTUGAL: PLAINS OF SOR AND RAIA

low-set, usually black tail •

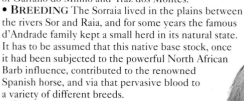

INFLUENCES

TARPAN
Primitive root stock provided constitutional soundness.

BARB
Improved movement, increased size, and added fiery character.

Colours Grey-dun	Uses Feral, Light Agricultural

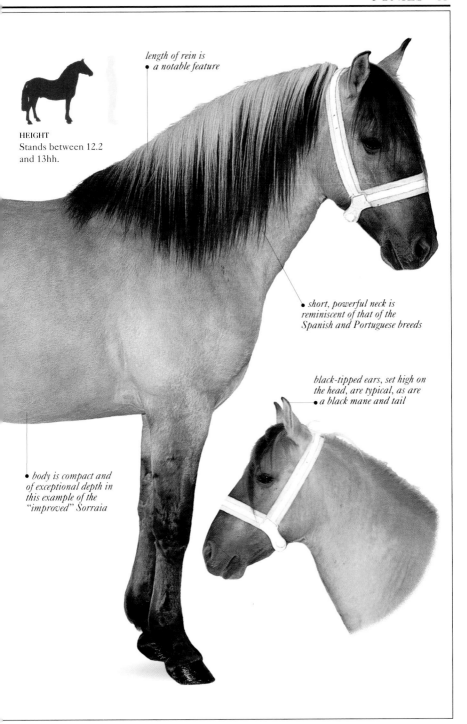

length of rein is a notable feature

HEIGHT
Stands between 12.2 and 13hh.

short, powerful neck is reminiscent of that of the Spanish and Portuguese breeds

black-tipped ears, set high on the head, are typical, as are a black mane and tail

body is compact and of exceptional depth in this example of the "improved" Sorraia

Environment Mediterranean	Origin Pre–Ice Age	Blood Warm

SKYRIAN HORSE

Skyros, in the Aegean Sea, has supported
ponies since ancient times. The ponies lived in
the mountains, being brought in to help with
the corn threshing. The modern pony, called
the Skyrian Horse by its breeders, has a
utilitarian role, but is also used for riding.

• **BREEDING** The proportions of the Skyrian
incline towards those of a horse, and it
resembles horses depicted in the statuary and
friezes of Ancient Greece. It is possible there
is a connection with the Thessalanian horse,
which would point towards Horse Type 4 as an
origin, although the coat pattern shows there
may be a relationship to the Tarpan.

• **CHARACTERISTICS** The Skyrian is
tough, hardy, good-tempered, willing and, in
relation to its size, it jumps well. It is straight
in the shoulders, usually cow-hocked, and
mean in the quarters. The coat is often marked
with an eel-stripe and zebra bars. The feet are
always black, a breed society requirement.

INFLUENCE

HORSE TYPE 4
Prototype Arab;
transmitted some
conformational
quality.

*neat head with
small, pointed ears* •

*narrow, sloping croup,
with quarters lacking
• in muscle*

*narrow body with •
generally upright
shoulders*

HEIGHT
Stands around 11hh.

GREECE: ISLAND
OF SKYROS

Colours Bay, Dun	Uses Saddle, Harness, Pack

Environment Mountain	Origin Pre–Ice Age	Blood Warm

PINDOS PONY

The Pindos Pony, larger than the Skyrian, comes from the mountainous areas of Thessaly and Epirus, the traditional horse lands of Ancient Greece. It is used as a sure-footed pack pony, in agricultural pursuits and forestry, and as a riding and driving pony. Pindos mares are often used for breeding mules.

• **BREEDING** The Pindos, in all probability, descends directly from the Thessalanian. Over the centuries, it is also likely to have been influenced by the ancient Peloponnese, Arcadian, and Epidaurian breeds.

• **CHARACTERISTICS** The Pindos Pony is tough, enduring, and can survive on minimal forage. The tail is set high (indicating Horse Type 4 in its ancestry), but the quarters are poor, with little second thigh. The feet are hard, narrow, and boxy, and are rarely, if ever, shod. The Pindos is noted for its stamina but has the reputation of being very stubborn.

INFLUENCE

HORSE TYPE 4
Prototype Arab; transmitted some conformational quality.

head is inclined to be long, but shows a certain quality •

back is strong in comparison to quarters; shoulders less upright than might be expected •

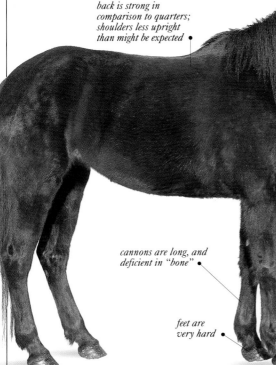

cannons are long, and deficient in "bone" •

feet are very hard •

HEIGHT
Stands around 13hh.

GREECE : THESSALONIKA

Colours Bay, Black, Brown	Uses Saddle, Harness, Pack

Environment Desert	Origin Prehistoric	Blood Hot

CASPIAN

The Caspian pony, in fact a miniature horse, may be the most ancient breed in existence and could, it is suggested, be the ancestor of the Arab. Caspians were "discovered" by Mrs Louise L. Firouz at Amol on the Caspian littoral, Iran, in 1965, and there are now Caspian societies in Britain, Australia, New Zealand, and the USA.

MIDDLE EAST: ARABIAN PENINSULA

• **BREEDING** The breed would seem to be the direct descendant of Horse Type 4 (see pp.14–15), described as the prototype Arab, which had its habitat in western Asia. Egyptian and Persian artefacts of the pre-Christian era (from 1,200–500BC) depict similar small horses of great refinement.

• **CHARACTERISTICS** The Caspian differs in physical character from other equines. For instance, there is a difference in the shape of the scapula and the formation of the parietal bones of the head. Although small, the Caspian is fast enough to keep up with much larger horses, and it is also an exceptional jumper.

• *body is narrow and light, with the proportions and length that are associated with speed*

feet are small, oval-shaped, very hard and strong, and not subject to disease •

Colours Bay, Chestnut	Uses Saddle, Harness

ears are not
longer than
11.5cm (4½in)

long, arched neck

withers are
relatively high
and sharp

head is short
and covered in
fine, thin skin

shoulders are
formed like those of a
horse and produce a
long, low stride

body, although deep,
is narrow in build and
thus very suitable for
young riders

HEIGHT
Stands between 10 and 12hh.

slim limbs, with little or
no feathering, are said
to have dense bone

INFLUENCE

HORSE TYPE 4
As the prototype
Arab, this horse
passed on many
Arab traits.

Environment Steppe-Savanna	Origin Pre-Ice Age	Blood Warm

BASHKIR

The Bashkir of the Russian steppe is an enormously tough pony. It is bred under state supervision as a pack, draught, and saddle animal, as well as for meat and milk. A mare may give up to 1,600 litres (350 gallons) during a lactation period which lasts seven to eight months. There are about 1,000 Bashkirs (called "Bashkir Curly" because of the curly coat) in the United States. They are reputed to have been popular with the native Americans of the north-western states.

• **BREEDING** The Bashkir, or Bashkirsky, evolved centuries ago around the southern foothills of the Urals in Bashkiria. Two types of Bashkir have since developed in the Russian Federation: a mountain pony and a steppe pony, the latter being more predominantly of harness type.

• **CHARACTERISTICS** Bashkirs are kept outside in herds, often in sub-zero temperatures, and are able to fend for themselves and find food in deep snow. This predominantly chestnut-coloured pony grows a thick, curly winter coat which can be spun to make cloth. Among the hardiest breeds, it can work hard without supplementary feed. A pair of Bashkirs is reputed to be able to pull a sleigh 120–140km (75–87 miles) in 24 hours, without being fed.

NORTHERN EURASIA:
RUSSIAN FEDERATION

feet are hard and need no shoes, which are unknown
• *on the steppe*

HEIGHT
Stands around 14hh.

INFLUENCES

TARPAN
A primitive influence which gave added freedom of action.

PRZEWALSKI'S HORSE
The dominant primitive gene; gave stamina.

Colours Chestnut, Bay	Uses Pack, Draught

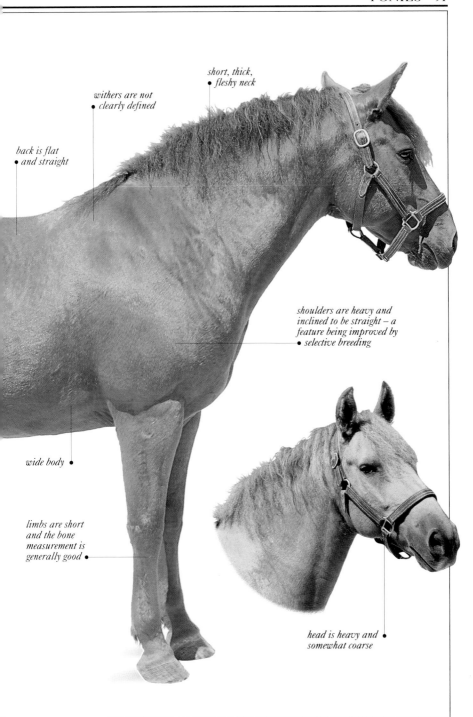

short, thick,
• fleshy neck

withers are not
• clearly defined

back is flat
• and straight

shoulders are heavy and
inclined to be straight – a
feature being improved by
• selective breeding

wide body •

limbs are short
and the bone
measurement is
generally good •

head is heavy and •
somewhat coarse

Environment Temperate grassland	Origin 20th century	Blood Warm

AUSTRALIAN PONY

The Australian Pony is now a breed in its own right. It is controlled by the Australian Pony Stud Book Society, a body formed in 1929 to produce children's riding ponies. The Association lays down a detailed standard of conformation.

• **BREEDING** The Australian Pony has evolved from an assortment of equine breeds and types, imported initially by the early settlers. The first pony import to arrive in Australia was in 1803, but by 1920 a pony of distinctive type had been established. Welsh Mountain Ponies provided much of the breeding stock, along with Shetland blood, as well as that of the Hackney, and also infusions of Arab and Thoroughbred.

• **CHARACTERISTICS** The Australian pony resembles the Welsh Mountain Pony more closely than any other breed. It is compact, well built, and strong, and is essentially a quality pony of correct conformation and very good free action. There is a pronounced pony character, very evident in the neat, refined head and the large eyes. It is considered to have the best of temperaments and has more in common with the British native ponies than with the specialized riding pony.

AUSTRALIA

quarters are generous and well-shaped •

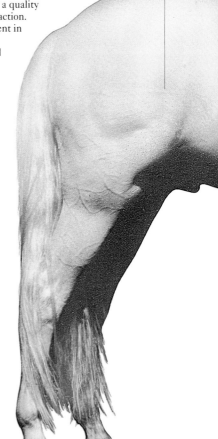

INFLUENCES

WELSH A
A dominant influence which contributed to pony character.

SHETLAND
Gave inherent hardiness and constitutional strength.

THOROUGHBRED
Improved action; provided extra scope and jumping ability.

HACKNEY
Added to brilliance of action; gave a particular spirit.

Colours All solid	Uses Saddle

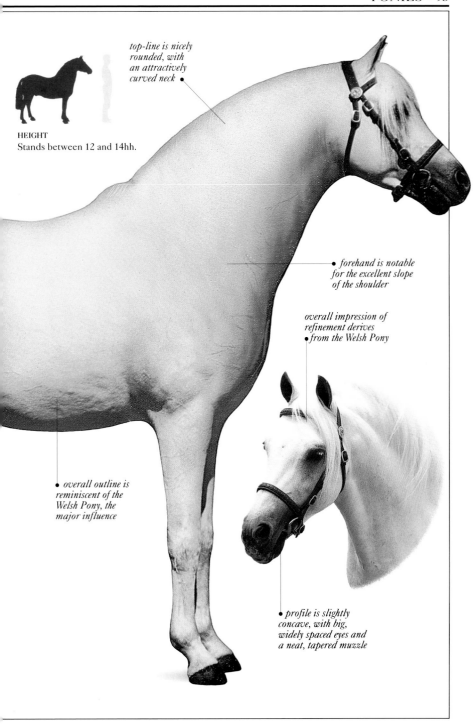

top-line is nicely
rounded, with
an attractively
curved neck •

HEIGHT
Stands between 12 and 14hh.

• forehand is notable
for the excellent slope
of the shoulder

overall impression of
refinement derives
• from the Welsh Pony

• overall outline is
reminiscent of the
Welsh Pony, the
major influence

• profile is slightly
concave, with big,
widely spaced eyes and
a neat, tapered muzzle

Environment Temperate, Controlled	Origin 20th century	Blood Warm

AMERICAN SHETLAND

The American Shetland is the most popular pony in North America. The first import from the Shetland Islands, off the coast of Scotland, was made in 1885. An American Shetland Pony Club was formed in 1888, but the American Shetland is an invented breed, bearing no resemblance to the distinctive, hardy Island pony.

• **BREEDING** America's new-look Shetland was created by crossing finer-built examples of the Island pony with Hackney Ponies, the subsequent progeny being given a particular character by further outcrossings to small Arabs and Thoroughbreds. Although the ponies do not retain the pure Shetland's legendary native hardiness and constitution, they are versatile. Primarily a show harness pony, it also races in harness, and those termed hunter-types are shown and jumped under saddle.

• **CHARACTERISTICS** The intelligent and good-natured American Shetland resembles the Hackney in outline and conformation. Narrower than the true Shetland Pony, it has greater length in the proportions. Although the relatively long head lacks pony character, the impression is of considerable refinement.

USA

broad, strong loins •

hair of tail and • mane is long and thick

stance is stretched • and typical of the harness pony

Colours All solid	Uses Harness

set of neck resembles
that of the Hackney •

• *relatively
long ears*

HEIGHT
Stands up to 11.2hh.

*long head and •
straight profile
show little pony
character*

• *frame is long and
narrow in relation
to overall size*

*characteristic long,
slim limbs, with
some tendency to
long cannons* •

INFLUENCES

HACKNEY
Imparted its
spirit and
spectacular
trotting action.

SHETLAND
The base stock
ensured small
stature and
soundness.

Environment Cool temperate	Origin 20th century	Blood Warm

ROCKY MOUNTAIN PONY

The American Rocky Mountain Pony is probably the latest
addition to the world's horse population. The registry was
opened as recently as 1986, but since then there has been a
steady development of this distinctive and attractive animal.
Further recognition of the Rocky Mountain Pony has been
given by the inclusion of a good specimen in the Breeds'
Barn at the Kentucky Horse Park in Lexington, USA.

USA: ROCKY MOUNTAINS

• **BREEDING** Visually, it is not difficult to see the connection
between the Rocky Mountain Pony and the Spanish imports
of early American history. However, credit for the development
of the Rocky Mountain belongs to Sam Tuttle of Stout Springs,
Kentucky, who held the riding concession at Natural Bridge
State Park. Tuttle's stallion, Old Tobe, was a favourite with
the riders because of his smooth and sure-footed lateral
gait (the amble or pace). He was a prepotent, prolific
sire who became the patriarch of a distinctive
group of horses which inherited his
conformation, action, and temperament.
• **CHARACTERISTICS** The gait and the unusual
colouring are the principal features of the Rocky
Mountain Pony. It ambles smoothly on rough
ground at about 11km/h (7mph), and can reach
speeds of 25km/h (16mph) for shorter distances
on the flat. The most prized coat-colouring is the
unusual rich chocolate shade accompanied by a
flaxen mane and tail. The breed is hardy and
able to tolerate severe mountain winters.

*full, flaxen tail
complements the rich
chocolate coat* •

HEIGHT
Stands between 14.2
and 15hh.

*pony is very sure-
footed and feet are
• hard and strong*

INFLUENCE

SPANISH
The influence
is evident in
the gait, colour,
and outline.

Colours Chocolate	Uses Saddle

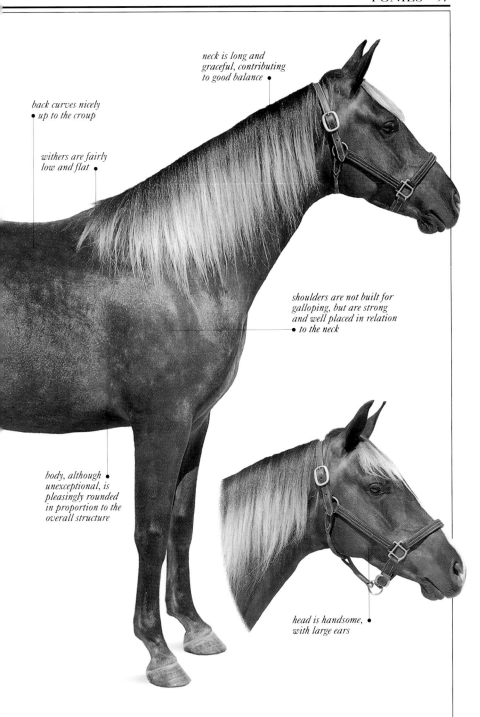

neck is long and
graceful, contributing
to good balance •

back curves nicely
• up to the croup

withers are fairly
low and flat •

shoulders are not built for
galloping, but are strong
and well placed in relation
• to the neck

body, although •
unexceptional, is
pleasingly rounded
in proportion to the
overall structure

head is handsome, •
with large ears

| Environment Cool temperate | Origin 16th century | Blood Warm |

CHINCOTEAGUE/ASSATEAGUE

Ponies living in the islands of Chincoteague and Assateague, off the coast of Virginia, USA, are some of the last wild stock in the world. Most of the 200 or so ponies live on Assateague, a national park, separated from the mainland by dramatic storms in 1933. Each year the Assateague ponies are rounded up and swum over the channel to Chincoteague, where the young stock are sold. The profits are used to manage the herds.

• **BREEDING** The ponies derive from stock that strayed or were abandoned in early colonial times, and which originated from the Spanish and North African imports. One story suggests that a ship carrying Barb horses from North Africa to Peru was wrecked, the horses swam ashore, and they have lived there ever since. But there is no evidence to support this.

• **CHARACTERISTICS** Although the ponies were improved by Pinto, Shetland, and Welsh pony blood, they would be regarded in European terms as degenerate in character, exhibiting the failings of scrub stock.

INFLUENCES

SPANISH Its inherent qualities were diluted by the harsh habitat.

withers are inclined to be lumpy and • shoulders heavy

HEIGHT
Stands around 12hh.

short, • compact body

usually light • feather on heels

USA: CHINCOTEAGUE AND ASSATEAGUE, VIRGINIA

| Colours All | Uses Feral, Saddle |

Environment Cool temperate	Origin 16th century	Blood Warm

SABLE ISLAND

Sable Island off Nova Scotia, Canada, is a
barren land, resembling a sandbank. For some
400 years it has supported herds of semi-wild
ponies, which are named after the island.
• **BREEDING** The present stock originated in
French horses believed to be of predominantly
Norman ancestry, which were probably brought
to the island by a Boston Huguenot in 1739.
• **CHARACTERISTICS** Although the ponies
are hardy and tough, their conformation is only
moderate. The
head is large, and
the quarters are
usually weak. The
ponies are said
to be docile and
easily managed
if they are trained
while still young.

CANADA: SABLE ISLAND,
OFF NOVA SCOTIA

INFLUENCE

NORMAN
Influenced the
overall size and
character of this
semi-wild breed.

HEIGHT
Stands between 14
and 15hh.

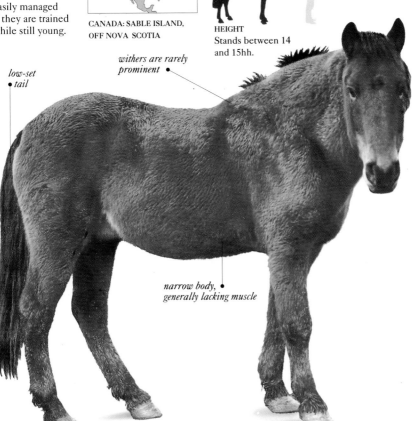

low-set
• *tail*

withers are rarely
prominent •

narrow body, •
generally lacking muscle

Colours Most solid	Uses Feral, Saddle

Environment Desert, Savanna	Origin 16th century	Blood Warm

GALICENO

The Galiceno pony of Mexico is another example of the Spanish legacy in the Americas. Since the 1950s, the Galiceno has spread northwards into the USA, being officially recognized as a breed in 1958. It is regarded as an ideal "in-between" mount for young riders who are making the transition from ponies to horses.

MEXICO

• **BREEDING** The Galiceno originated in Galicia in north-west Spain and takes its name from that area. Throughout Europe, from the earliest times, Galicia was famed for its smooth-gaited horses. The modern Galiceno is still distinguished by the swift running-walk that was so much prized in Elizabethan England. The ancestors of these small horses would have been among those brought by the Spaniards from Hispaniola in the 16th century, and those horses, in turn, are likely to have been descendants of the indigenous Sorraias and Garranos (the same equine under different names) of the Iberian Peninsula.

• **CHARACTERISTICS** The tough and hardy Galiceno is said to be tractable, intelligent, and versatile. The pony's natural agility and speed ensure its popularity as a ranch and competition pony. It is also used in harness and as an everyday means of transport.

fine head has a distinctive • character

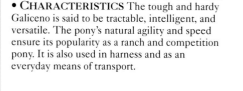

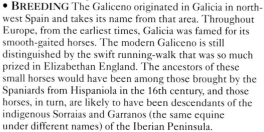

• intelligent eyes are large and widely spaced

Colours All solid	Uses Saddle, Harness

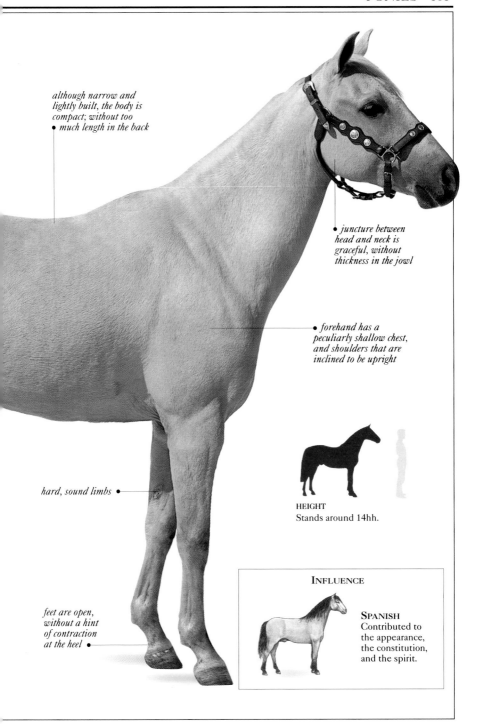

although narrow and
lightly built, the body is
compact; without too
• much length in the back

• juncture between
head and neck is
graceful, without
thickness in the jowl

• forehand has a
peculiarly shallow chest,
and shoulders that are
inclined to be upright

hard, sound limbs •

HEIGHT
Stands around 14hh.

feet are open,
without a hint
of contraction
at the heel •

INFLUENCE

SPANISH
Contributed to
the appearance,
the constitution,
and the spirit.

Environment Temperate, Controlled	Origin 20th century	Blood Warm

FALABELLA

The natural reasons for small stature in equines are environmental – severe climatic conditions combined with low feed availability. However, it is possible to breed miniatures or, conversely, very large horses deliberately. Miniature horses have been bred as pets and for their curiosity value throughout history. Today, the best-known example is the Falabella, claimed to be a miniature horse, rather than a pony, on account of its proportions and character.

• **BREEDING** The Falabella takes its name from the Falabella family, who developed the breed at the Recreo de Roca Ranch, outside Buenos Aires, Argentina. They crossed the smallest Shetlands with a very small Thoroughbred, thereafter deliberately breeding down by crossing the smallest animals and practising close in-breeding. The aim was to produce a near-perfect equine specimen in miniature, but in-breeding often results in conformational weaknesses and a loss of vigour. It is said that Falabellas can be used in harness, but they are considered unsuitable for riding. One of the smallest miniatures bred was a mare called Sugar Dumpling, belonging to Smith McCoy of Roderfield, West Virginia, USA. She was only 51cm (20in) high and weighed 13.6kg (30lb).

• **CHARACTERISTICS** Conformational defects, such as weak hocks, crooked limbs, and heavy heads, are fairly common in miniature stock. However, the best exhibit many of the qualities of a good Shetland. As pets, Falabellas are said to be friendly and intelligent, and some attractive coat colours occur in the breed, including spot patterns.

ARGENTINA: BUENOS AIRES

quarters have a tendency to drop away, • with tail set low

hocks are sometimes • weak and not straight

HEIGHT
Stands up to 7hh.

INFLUENCE

SHETLAND
The base was very small Shetlands, crossed with small Thoroughbreds.

Colours All, including part	Uses Novelty

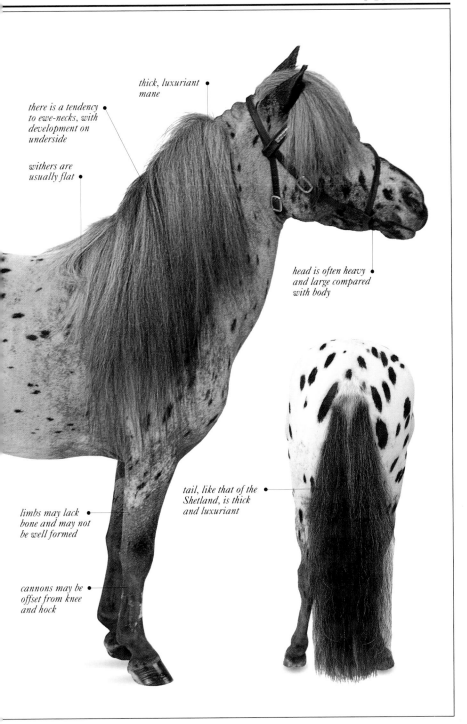

thick, luxuriant mane

there is a tendency to ewe-necks, with development on underside

withers are usually flat

head is often heavy and large compared with body

limbs may lack bone and may not be well formed

tail, like that of the Shetland, is thick and luxuriant

cannons may be offset from knee and hock

HORSES

Environment Cool temperate	Origin 19th century	Blood Warm

DØLE GUDBRANDSDAL

Comprising nearly half of the Norwegian horse population, the Døle Gudbrandsdal resembles British Dales and Fell ponies. All three derive from the same prehistoric wild stock.

• **BREEDING** Bred in the great central valley of Gudbrandsdal, Norway, the horses were used in pack and in agriculture. The breed is noted for its speed at the trot and, although the heavier, draught-type was retained, a lighter Døle Trotter was developed for harness racing. The Thoroughbred stallion, Odin, imported in 1834, had the most significant influence on the Trotter. State breeding centres were established in 1962, and the stallions are performance-tested over 1,000m (1,094yd) with a three-minute time limit.

• **CHARACTERISTICS** The Døle Gudbrandsdal is hardy, and very powerful in relation to its size.

NORWAY: GUDBRANDSDAL VALLEY

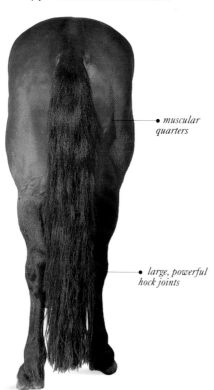

• *muscular quarters*

• *large, powerful hock joints*

Colours Black, Brown	Uses Light Draught

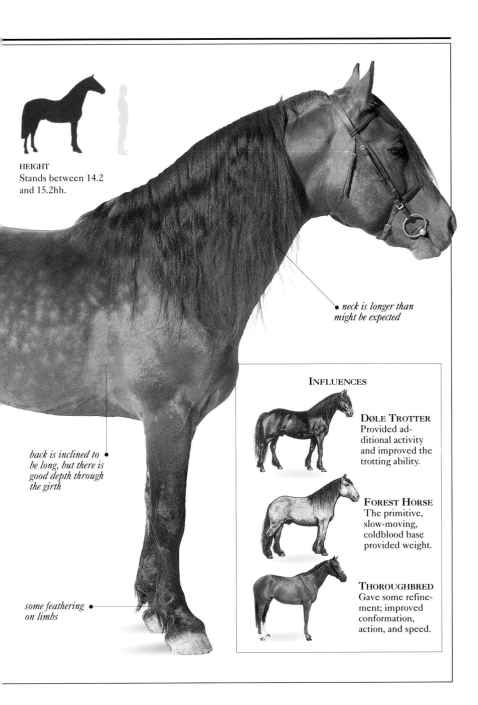

HEIGHT
Stands between 14.2
and 15.2hh.

*neck is longer than
might be expected*

*back is inclined to
be long, but there is
good depth through
the girth*

*some feathering
on limbs*

INFLUENCES

DØLE TROTTER
Provided additional activity
and improved the
trotting ability.

FOREST HORSE
The primitive,
slow-moving,
coldblood base
provided weight.

THOROUGHBRED
Gave some refinement; improved
conformation,
action, and speed.

Environment Taiga	Origin Pre-Ice Age	Blood Cold

FINNISH HORSE

In times past there were two Finnish breeds, the Finnish
Draught and the Finnish Universal, both of which were
bred for performance rather than for their appearance.
The Draught horse, the heavier of the two, was a sturdy,
powerfully built animal, fairly common in its appearance
but with quick, active paces. The lighter Universal was a
general-purpose animal which could be ridden, used for
light transport and, importantly, for harness racing. Since
the 1970s, emphasis has shifted towards the lighter
utility horse, although there is still a need for horses in
agriculture and, particularly, in the forest industry.
• **BREEDING** The Finnish Horse is probably a
descendant of the ancient breeds of both heavy and
light horses in Europe, crossed with both cold- and
warmblood breeds. A stud book was opened in
1907, for both the heavier and lighter types, and
rigorous performance testing was instituted.
• **CHARACTERISTICS** The even-tempered
Finnish Horse, despite its relatively small frame,
has the draught power of a heavy horse combined
with the speed, character, and agility of the light
horse breeds. It is long-lived, very enduring, and
possessed of remarkable stamina. Needless
to say, the breed is noted for its excellent
constitution. The slope of the quarters from the
croup, combined with some length in the body,
is characteristic of the harness racing horse,
and is a reflection of the shift in emphasis
in the breeding of the Finnish Horse.

FINLAND

*slope of the quarters from the
croup is characteristic of the
• harness racing horse*

*legs are clean,
with little or no
• feathering at heels*

INFLUENCES

FINNISH PONY
Native ponies
provided a hardy,
enduring base
for outcrosses.

OLDENBURG
Fixed the char-
acter and gave
additional size
and action.

Colours All	Uses Light Draught

HEIGHT
Stands around 15.2hh.

outline is characterised by a straight, harness-type back

shoulders are strong and more suited to harness work than to riding

nbs are niformly rrect

head is inclined to plainness, but is otherwise honest and workmanlike, reflecting the breed's pleasant disposition

Environment Temperate, Controlled	Origin 17th century	Blood Warm

SWEDISH WARMBLOOD

The Swedish Warmblood was bred originally as a cavalry horse of above average quality. More recently, breeders have concentrated on producing a competition horse that is capable of performing internationally in the three principal mounted disciplines – jumping, dressage, and eventing.
• **BREEDING** The breed descends from Spanish, oriental, and Friesian stallions imported some 300 years ago, and is the result of carefully supervised breeding policies that go back to that time. The crossing of these horses with local stock at the great studs of Stromsholm (founded 1621) and Flyinge (founded 1658) provided a base for the use of Trakehners, Hanoverians, Arabs, and Thoroughbreds. Stock is rigorously tested and exports are worldwide.
• **CHARACTERISTICS** The Swedish Warmblood is a big, imposing horse. It is sound, of good conformation, and has a sensible temperament, which makes it particularly suitable for dressage. Otherwise it is in demand for jumping, eventing, and driving.

SWEDEN

• *short, strong limbs*

• *sound feet*

INFLUENCES

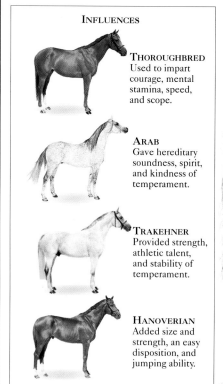

THOROUGHBRED
Used to impart courage, mental stamina, speed, and scope.

ARAB
Gave hereditary soundness, spirit, and kindness of temperament.

TRAKEHNER
Provided strength, athletic talent, and stability of temperament.

HANOVERIAN
Added size and strength, an easy disposition, and jumping ability.

Colours All solid	Uses Saddle

HEIGHT
Stands around 16.2hh.

strong shoulders allow good movement

compact body with a deep enough girth and well-sprung ribs

good joints

head is pleasant and "hunter-like", with a sensible expression

Environment Cool temperate	Origin 16th century	Blood Warm

FREDERIKSBORG

In the 16th century, Denmark was a principal source for elegant, active saddle horses and quality military chargers. These horses, called Frederiksborgs, were the product of a stud founded by King Frederik II in 1562. Pluto, a white horse and founder of the Lipizzaner line that carries his name, was a Frederiksborg, foaled at the Royal Danish Court Stud in 1765.

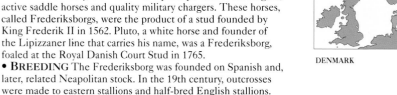

DENMARK

• **BREEDING** The Frederiksborg was founded on Spanish and, later, related Neapolitan stock. In the 19th century, outcrosses were made to eastern stallions and half-bred English stallions. The result was an impressive, lively riding horse with a vigorous action. The breed was also used extensively to improve other stock, including the Jutland (see pp.216–217). Heavy exportation seriously depleted the old stock and, in 1839, the Stud turned to producing Thoroughbred-type animals and the original breed almost disappeared. For a while, private individuals continued to raise Frederiksborgs as smart carriage horses but, as the demand for riding horses grew, Thoroughbreds were used increasingly. It is unlikely that many of the old-type Frederiksborgs survive.

• **CHARACTERISTICS** Although a riding horse, the Frederiksborg always retained a high carriage action described as being "strong and sweeping".

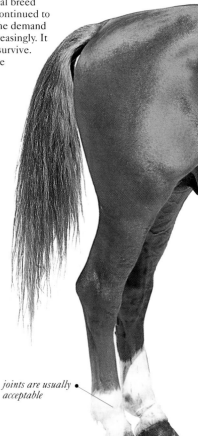

joints are usually acceptable

• head has an intelligent expression but is otherwise plain and plebeian

Colours Chestnut	Uses Saddle

neck is short and
upright, and
characteristic of the
carriage horse •

withers are flat, and
overall the whole
forehand is suited
to use in harness •

front is short and
shoulders are upright,
which results in a
• strong, high action

body is relatively •
long and girth is
acceptable, but horse
is "on the leg"

HEIGHT
Stands around 15.3hh.

feet are strong and
well shaped •

INFLUENCE

SPANISH
The source of
great elegance,
showy action, and
imposing presence.

Environment Cool temperate	Origin 19th century	Blood Warm

KNABSTRUP

Spotted coat patterns were evident in the cave drawings
of Cro-Magnon man 30,000 years ago, and such horses were
frequently much revered in the ancient world. Denmark's
Knabstrup, however, is of more recent origin, the breed
being founded on a Spanish mare in 1808. Spotted strains
occurred in Spanish horses well into the 19th century.

DENMARK

• **BREEDING** The Knabstrup foundation mare was
Flaebehoppen, a Spanish mare bought by Judge Lunn
from a butcher named Flaebe (*Flaebehoppen* means Flaebe's
horse). Lunn bred her to Frederiksborgs
and she founded a line of spotted horses,
largely through her grandson Mikkel.
• **CHARACTERISTICS** The old
Knabstrups were tough, rawboned horses.
They were intelligent, tractable, and
quick to learn. They deteriorated as a
result of injudicious breeding for
colour, and now hardly exist. The
modern type, closer in character to
the Appaloosa, is a quality animal
of some substance and with a
greater range of colours.

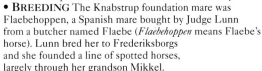

*spotted colouring
extends down the legs,
which are usually
conformationally
• correct*

*hooves marked by
vertical stripes are
characteristic of all
• spotted horses*

*• head reflects the
traditional kindliness
and intelligence of the
spotted horse strains*

Colours Spotted	Uses Saddle

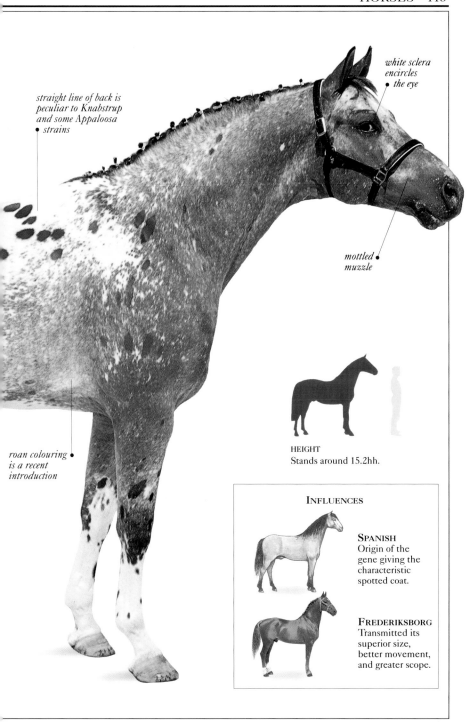

straight line of back is peculiar to Knabstrup and some Appaloosa • *strains*

white sclera encircles • *the eye*

mottled • *muzzle*

roan colouring • *is a recent introduction*

HEIGHT
Stands around 15.2hh.

INFLUENCES

SPANISH
Origin of the gene giving the characteristic spotted coat.

FREDERIKSBORG
Transmitted its superior size, better movement, and greater scope.

Environment Temperate, Controlled	Origin 20th century	Blood Warm

DANISH WARMBLOOD

One of the more recent of the European, purpose-bred competition horses is the Danish Warmblood, whose stud book was not opened until the 1960s. In a relatively short space of time, however, Danish breeders have succeeded in producing a competition horse of superior quality and more versatility than many of the European breeds.

DENMARK

• **BREEDING** Denmark has an ancient equestrian tradition. Cistercian monks in 14th-century Holstein (a Danish Duchy until 1864) crossed the best Spanish stock with big north German mares. One of the results was Denmark's Frederiksborg. The Danish Warmblood was founded on Frederiksborg stock, crossed with the Thoroughbred. The resultant local mares were put to Anglo-Norman (virtually Selle Français) stallions, Thoroughbreds, and Trakehners. The mix was adjusted to produce a sound horse of excellent conformation, relatively fixed in type, and with scope and galloping ability. The Hanoverian influence is absent in the Danish Warmblood, which may account for its distinctive character compared to other warmbloods.

• **CHARACTERISTICS** The best Danish horses have a Thoroughbred outline that is combined with substance, strength, and good limbs. They are courageous and spirited, have excellent temperaments, and good, free action. They are brilliant dressage horses and first-class performers across country.

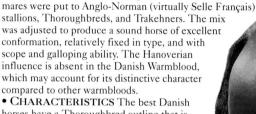

INFLUENCES

FREDERIKSBORG The base stock, a showy carriage and riding horse of some elegance.

TRAKEHNER Used for its fixed type, correct conformation, and proven ability.

THOROUGHBRED An upgrading influence; gave quality, speed, and improved action.

shape of foot and corresponding slope of pastern are
• *entirely correct*

Colours All solid	Uses Saddle

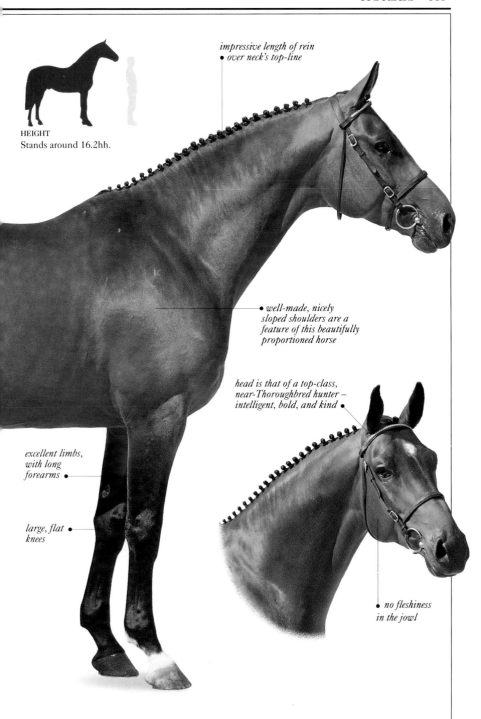

impressive length of rein
over neck's top-line

HEIGHT
Stands around 16.2hh.

well-made, nicely
sloped shoulders are a
feature of this beautifully
proportioned horse

head is that of a top-class,
near-Thoroughbred hunter –
intelligent, bold, and kind

excellent limbs,
with long
forearms

large, flat
knees

no fleshiness
in the jowl

Environment Cool temperate	Origin Pre-Christian	Blood Cold

FRIESIAN

The black Friesian is a coldblood horse of ancient origin. In
its own land it arouses much the same admiration, and even
adulation, as that given to the massive Shire horse in Britain.
Although it is ridden and displays great agility under saddle,
the modern Friesian excels as an impressive, free-moving
harness horse. Its temperament and appearance made it
popular with circus trainers, and its presence and colour
ensured a market for it in the funeral business.

• **BREEDING** The Friesian, which descends from the
"primitive" Forest Horse of Europe, is bred principally in
Friesland on the northern Netherlands coast. It carried the
German and Friesian Knights to the Crusades, and was used
as an all-purpose warhorse. At first it was improved by
crossings with oriental horses, and thereafter, up to the
Netherlands becoming independent of Spain in 1609,
it was much influenced by the pervading Spanish
blood. As the flank-guard of the Roman legions,
Friesian horses played a role in the development
of the British Dales and Fell ponies. Thereafter,
through the Old English Black, they influenced
the Shire. Both the Oldenburg and the Døle
Gudbrandsdal have strong Friesian connections.

• **CHARACTERISTICS** The Friesian is noted
for its lovable character and easy temperament.
Constitutionally, it is robust and it can
be kept very economically.

NETHERLANDS: FRIESLAND

*luxuriant
feathering
grows on
• lower limbs*

*hooves are of
blue horn and
• very hard*

INFLUENCES

SPANISH
Much improved
the carriage and
added quality
and refinement.

BARB
Transmitted its
great stamina,
fiery character,
and endurance.

FOREST HORSE
Passed on the
typical, primitive,
heavy base stock
characteristics.

Colours Black	Uses Harness

HEIGHT
Stands at 15hh or more.

neck is arched and carried proudly

strong shoulders are characteristic

thick, full mane

head is long, ears are short, and expression is alert and kindly

Environment Cool temperate	Origin 19th century	Blood Warm

GELDERLANDER

Of the two principal components in the make-up of the
Dutch Warmblood, the Groningen and the Gelderlander,
the latter is the more attractive. The marketwise breeders
of Holland's Gelder province created it to fulfil their own
needs, and at the same time to be attractive to their
neighbours and remain a distinctive type.

NETHERLANDS: GELDER
PROVINCE

• **BREEDING** About a century ago, the Gelder breeders
saw a market for a showy carriage horse of presence that
would do light work on the farm and could also be used as
a sensible saddle horse. To obtain this, while retaining the
essential docility of character, they introduced a variety
of bloods to their common native mares. They used the
Norfolk Roadster, as well as German, Polish, Hanoverian,
and Russian outcrosses (the latter predominantly eastern).
When they had fixed the type, they added Cleveland Bay,
Oldenburg, and Anglo-Norman blood. Then, to improve
quality, they introduced Thoroughbred and Arab.
• **CHARACTERISTICS** The modern Gelderlander
is both an upstanding, powerful carriage horse of the
best type and a useful heavyweight riding horse
with some jumping ability.

*short, strong limbs
have no feathering
• at the heel*

*head is not •
beautiful, but
has an honest
outlook, with a
calm, intelligent
expression*

Colours Chestnut	Uses Saddle, Light Draught, Carriage

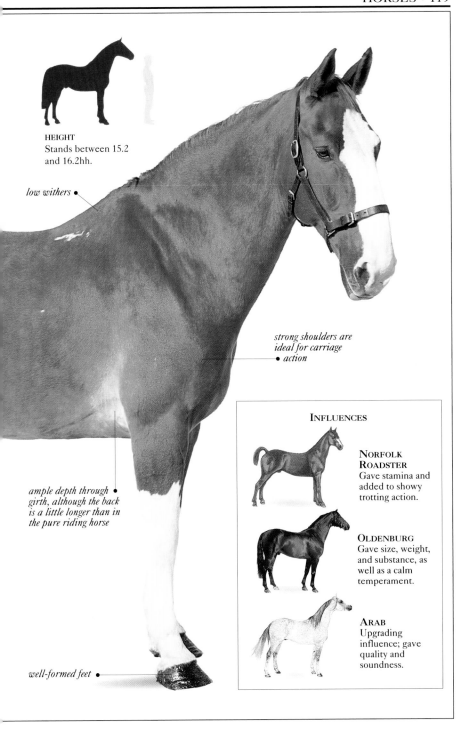

HEIGHT
Stands between 15.2
and 16.2hh.

low withers •

*strong shoulders are
ideal for carriage
• action*

ample depth through •
*girth, although the back
is a little longer than in
the pure riding horse*

well-formed feet •

INFLUENCES

**NORFOLK
ROADSTER**
Gave stamina and
added to showy
trotting action.

OLDENBURG
Gave size, weight,
and substance, as
well as a calm
temperament.

ARAB
Upgrading
influence; gave
quality and
soundness.

Environment Cool temperate	Origin 19th century	Blood Warm

GRONINGEN

The Groningen has the distinction of providing, along with the Gelderlander, the base stock for the evolution of the very successful Dutch Warmblood. Today, it can hardly be said to still exist in its old form but, in its time, the Groningen was an essentially practical animal which was bred to meet the specific agricultural needs of the region.

• **BREEDING** The breed originated in the Groningen region of the Netherlands. Up to 1945, the Groningen was a heavy farm-horse type that could double as a steady, but not spectacular, coach horse. It was noted for the strength of its quarters, but was not distinguished by the freedom of its action. Thereafter, it was improved and lightened as the demand for a more active, versatile horse increased.

• **CHARACTERISTICS** The old Groningen breed relied heavily on its famous neighbour, the Friesian, and the powerful, temperate Oldenburg. From these two it inherited its calm character and willing disposition. The roomy Groningen mares, when crossed with quality sires, produced strong stock, passing on both their size and good bone.

NETHERLANDS:
GRONINGEN REGION

like many coach-type horses, it is fairly long in body and back

plain, honest head is carried on a short, strong neck, which characterizes the heavier carriage horse

Colours Bay, Brown	Uses Light Draught, Coach

HEIGHT
Stands between 15.2 and 16.2hh.

*originally not a good-fronted
horse, it was much improved
• in this respect after 1945*

*joints were once
inclined to be round
and fleshy, but there
was ample bone •*

INFLUENCES

FRIESIAN
Gave endurance
and better limbs
to the common
Dutch mares.

OLDENBURG
Passed on size,
strength, bone,
and power in
the quarters.

Environment Cool temperate	Origin 20th century	Blood Warm

DUTCH WARMBLOOD

The Dutch Warmblood is one of the most successful of
the post-war competition horses, and one of the most
skilfully promoted. Marius, sire of the fabulous Milton,
was an exceptional representative of the breed and has to
be regarded as one of the great show jumping stallions of
recent years. Dutch Courage, the dressage horse produced
by the British Olympic rider Jennie Loriston-Clarke, was
significant in establishing the breed's reputation in Britain.
• **BREEDING** Essentially, the Dutch Warmblood is the
product of an amalgamation of two of Holland's indigenous
breeds, the Gelderlander and the Groningen. The former
is a good-moving carriage horse of presence that can also
be used under saddle; the latter is heavier and has very
powerful quarters. When they were combined, a base for
a competition horse was created. This base was refined
with Thoroughbred blood, and the mix was subsequently
adjusted, in respect of temperament and conformation,
by outcrosses to French and German warmbloods.
• **CHARACTERISTICS** A proven performer as
a show jumper and dressage horse, the Dutch
Warmblood is noted for its good limbs and feet.
Although not fast, the breed is athletic with
pronounced gymnastic ability. Breeders put
much emphasis on the correctness of the
action and the even temperament.

NETHERLANDS

• *good, sound limbs
are a feature of the
breed, along with
adequate bone*

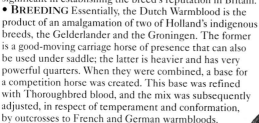

INFLUENCES

GELDERLANDER
Gave size, strength
of shoulder,
presence, and a
showy action.

GRONINGEN
Increased sub-
stance, adding
to the power of
the quarters.

THOROUGHBRED
Shortened carriage
back, improved
conformation, and
added courage.

Colours All solid	Uses Saddle

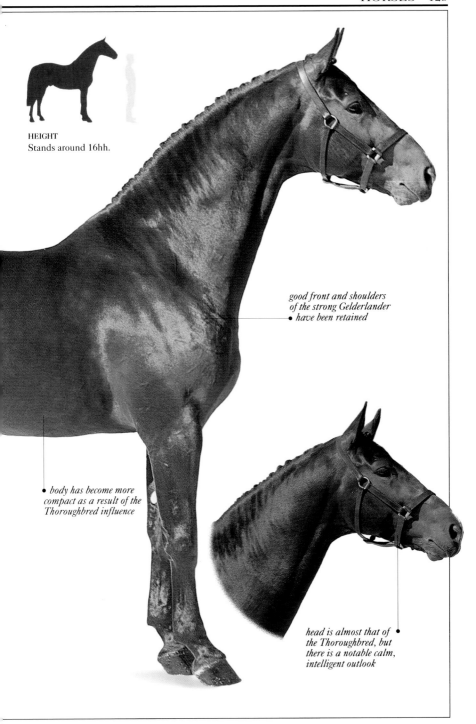

HEIGHT
Stands around 16hh.

*good front and shoulders
of the strong Gelderlander
• have been retained*

*• body has become more
compact as a result of the
Thoroughbred influence*

*head is almost that of •
the Thoroughbred, but
there is a notable calm,
intelligent outlook*

Environment Cool temperate	Origin 20th century	Blood Warm

BELGIAN WARMBLOOD

The Belgian Warmblood is a relatively recent development.
Purpose-bred for competition, it excels as a dressage or
jumping horse. Traditionally, Belgium specialized in the
production of heavy agricultural horses, but now upwards
of 4,500 Belgian Warmblood foals are born each year.
• **BREEDING** The history of the breed began in the 1950s,
when lighter agricultural horses were crossed with imported
Gelderlanders to produce riding horses. Ten years later, the
Gelderlanders were replaced by the more wiry and athletic
Selle Français and some Hanoverian sires. The importance
of Thoroughbred and Anglo-Arab blood was recognized as a
means of giving quality, and some use is also made of Dutch
Warmblood stallions, horses with impressive performance
records, noted for their equable disposition.
• **CHARACTERISTICS** The amalgam of the various
bloods has resulted in powerful, straight-moving horses
of great agility and excellent temperaments. Belgian
Warmblood breeders enjoy a considerable demand for
these reliable horses and they have developed
flourishing export markets.

BELGIUM

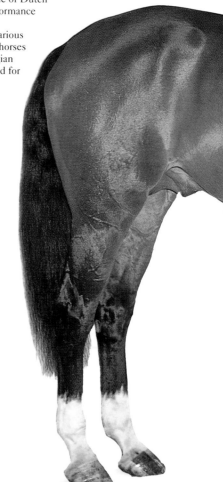

INFLUENCES

GELDERLANDER
Provided size,
strength, and
substance, as
well as bone.

**SELLE
FRANÇAIS**
Gave athletic
ability, stamina,
and hardiness.

HANOVERIAN
Gave correctness
of movement,
size, and equable
temperament.

THOROUGHBRED
Improved speed,
conformation, and
freedom of action;
gave high courage.

Colours All solid	Uses Saddle

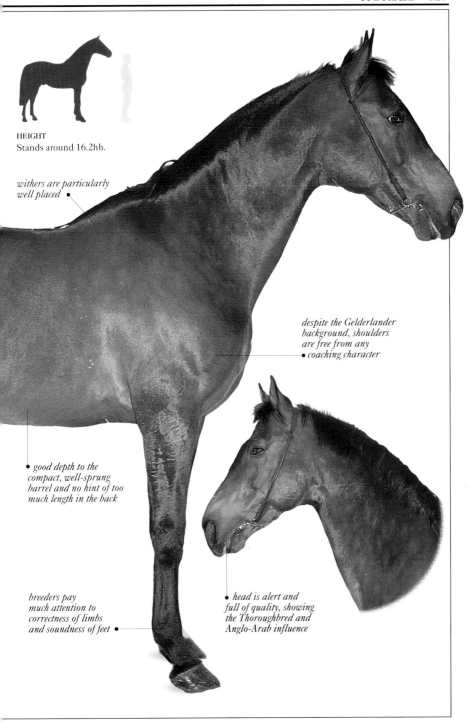

HEIGHT
Stands around 16.2hh.

*withers are particularly
well placed* •

*despite the Gelderlander
background, shoulders
are free from any
• coaching character*

• *good depth to the
compact, well-sprung
barrel and no hint of too
much length in the back*

*breeders pay
much attention to
correctness of limbs
and soundness of feet* •

• *head is alert and
full of quality, showing
the Thoroughbred and
Anglo-Arab influence*

Environment Cool temperate	Origin 13th century	Blood Warm

TRAKEHNER

Many consider the Trakehner to be Europe's finest warmblood and the ideal competition horse. During the Second World War, 1,200 Trakehners, out of 25,000 registered in the East Prussian stud book, were trekked 1,450km (900 miles) across Europe to prevent them from falling into Soviet hands. Using this nucleus, German breeders have been able to preserve the breed.

• **BREEDING** The Trakehner originated in the 13th-century studs of the Teutonic Knights, in what used to be East Prussia. They used indigenous Schweiken ponies, descendants of the Tarpan, as a base. The Royal Trakehner Stud was founded by Friedrich Wilhelm I of Prussia in 1732, and aimed to produce active coach horses. Within 50 years, more emphasis was placed on breeding cavalry remounts. As a result, Thoroughbreds and Arabs were used. The greatest Thoroughbred influence was that of Perfectionist, son of the 1896 Derby and St Leger winner, Persimmon. Perfectionist's son, Tempelhuter, provided a powerful line for the Trakehner. Tempelhuter daughters are the base of Dingo, the other important Trakehner line.

• **CHARACTERISTICS** Selective breeding has ensured excellent conformation. The Trakehner has the appearance of a top-class middleweight hunter, and is courageous across country. It excels at dressage and show jumping.

POLAND: EAST

• *good, strong limbs and joints*

INFLUENCES

ARAB
The upgrading influence that ensured a good temperament.

THOROUGHBRED
Improved the size, also giving the Trakehner greater speed and scope.

SCHWEIKEN
The indigenous base stock, passing on primitive vigour.

Colours All solid	Uses Saddle

HEIGHT
Stands between
16 and 17.2hh.

strong, sloped
shoulders and long,
elegant neck are
• particularly notable

• outline of strong body
inclines towards the
Thoroughbred and
indicates speed and
athletic ability

feet are harder and
pasterns more correctly
sloped than in many
other warmbloods •

head reflects strong •
Thoroughbred element
and is full of quality
and very expressive

Environment Cool temperate	Origin 20th century	Blood Warm

WIELKOPOLSKI

The Wielkopolski embraces the two older, dual-purpose
warmblood horses of central and western Poland – the
Poznan and the Masuren, neither of which now exists
officially. It is typical of Poland's long horse tradition, being
practical, economical, and depending to a degree on the
Arab blood that is so much a part of the Polish heritage.
• **BREEDING** The Poznan Horse, a breed established in
the state studs about 150 years ago, was an amalgam of Arab,
Thoroughbred, and Hanoverian blood, with a later cross to
the Trakehner. The Masuren, bred in the Masury district
was, to all intents, Trakehner in origin. The two distinctive
strains were combined in the Wielkopolski, and outcrosses
were made to the Thoroughbred, Arab, and Anglo-Arab.
• **CHARACTERISTICS** The Wielkopolski is a strong,
quality horse that can be used in harness or under
saddle. Heavier specimens, combining activity and
the characteristic good temperament, can be used
as farm horses. The handsome Wielkopolski is
noted for its paces: long, easy walk; low, level trot;
and ground-covering canter and gallop.

POLAND: CENTRAL AND
WESTERN

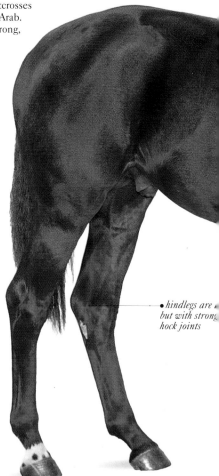

• *hindlegs are*
but with strong
hock joints

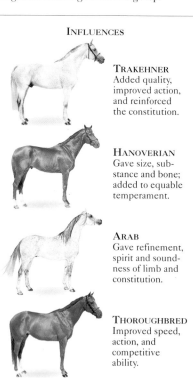

INFLUENCES

TRAKEHNER
Added quality,
improved action,
and reinforced
the constitution.

HANOVERIAN
Gave size, sub-
stance and bone;
added to equable
temperament.

ARAB
Gave refinement,
spirit and sound-
ness of limb and
constitution.

THOROUGHBRED
Improved speed,
action, and
competitive
ability.

Colours All solid	Uses Saddle, Harness, Light Draught

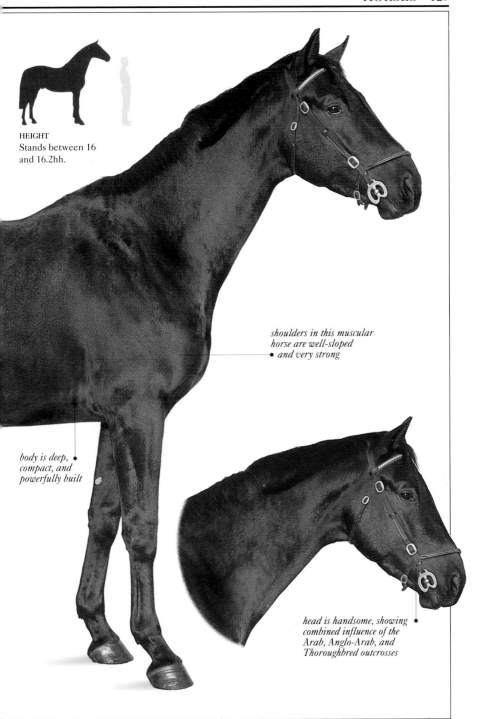

HEIGHT
Stands between 16
and 16.2hh.

shoulders in this muscular
horse are well-sloped
• and very strong

body is deep, •
compact, and
powerfully built

head is handsome, showing •
combined influence of the
Arab, Anglo-Arab, and
Thoroughbred outcrosses

Environment Cool temperate	Origin 10th–11th centuries	Blood Warm

Bavarian Warmblood

The Bavarian is not the best known of the German warmbloods but it is one of the oldest, and its origins trace back to the Crusades. At the time of the Crusades, it was known as the Rottaler, the chestnut warhorse of the Rott Valley in Germany, a noted breeding area.

• **BREEDING** The horses were bred at the monastery studs during the 16th century, and 200 years later stock was being upgraded by imported half-bred English stallions, Cleveland Bays, and some Normans. A century after, the Oldenburg was used to increase the substance of the breed, laying the foundation for the modern, more scopy, competition horse.

• **CHARACTERISTICS** The Bavarian is of medium size with great depth and width, in proportion. Breeders place great emphasis on temperament, and the stock is tested carefully for performance.

INFLUENCES

CLEVELAND
Provided size, strength, substance, and stamina.

OLDENBURG
Gave substance and improved correctness of limb.

THOROUGHBRED
Gave additional speed, quality, and courage; improved scope.

HEIGHT
Stands around 16hh.

GERMANY: ROTT VALLEY, BAVARIA

• *strongly built body combines bone, substance, and depth through girth*

Colours Chestnut	Uses Saddle

Environment Cool temperate	Origin 18th century	Blood Warm

HANOVERIAN

Foremost among the German competition horses is the Hanoverian, a great show-jumping breed and a dressage performer of note.
• **BREEDING** Selective breeding began in 1735, when George II, Elector of Hanover and King of England, founded the Celle stud. Initially, 14 Holstein stallions were used with local mares to produce all-round farm horses. Then, Thoroughbreds were used to produce a better quality horse. After the Second World War, emphasis changed towards competition, and both Trakehner and Thoroughbred blood was employed to obtain further refinement, but outcrossing was carefully controlled.
• **CHARACTERISTICS** The policy of strict selection produces a horse of exceptional strength with notably correct movement, and a particularly good temperament.

INFLUENCES

THOROUGHBRED Gave courage, and improved speed, conformation, and movement.

HOLSTEIN Fulfilled the original need for size, strength, and substance.

TRAKEHNER Passed on strength of constitution and stamina.

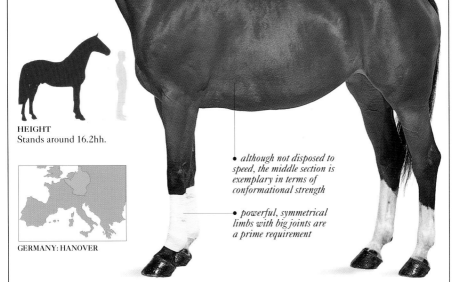

HEIGHT
Stands around 16.2hh.

GERMANY: HANOVER

• *although not disposed to speed, the middle section is exemplary in terms of conformational strength*

• *powerful, symmetrical limbs with big joints are a prime requirement*

Colours All solid	Uses Saddle

Environment Cool temperate	Origin 17th–19th century	Blood Warm

HOLSTEIN

The Holstein has been refined by the increasing use of the Thoroughbred outcross, and is probably the best cross-country prospect of the carefully bred German warmbloods. The Holstein is also an impressive dressage horse, and some of the best post-war German show jumpers have been Holsteins.

• **BREEDING** During the 17th century, the Holstein was in demand as a heavy, but not inelegant, coach horse. The horses of that time were an amalgam of German and Spanish blood, topped up with an oriental infusion. In the 19th century, the Yorkshire Coach Horse was introduced. After this, as more emphasis was placed on producing a riding horse, more reliance was put on Thoroughbred outcrosses.

• **CHARACTERISTICS** The modern Holstein exhibits very correct, straight, and rhythmic paces. Some knee action, however, is acceptable. The heaviness that typified the old Holstein has disappeared. The tractable, intelligent, and reliable Holstein is also a bold jumper.

GERMANY: HOLSTEIN

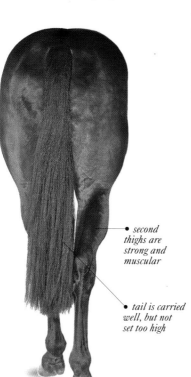

• *second thighs are strong and muscular*

• *tail is carried well, but not set too high*

Colours All solid	Uses Saddle

shoulder blades are
not widely spaced •

withers are
relatively high •

• throat should be
clean, with no
fleshiness in the jowl

• neck is long and
slightly arched

HEIGHT
Stands between 16 and 17hh.

correct limbs and a
good foot structure
are always sought by
Holstein breeders •

INFLUENCES

THOROUGHBRED
Courage, speed,
and improved
action were all
introduced.

YORKSHIRE
COACH HORSE
Gave substance,
bone, size, and
greater strength.

Environment Temperate, Controlled	Origin 17th century	Blood Warm

OLDENBURG

The Oldenburg was developed in the 17th century as a coach horse, able to cope with rough roadways, and capable of doing a variety of agricultural jobs. Since then the breed has been continually adapted by skilful and controlled breeding to meet changing requirements. Still the most powerfully built of the warmbloods, the Oldenburg is a competition horse, particularly suited to dressage and driving.

GERMANY: OLDENBURG

• **BREEDING** The breed, based on Friesian stock, originated in the provinces of Oldenburg and East Friesland, now in Germany. It was developed by Count Anton Gunther von Oldenburg (1603–1667), who used Spanish and Neapolitan blood. Half-bred English stallions were introduced at the end of the 18th century, and then Thoroughbreds and some Cleveland Bays around 1897. An important outcross was Normann 700, a Norman from Norfolk Roadster and English half-bred lines. When emphasis shifted to the riding horse, another Norman, Condor, was used, as well as the Thoroughbred, Lupus. Recent crosses have also been Thoroughbred, with occasional recourse to the Hanoverian.

• **CHARACTERISTICS** The modern Oldenburg is an impressive horse, with an equable temper. It retains some knee action, but has correct, rhythmic paces. Surprisingly for such a large-framed horse, the breed matures early.

feet are uniformly well-shaped and in proportion •

INFLUENCES

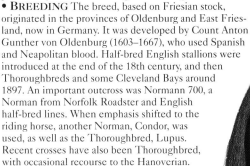

NORMAN Transmitted the qualities of the English half-bred stallions.

THOROUGHBRED Used to upgrade and lighten the somewhat heavy Oldenburgs.

FRIESIAN The hardy, economical, and easily-managed base stock.

Colours All solid	Uses Saddle, Harness

HEIGHT
Stands between 16.2 and
17.2hh.

• *some
thickness in
the jowl*

• *strong neck and long
shoulders still incline
towards coach-horse
conformation*

• *chest is both
broad and wide*

• *exceptionally
powerful body*

*head has a kind, genuine
appearance and profile is
straight or inclined to a
Roman nose* •

Environment Cool temperate	Origin 16th century	Blood Warm

WURTTEMBURG

The Württemburg is one of Germany's classic warmblood breeds and has been bred systematically for over a century at the oldest of the German state-owned stud farms at Marbach. This stud was founded in 1573 by Duke Christoph von Wirttemburg, and in the early 19th century had a horse complement exceeding 81,000.

• **BREEDING** The first influence of note was the Arab crossed with local warmblood mares of mixed origin. In the 17th century, Barb and Spanish mares were brought in, as well as some of the heavier Friesian stallions. Anglo-Norman and East Prussian blood were helpful in fixing a stocky, all-round type. An Anglo-Norman of the Cob type, called Faust, created the prototype Württemburg. The greatest improvement to the breed was made by Trakehners, and notable among these was Julmond, who died at Marbach in 1965. An interesting feature of the Württemburg, which is not found in the other German warmbloods, is the powerful influence of the famous Marbach herd of Arabs. Although it was originally bred as a light utility horse, more emphasis is now placed on it being suitable for ridden competition.

• **CHARACTERISTICS** The Württemburg is a stocky riding horse with great depth through the girth. It is noted for its sound limbs, excellent action, and faultless disposition. A very hardy horse, it is long-lived and exceptionally economical to feed.

GERMANY: MARBACH, WURTTEMBURG

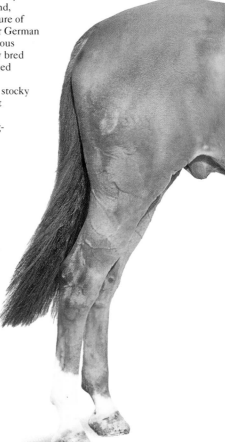

INFLUENCES

ANGLO-NORMAN
Gave substance and helped to create the type.

ARAB
The refining influence, produced the basic type.

TRAKEHNER
Gave distinctive size, character, scope, and movement.

Colours Brown, Bay, Chestnut	Uses Saddle

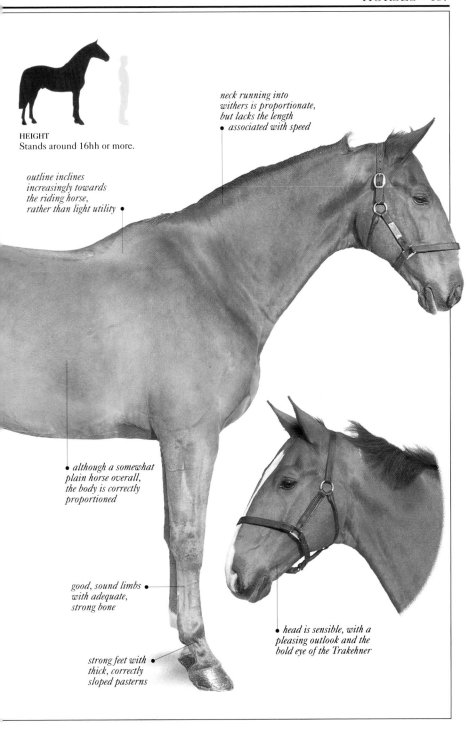

HEIGHT
Stands around 16hh or more.

outline inclines increasingly towards the riding horse, rather than light utility •

neck running into withers is proportionate, but lacks the length
• *associated with speed*

• *although a somewhat plain horse overall, the body is correctly proportioned*

good, sound limbs • *with adequate, strong bone*

strong feet with • *thick, correctly sloped pasterns*

• *head is sensible, with a pleasing outlook and the bold eye of the Trakehner*

Environment Cool temperate	Origin 1960s–1970s	Blood Warm

RHINELANDER

The old Rhenish-German or Rhineland heavy draught horse owed much to Brabant blood and was once a popular workhorse throughout the Rhineland, Westphalia, and Saxony. But modern agricultural practice has long since made this breed redundant and it is no longer recognized. However, the Rhenish Stud Book has moved towards a warmblood riding horse based on the old heavy draught, particularly the lighter specimens.

• **BREEDING** In the 1970s, breeding programmes specifically designed to produce a recognizable saddle- or riding-horse type took place. These horses were sired by stallions within the Hanover-Westphalia area, from warmbloods that had Thoroughbred, Trakehner, and Hanoverian blood and that derived, if tenuously, from the old Rhenish background. The modern Rhinelander developed from selected half-bred stallions which were produced from this amalgam.

• **CHARACTERISTICS** The breeders have concentrated on action and conformation, possibly the hallmark of the German warmbloods, along with the insistence on an equable temperament. Early specimens, however, were said to be lacking in bone, a failure that breeders continually strive to eradicate. The modern Rhinelander is a useful riding horse, although perhaps not, as yet, in the same class as the older established breeds such as the Hanoverian and the Holstein.

GERMANY: RHINELAND
AND WESTPHALIA

INFLUENCES

RHINELAND DRAUGHT
As the base stock, it was responsible for size.

HANOVERIAN
Gave correct movement, good temperament, and riding character.

THOROUGHBRED
Increased scope and speed; acted as an upgrading influence.

Colours All solid, esp. Chestnut	Uses Saddle

HEIGHT
Stands around 16.2hh.

neck is light and fairly short •

• in this specimen, the neck runs into a "bosomy" chest

outline is that of a • typical riding horse and, if undistinguished, is not unattractive

head is sensible, not without • quality, and reflects equable temperament

Environment Cool temperate	Origin 19th century	Blood Warm

NONIUS

The Nonius evolved in the 19th century, when the studs of the vast Austro-Hungarian Empire, then at its zenith, provided cavalry remounts throughout Europe.
• **BREEDING** The breed was founded on Nonius Senior. He was foaled at Calvados, Normandy, in 1810 and captured by the Hungarians in 1813. He was by Orion, an English half-bred with Norfolk Roadster blood, out of a common Norman mare. The type was obtained by mating the progeny of Arab, Lipizzaner, Norman, and English mares by Nonius, back to their sire. In the 1860s, more Thoroughbred blood was introduced. Today, Nonius horses are bred in Hortobagy in Hungary and Topolçianky in Czechoslovakia.
• **CHARACTERISTICS** The Nonius is a sound, well-built horse. Neither carriage nor saddle types are fast, but are good all-rounders.

INFLUENCES

ARAB Transmitted its refinement and equable temperament.

NORMAN Resulted in increased size and substance in the Nonius.

ENGLISH HALF-BRED Gave improved constitution and performance.

HEIGHT
Stands between 15.3 and 16.2hh.

HUNGARY: HORTOBAGY

bone below knee is adequate and limbs are strongly
• *proportioned*

• *hard feet*

Colours Bay, Brown	Uses Saddle, Harness

Environment Cool temperate	Origin 19th century	Blood Warm

FURIOSO

The Furioso is closely related to the Nonius and is bred over Europe, from Austria to Poland. The Furioso was also bred as a cavalry horse, but it is more refined than the Nonius.
• **BREEDING** The Furioso was founded on two English horses, Furioso and North Star, who were put to Nonius mares. Furioso, imported in about 1840, was a Thoroughbred. North Star, imported three years later, was the son of the 1834 St Leger winner, Touchstone, but also had strong Norfolk Roadster connections. He sired many good harness racers. Later, more Thoroughbreds were used. The two lines were cross-bred after 1885, when the Furioso strain became more prominent.
• **CHARACTERISTICS** The Furioso is a riding horse of sufficient ability to compete in the major disciplines, including steeplechasing, at European level. It also goes well in harness.

INFLUENCES

NONIUS Provided the base stock for the development of the breed.

THOROUGHBRED An upgrading influence; added size, speed, and improved action.

NORFOLK ROADSTER Ensured stamina, strength, and soundness.

HEIGHT
Stands around 16hh.

HUNGARY: APAJPUSZTA

• *body is compact, and strongly built, with depth through the girth*

hindlegs are strong, • with hocks close to the ground, but they are not built for speed

Colours Black, Brown	Uses Saddle, Harness

Environment Desert	Origin 19th century	Blood Hot

SHAGYA ARAB

The most famous product of the great Hungarian studs
of the 19th century is the Shagya Arab, which was bred
specifically as a riding horse of quality and substance for
the incomparable light cavalry of Hungary. The modern
Shagya Arab is just as practical as its forebears, and
performs equally as well in harness as it does under
saddle. Some of the strains are suitable for use in
competitions, including jumping.

• **BREEDING** The centre of Shagya breeding is the
Babolna Stud, founded in 1789. After 1816, Babolna
concentrated on the breeding of pure "desert" Arabs and
then, increasingly, on part-breds of "Arabian Race". These
were by pure-bred stallions out of predominantly Arab
mares carrying strains of Spanish, Hungarian, and
Thoroughbred blood, and took the name of the
breed's foundation stallion, Shagya. This cream-
coloured horse of Kehil/Siglavi strain was larger than
is usual for an Arab, being 15.2½hh. He arrived at
Babolna from Syria in 1836, and his descendants
are still at Babolna and other studs in Europe.

• **CHARACTERISTICS** The Shagya is
wholly Arab in outline and character, but it is
bigger and has more substance and bone
than many of the modern Arabs. The
withers are more pronounced and the strong
shoulders are more oblique. The hindlegs,
often a matter for criticism in the Arab, are
notably correct in the Shagya.

HUNGARY: BABOLNA

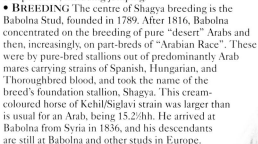

• *remarkably
wide forehead*

*hindlegs are
notably correct* •

• *beautiful head,
dominated by
large eyes*

Colours All solid	Uses Saddle, Harness

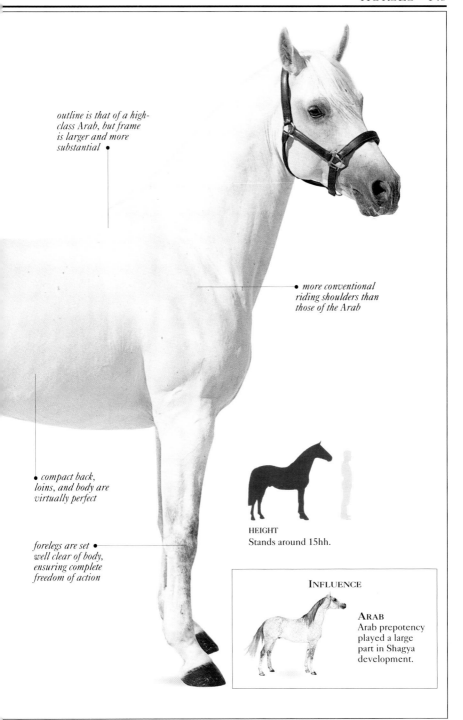

outline is that of a high-class Arab, but frame is larger and more substantial •

• *more conventional riding shoulders than those of the Arab*

• *compact back, loins, and body are virtually perfect*

forelegs are set • *well clear of body, ensuring complete freedom of action*

HEIGHT
Stands around 15hh.

INFLUENCE

ARAB
Arab prepotency played a large part in Shagya development.

Environment Cool temperate	Origin 16th century	Blood Warm

LIPIZZANER

The Lipizzaner is associated with Vienna's Spanish Riding School, the School horses being raised at Piber, near Graz in Austria. It is also bred extensively in Hungary, Romania, Czechoslovakia, and Slovenia, each country producing its own type, and in lesser numbers elsewhere in Europe.

• **BREEDING** The Lipizzaner descends from Spanish horses, taking its name from the stud at Lipica, in Slovenia. The stud was founded in 1580, when the Hapsburg Archduke, Charles II, imported nine stallions and 24 mares from the Iberian Peninsula. He wanted to ensure a supply of showy, predominantly white horses for the ducal stables at Graz and the court stables in Vienna. The Spanish School, so called because it used only "Spanish" horses, was founded for the instruction of the nobility in 1572. The present School, the Winter Riding Hall, was completed in 1735.

• **CHARACTERISTICS** The conformation of the Lipizzaner is that of a useful, all-round cob. Today, many Lipizzaners are used as much in harness as under saddle. The Hungarian-bred horses are superb carriage horses and, due to Thoroughbred influence, have more scope and freedom of movement. The breed is long-lived, many School horses continuing to perform difficult movements in their twenties.

SLOVENIA: LIPICA

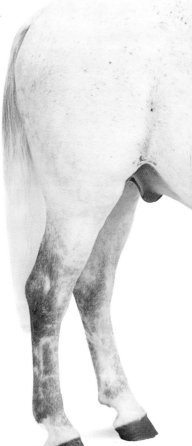

head shows Arab influence, but retains something of the hawk-like profile of the old Spanish Horse

Colours Grey	Uses Saddle, Harness

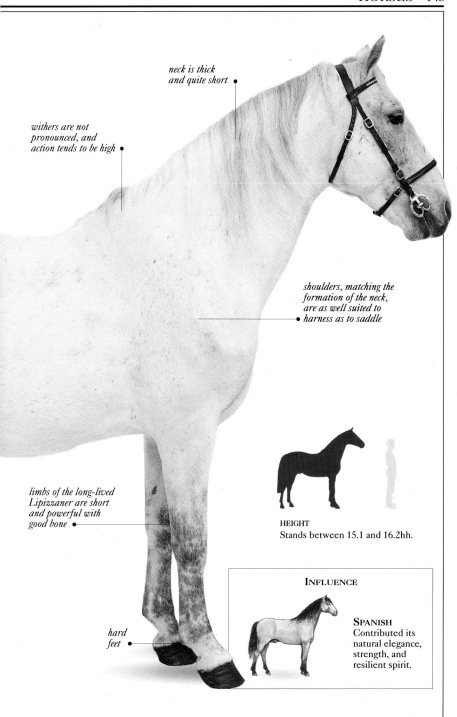

neck is thick
and quite short

withers are not
pronounced, and
action tends to be high

shoulders, matching the
formation of the neck,
are as well suited to
harness as to saddle

limbs of the long-lived
Lipizzaner are short
and powerful with
good bone

HEIGHT
Stands between 15.1 and 16.2hh.

hard
feet

INFLUENCE

SPANISH
Contributed its
natural elegance,
strength, and
resilient spirit.

Environment Cool temperate	Origin 19th–20th century	Blood Warm

SELLE FRANCAIS

The French warmblood, called *le cheval de selle Français*, is one of the toughest and most versatile European competition horse breeds.

• **BREEDING** During the 19th century, Norman breeders imported Thoroughbred and half-bred stallions from England to cross with their useful, but common, Norman stock. This produced the forerunners of the present French Trotter and the Selle Français breeds. After the Second World War, the Selle Français was further developed using Trotters, Thoroughbreds, Arabs, and Anglo-Arabs.

• **CHARACTERISTICS** The Selle Français was developed as a show jumper and has, perhaps as a result of the Trotter influence, great ability in this field. It is also a highly courageous horse, well able to compete in cross-country racing and eventing.

INFLUENCES

NORMAN
The base stock which passed on its constitution and added size.

ARAB
Added refinement; gave spirit and greater physical soundness.

THOROUGHBRED
Contributed to speed; improved action and overall mental stamina.

HEIGHT
Stands around 16hh.

very strong limbs have bone measurement of not less than 20cm (8in)

FRANCE: NORMANDY

Colours All solid	Uses Saddle

Environment Cool temperate	Origin 19th century	Blood Warm

FRENCH TROTTER

The sport of trotting was established in France in the 19th century, encouraging the evolution of the French Trotter.

• **BREEDING** The utilitarian Norman horse provided the base for the Trotter strains. The principal outside influences were The Norfolk Phenomenon, a Norfolk Roadster; Young Rattler, a Thoroughbred/Roadster cross; and, to a lesser extent, Heir of Linne, a Thoroughbred. Later, to improve the speed, crosses were made to the American Standardbred.

• **CHARACTERISTICS** This tough breed races in the diagonal gait and is able to take on the best harness racers. In 1989, the qualifying standard for four-year-olds and over was 1 minute 22 seconds over 1km (⅗ mile). Bigger Trotters are also raced under saddle.

INFLUENCES

NORFOLK ROADSTER
Gave stamina, robust constitution, trotting ability.

NORMAN
Base stock; gave size, versatility, and equable temperament.

THOROUGHBRED
Contributed to speed, improved action, and overall mental stamina.

fairly flat, trotting withers •

modern French Trotter has good harness shoulders •

HEIGHT
Stands around 16.2hh.

immensely powerful quarters •

limbs and feet are exceptionally hard, strong, and enduring •

FRANCE: NORMANDY

Colours All solid	Uses Harness

Environment Salt marshland	Origin Prehistoric	Blood Warm

CAMARGUE

Camargue horses, known as "the white horses of the sea", are indigenous to the Rhône delta in southern France. Here the *manades* (semi-wild herds) live in much the same way as they have done for thousands of years on the wild, watery wasteland dominated by the *mistral* (the salt-laden wind). Camargue horses are the traditional mounts of the *gardian* (Camargue cowboy), and are indispensable for working the wild, black bulls of the Camargue.

• **BREEDING** It is possible that the Camargue horses are descendants of the prehistoric animals whose remains were discovered at Solutré in the 19th century. Certainly, the breed bears a resemblance to the primitive horses depicted in the Lascaux cave drawings, dated around 15,000BC. The indigenous horse was undoubtedly influenced by Barbs, brought over from North Africa with the Moorish invaders. Since then, the isolation of the region has ensured that the *manades* have been untouched by outside influences.

• **CHARACTERISTICS** Although hardly a model of conformation, the breed is strong and enduring, and is fiery and courageous under saddle. It is also incredibly hardy and able to exist on the feed offered by stunted reed beds. The action is peculiar – walk, canter, and gallop are free and active, while the trot is so stilted that it is rarely employed.

FRANCE: CAMARGUE

sloped croup and
• *low-set tail*

• *quarters are generally powerful*

HEIGHT
Stands up to 14.2hh.

INFLUENCE

BARB
The powerful genes contributed by the Barb are in evidence.

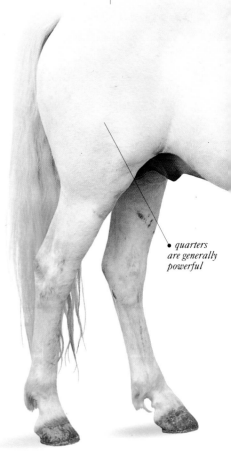

Colours Grey, White	Uses Saddle

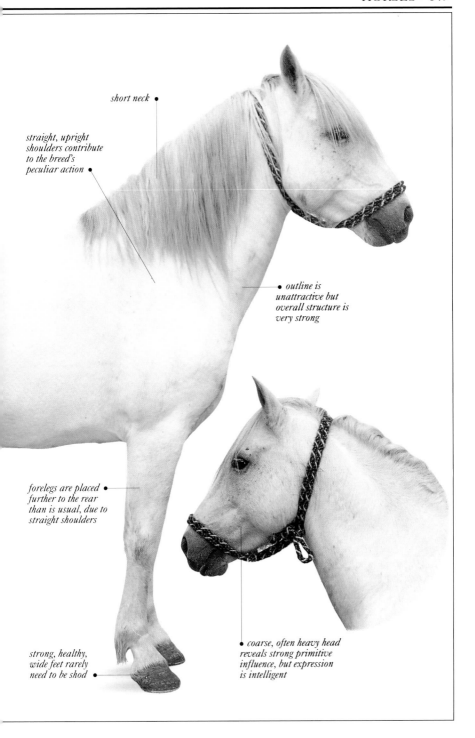

short neck •

straight, upright
shoulders contribute
to the breed's
peculiar action •

• outline is
unattractive but
overall structure is
very strong

forelegs are placed •
further to the rear
than is usual, due to
straight shoulders

strong, healthy,
wide feet rarely
need to be shod •

• coarse, often heavy head
reveals strong primitive
influence, but expression
is intelligent

Environment Temperate, Controlled	Origin 19th century	Blood Hot

ANGLO-ARAB

The Anglo-Arab is an offshoot of the Arab and its derivative, the Thoroughbred. It is a horse that should combine the best of both. Such a cross might be expected to inherit some of the Arab's qualities of soundness and stamina while incorporating the speed and scope of the Thoroughbred, without its sometimes excitable temperament.

• **BREEDING** The breed may be said to have originated in Britain and to have been perfected in France, where Anglo-Arabs have been bred systematically at the great studs of Pau, Pompadour, Tarbes, and Gelos for over 150 years. Britain has produced some good Anglo-Arabs, but their influence on breeding generally is insignificant in comparison with the French product. The British Anglo-Arab is a cross between a Thoroughbred horse and an Arab mare or vice versa, with their subsequent re-crossings. In 1836, French Anglo-Arab breeding was based on two Arab stallions – Massoud and Aslan, and three Thoroughbred mares – Dair, Common Mare, and Selim Mare. Entry to the stud book is now confined to horses with a minimum of 25 per cent Arab blood, and ancestors must be Arab, Thoroughbred, or Anglo-Arab.

• **CHARACTERISTICS** The Anglo-Arab tends more towards the Thoroughbred than the Arab in appearance. The profile is straight, the shoulders are sloped, and the withers are prominent. Although the Anglo-Arab is not as fast as the Thoroughbred, the proportions, particularly of its hindlegs, are those associated with galloping ability. Overall, the Anglo-Arab is much bigger and more substantial than the Arab. In France, Anglo-Arabs have special races; they also jump, event, and compete in dressage competitions at international standard.

UK, AND FRANCE:
SOUTH-WEST

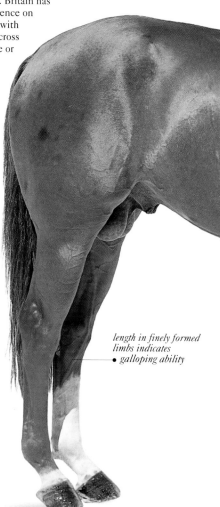

length in finely formed limbs indicates
• *galloping ability*

INFLUENCES

THOROUGHBRED
Imparted size, scope, galloping ability, and competitive potential.

ARAB
Gave soundness, stamina, and endurance, with a kindly temper.

Colours Bay to Chestnut	Uses Saddle

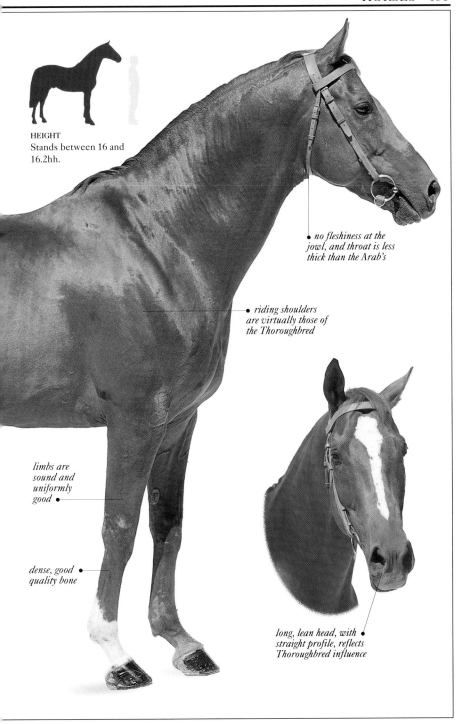

HEIGHT
Stands between 16 and
16.2hh.

no fleshiness at the
jowl, and throat is less
thick than the Arab's

riding shoulders
are virtually those of
the Thoroughbred

limbs are
sound and
uniformly
good

dense, good
quality bone

long, lean head, with
straight profile, reflects
Thoroughbred influence

Environment Cool temperate	Origin 17th–18th century	Blood Hot

THOROUGHBRED

The Thoroughbred is the fastest and most valuable of the world's horses and supports a huge, multinational breeding and racing industry. The Thoroughbred is also the essential element in the production of competition horses, and the principal means of improving many other breeds.

• **BREEDING** The breed evolved in England in the 17th and 18th centuries when native "running horses" were crossed with oriental stallions. The foundation horses were the Byerley Turk (1689), the Darley Arabian (1704), and the Godolphin Arabian (1728). They produced the four principal Thoroughbred lines: Herod, Eclipse, Matchem, and Highflyer, who was Herod's son.

• **CHARACTERISTICS** A horse of great quality, the Thoroughbred has near-perfect proportions, which are long compared to those of more heavily built breeds. It has great athletic ability, and physical and mental stamina. Thoroughbreds are courageous in the extreme, but they are highly strung and sometimes have difficult temperaments.

UK: ENGLAND

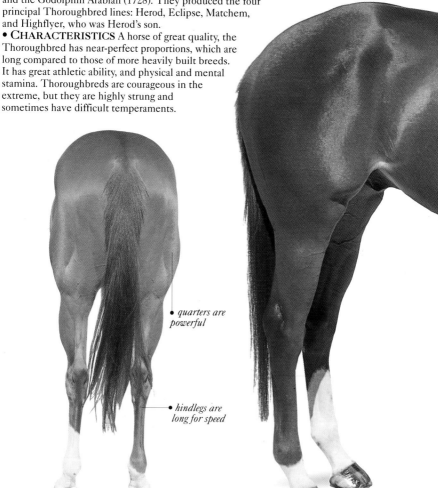

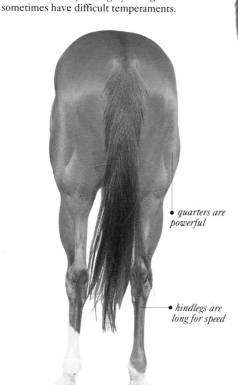

• *quarters are powerful*

• *hindlegs are long for speed*

Colours All solid	Uses Saddle

long, sloping shoulders, complemented by a graceful neck, produce long, low galloping action

HEIGHT
Stands between 16 and 16.2hh.

there should be depth through the girth to allow for maximum lung expansion

limbs are fine, with large, flat joints

bone below the knee measures 20cm (8in)

INFLUENCES

ARAB
Added quality, spirit, hereditary soundness, and great prepotence.

SPANISH
Another element that contributed to the excellence of the base stock.

GALLOWAY
Formed one part of the base stock for English "running horses".

Environment Cool temperate	Origin 19th century	Blood Warm

HACKNEY HORSE

The modern Hackney Horse is the most spectacular show-ring harness horse, although it also takes part successfully in competitive driving events at international level. It is an English breed, derived from the renowned Norfolk and Yorkshire Roadsters, and has been exported all over Europe as well as to the Americas, South Africa, and Australia. The origin of the word Hackney, used with a capital letter after the foundation of the Hackney Horse Society in 1883, is open to question. It probably comes from the French *haquenée*, which means a "nag" or gelding. Hackney, without the capital letter, was used to describe a riding horse from the Middle Ages onwards.
• **BREEDING** Both Yorkshire and Norfolk Roadsters shared a common ancestor in Original Shales, who was by Blaze (foaled in 1733), out of a Norfolk mare. Blaze was a son of the first great racehorse, Flying Childers, and a grandson of the Darley Arabian, one of the foundation sires of the Thoroughbred. The modern Hackney has a strong connection to the Thoroughbred, though its emphasis is on trotting, rather than galloping.
• **CHARACTERISTICS** The Yorkshire and Norfolk Roadsters were used as much under saddle as in harness, and were able to travel long distances at 26–27km/h (16–17mph), carrying heavy weights. The main characteristic of the breed is the brilliance of the high, floating action, described by the breed society standard as "effortless, electrical, and snappy at its zenith".

UK: NORFOLK, ENGLAND

*tail is set and
• carried high*

*• hocks have
maximum flexion*

*• limbs are
relatively short,
with joints not
carried high off
the ground*

HEIGHT
Stands around 15.3hh.

INFLUENCE

NORFOLK
TROTTER
Passed on stamina,
trotting ability, and
robust constitution.

Colours All solid	Uses Harness

great depth
through chest •

low withers •

• long, graceful neck
rises almost vertically
from powerful shoulders,
which are ideally formed
to take a collar

compact body •

forelegs have a very •
elevated action, being
thrown well forward,
with a slight moment
of suspension at
each stride

head is small and convex, •
with small muzzle, small
ears, and large eyes

Environment Cool temperate	Origin Middle Ages	Blood Warm

CLEVELAND BAY

The Cleveland Bay is the oldest and purest of the indigenous British horse breeds and was used in the 18th and 19th centuries to upgrade many European breeds. In Britain, it has enjoyed royal patronage for over 200 years. The shortage of pure-bred mares has caused the Rare Breeds Trust to classify the Cleveland Bay situation as "critical".

• **BREEDING** The breed evolved in the Middle Ages from the bay-coloured Chapman horses of Cleveland in northern England. Apart from the addition of Spanish and Barb blood in the 17th century, the Cleveland was free from outside influence. The result was a powerful coach horse that could work in heavy clay and carry men hunting in all conditions.

• **CHARACTERISTICS** The breed is long-lived and remarkably prepotent, transmitting size, bone, constitutional hardiness, and usually jumping ability when crossed with the Thoroughbred. It is a magnificent coach horse and is employed as such in the Royal stables.

INFLUENCE

SPANISH
Lightened base stock, endowing elegance, spirit, and strength.

HEIGHT
Stands around 16.2hh.

immensely powerful quarters contribute to • jumping ability

strong neck and shoulders are ideal for carriage work •

measurement from • wither to elbow equals or exceeds that from elbow to ground

bone measures • 22cm (9in) or more

legs are clean and without • feathering

UK: CLEVELAND, ENGLAND

Colours Bay	Uses Saddle, Harness

Environment Cool temperate	Origin 12th century	Blood Warm

IRISH DRAUGHT

The Irish Draught, the "horse of the country-side", was used for every sort of work on small Irish farms. Although not fast, it was ridden, and it developed an ability to negotiate tricky obstacles across country. Crossed with the Thoroughbred, it produces the world's best cross-country horse – the Irish hunter. This cross also produces horses that are successful in the show ring and the major ridden disciplines.

• **BREEDING** The size of the indigenous stock was increased by French and Flemish heavy horses in the 12th century, and the type was later upgraded by Spanish horses. The limestone pastures and mild climate of Ireland contribute to the bone and substance.

• **CHARACTERISTICS**
The Irish Draught is a natural, athletic jumper with an equable temper, and is amazingly economical to keep.

INFLUENCES

SPANISH
The upgrading and refining action on the native stock.

FLANDERS
Gave the breed its overall size, weight, and substance.

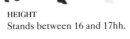

HEIGHT
Stands between 16 and 17hh.

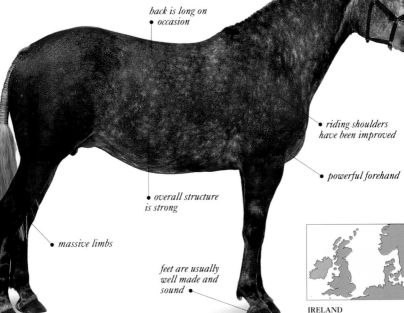

back is long on
• occasion

• riding shoulders
have been improved

• powerful forehand

• overall structure
is strong

• massive limbs

feet are usually
well made and
sound •

IRELAND

Colours All solid	Uses Saddle, Light Draught

Environment Cool temperate	Origin 11th–12th century	Blood Warm

WELSH COB

The Welsh Cob, with its explosive trotting action, arouses as much fervour in its native land as do the Welsh choirs or rugby football at Cardiff Arms Park. It is the natural successor to the great trotting tradition of the Norfolk Roadster, which played a part in its evolution. As a harness horse, it is unsurpassed in stamina and courage and, under saddle, it is a bold ride with great jumping ability.

- **BREEDING** The Welsh Cob (Section D in the stud book) is, in perfection, a larger version of the Welsh Mountain Pony, which represents its base. These ponies were crossed with Roman imports and then, in the 11th and 12th centuries, with Spanish horses to produce the Powys Cob and a heavier animal, the Welsh Cart Horse. In the 18th and 19th centuries, outcrosses to Norfolk Roadsters and Yorkshire Coach Horses, with an admixture of Arab blood, resulted in the modern Cob. In the past, there was a big market for the Cobs as gun horses and troopers for mounted infantry. Until the 1960s, Cobs were employed in large numbers on milk, bread, and general delivery rounds in the big cities.
- **CHARACTERISTICS** The Welsh Cob is in demand as a harness and saddle horse, and as a cross with the Thoroughbred to produce competition horses. The Cob is economical to keep, exceptionally hardy, robust in constitution, and inherently sound.

UK: WALES

• powerful quarters

• extraordinary flexion in hock joints contributes to brilliant action

---

INFLUENCES

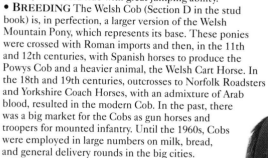

WELSH A
The base of Cob breeding; gave movement and soundness.

SPANISH
Improved size and strength, and contributed to horse's carriage.

NORFOLK ROADSTER
Established good trotting ability and gave stamina.

Colours All solid	Uses Harness, Saddle

HEIGHT
Stands between 14.2
and 15.2hh.

strong, arched neck
joins smoothly with
powerful shoulders

head is neat, with
small, pony ears and,
despite the Cob's size, is
full of pony character

there is depth through
the girth, and body is
compact, well sprung in
the ribs, and very strong

some silky
feathering at
the heel is
permissible

Environment Mediterranean	Origin 18th century	Blood Warm

SALERNO

The Salerno, although now much reduced in number, is one of the most attractive of the Italian warmbloods. The homeland of the breed is in the Campania region of Italy, adjoining Puglia. Some notable horses were produced at the Morese Stud, including two of the greatest Italian show jumpers, Merano and Posillipo, both ridden by the Italian Raimondo d'Inzeo.

ITALY: CAMPANIA

• **BREEDING** The Morese Stud is close to where the Bourbon Charles III, King of Naples and then of Spain, founded the stud of Persano in the first half of the 18th century, and it was from this stud that the Salerno evolved. The horses, bred at Persano and called by that name, were based on the Neapolitan. Neapolitans were bred near Sorrento and Naples, and were full of Spanish and Barb blood. They were regarded as the finest school horses of the day and were much admired for their high, fiery action and exceptional strength of limb. These horses were crossed with the local horses of the Salerno and Ofanto valleys, and then use was made of Arab and Spanish imports to produce a distinctive, quality riding horse. The stud was closed after the establishment of the Italian Republic, and when breeding was revived in 1900, the old name lapsed, the breed being increasingly referred to as the Salerno.

• **CHARACTERISTICS** The introduction of Thoroughbred blood improved the stock and the result was a good type of cavalry horse, bigger than its predecessors, attractive in appearance, with good conformation, and a pronounced aptitude for jumping.

INFLUENCES

SPANISH
Gave strength, agility, improved conformation, and spirit.

THOROUGHBRED
Added size, quality, courage, and greater freedom of action.

Colours All solid	Uses Saddle

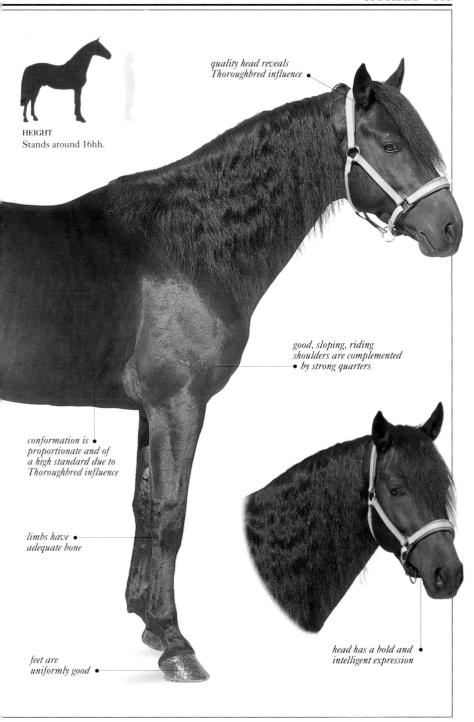

HEIGHT
Stands around 16hh.

*quality head reveals
Thoroughbred influence* •

*good, sloping, riding
shoulders are complemented
• by strong quarters*

conformation is •
*proportionate and of
a high standard due to
Thoroughbred influence*

limbs have •
adequate bone

*feet are
uniformly good* •

head has a bold and •
intelligent expression

Environment Mediterranean	Origin 16th century	Blood Warm

SARDINIAN

Like so many of the Italian breeds, there is little
discernible order in the breeding of the Sardinian horse,
although for centuries Sardinia was a principal importer
of horses. In 1918, the island's horse population was
estimated to be 60,000; some 40 years later the
figure had dropped to about 24,000.

• **BREEDING** Without doubt, the breed was founded on
crosses between the Barb horses of North Africa, and Arabs.
Ferdinand the Catholic (1452–1516) introduced Andalucian
blood. He established a stud of Spanish horses near
Abbasanta and made them available to Sardinian breeders.
Studs dedicated to producing a Sardinian horse were
founded at Padromannu, Mores, and Monte Minerva,
and a distinct type began to appear. However, horse
breeding went into a decline when Sardinia passed to
the House of Savoy in 1720. In 1908, Arab stallions
were imported to upgrade the stock, with the object
of once more producing the tough, enduring
saddle horses for which Sardinia had been famed.

• **CHARACTERISTICS** The Sardinian horse
was prized for its hardiness and stamina. In
appearance, it is oriental, the best horses having
good conformation. Others, because of a lack of
systematic breeding policies, are far less well-
made. It is said that a good Sardinian is bold,
intelligent, and jumps well.

ITALY: SARDINIA

*quarters are light but the
tail is well positioned* •

• *hocks are carried
fairly high*

• *hindlegs lack
some symmetry*

HEIGHT
Stands around 15.2hh.

INFLUENCE

ARAB
The Arab was the
greatest outside
influence in the
20th century.

Colours Bay, Brown	Uses Saddle

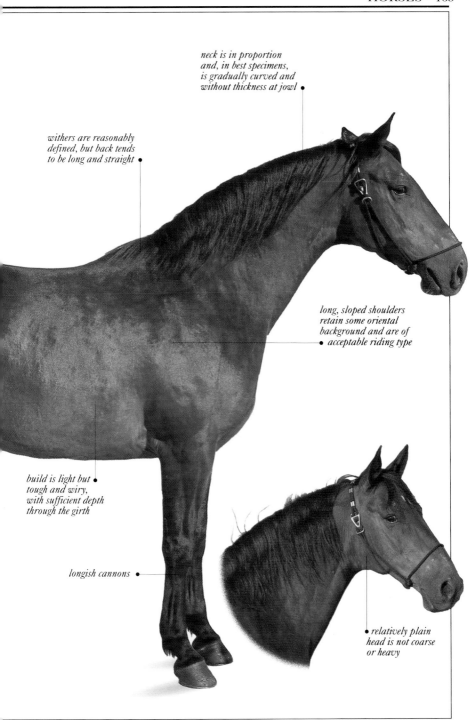

neck is in proportion
and, in best specimens,
is gradually curved and
without thickness at jowl •

withers are reasonably
defined, but back tends
to be long and straight •

long, sloped shoulders
retain some oriental
background and are of
• acceptable riding type

build is light but •
tough and wiry,
with sufficient depth
through the girth

longish cannons •

• relatively plain
head is not coarse
or heavy

Environment Mediterranean	Origin 19th century	Blood Warm

MAREMMANA

The Maremmana is the utility horse of Tuscany. As a result of its endurance, good temper, and ability to work cattle, it is the favoured mount of the *butteri*, the Italian cowboy. It is also employed in agriculture and was once bred as a troop and police horse.

• **BREEDING** The Maremmana is not a horse of an entirely fixed type, nor is it indigenous to Italy. There has been much cross-breeding against an early background of Neapolitan blood and, during the 19th century, there were infusions of English stock, some of it being of Norfolk Roadster extraction.

• **CHARACTERISTICS** Despite the lack of any planned breeding, the Maremmana has some particular qualities. Although it is not very handsome, it is a solid, steady, and serviceable animal, and it is very versatile and economical to keep.

INFLUENCES

SPANISH
Improved the quality of the base stock and added size.

BARB
Contributed its tenacious spirit, hardiness, and great stamina.

NORFOLK ROADSTER
Improved action and soundness of the Maremmana.

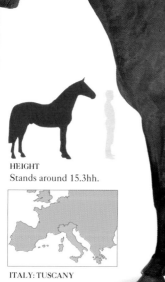

HEIGHT
Stands around 15.3hh.

ITALY: TUSCANY

• *conformation is not generally impressive but the best are well suited for varied work*

limbs have adequate • bone, and hock and knee joints are well defined

Colours All solid	Uses Saddle, Light Draught

Environment Mediterranean	Origin 15th–16th century	Blood Warm

MURGESE

The modern Murgese, a light draught horse of variable type, was developed in the 1920s from an earlier form. Some regard it as the Italian equivalent of the Irish Draught, though inferior.
• **BREEDING** The breed is from Murge, near Puglia in Italy, a region once famed for its horses. There is a background of Neapolitan and probably also Avelignese and Italian Draught.
• **CHARACTERISTICS** The Murgese is a useful, easily managed agricultural horse and a willing worker. It can be used as a base for better quality riding horses as it has active movement, despite its short stride. The mares are used to breed strong mules.

INFLUENCES

NEAPOLITAN Imparted spirit, overall physical soundness, and useful strength.

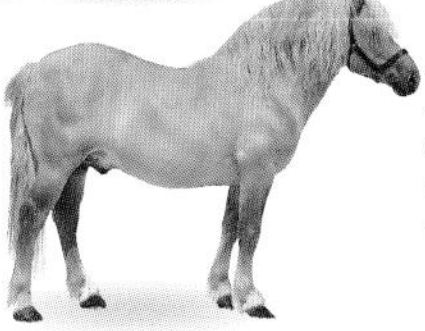

AVELIGNESE Added size and strength, and ensured equable temperament.

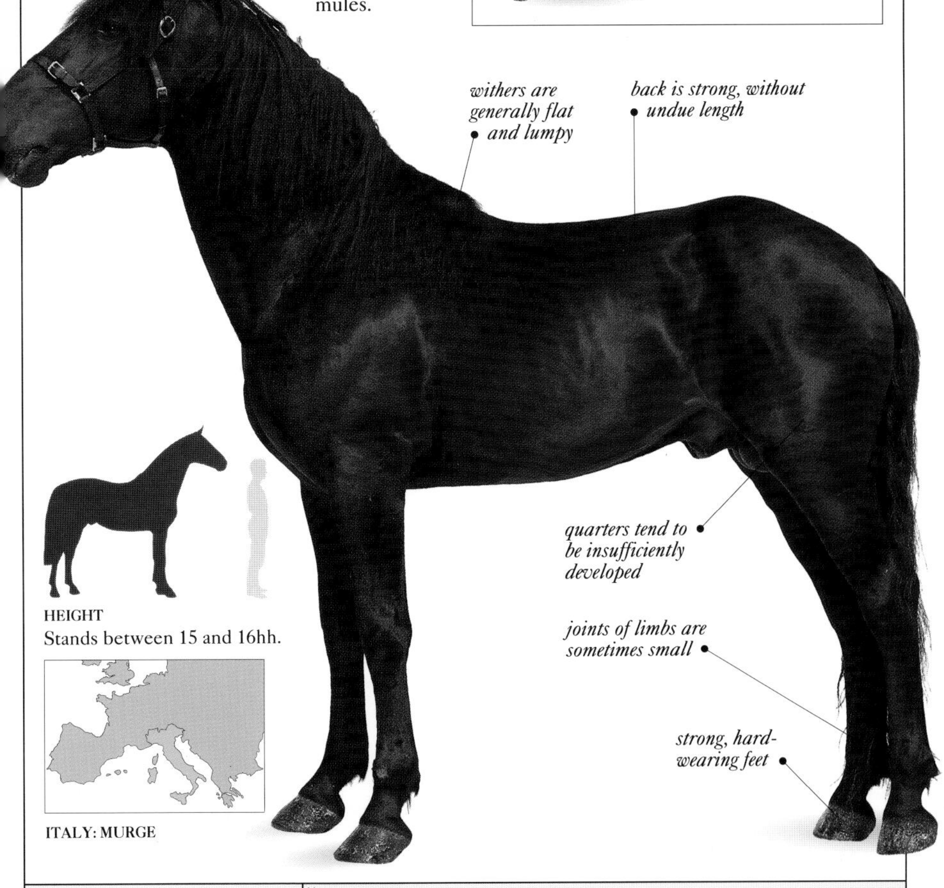

withers are generally flat and lumpy

back is strong, without undue length

quarters tend to be insufficiently developed

joints of limbs are sometimes small

strong, hard-wearing feet

HEIGHT
Stands between 15 and 16hh.

ITALY: MURGE

Colours Chestnut	Uses Light Draught

Environment Hot temperate	Origin Pre-Ice Age	Blood Warm

ANDALUCIAN

The modern Andalucian is the descendant of the Spanish Horse which, along with the Arab and the Barb, has exerted the greatest influence on the world horse population. Until the 19th century, the Spanish Horse was the first horse of Europe, and the one on which the classical equitation of the Renaissance schools was based. The Spanish Riding School of Vienna was named after Spanish horses used there, and the famous white Lipizzaners derive directly from horses exported from Spain to Lipica (in Slovenia) during the 16th century. The Spanish Horse was a major influence on almost every breed and is the foundation for most American stock.

• **BREEDING** Andalucian breeding is centred on Jerez de la Frontera, Cordoba, and Seville, where it was preserved by the Carthusian monasteries. The Spanish Horse may have derived from a mix of the indigenous Sorraia stock, with its Tarpan connection, and the Barb horses of the Berber invaders from North Africa.

• **CHARACTERISTICS** The Andalucian is a horse of great presence, and although not fast, it is agile and athletic. It has a noble head, with a characteristic hawk-like profile, and the mane and tail are long, luxuriant, and frequently wavy.

SPAIN: JEREZ

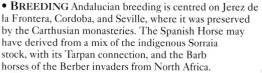

HEIGHT
Stands around 15.2hh.

INFLUENCES

BARB
Passed on fiery, courageous spirit, strength, stamina, and great agility.

SORRAIA
The "primitive" base stock gave hardiness and noted endurance.

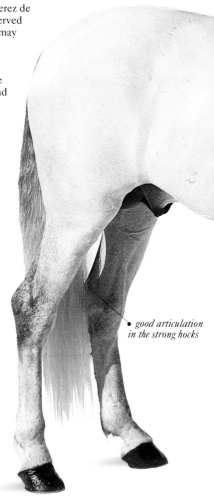

• *good articulation in the strong hocks*

Colours Bay, Grey	Uses Saddle

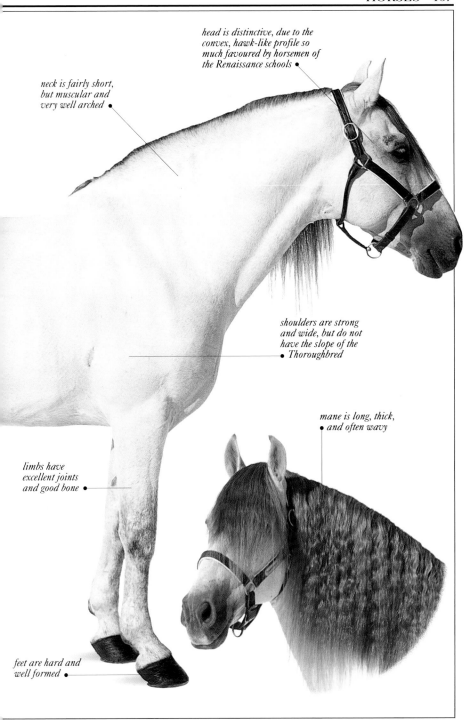

head is distinctive, due to the convex, hawk-like profile so much favoured by horsemen of the Renaissance schools •

neck is fairly short, but muscular and very well arched •

shoulders are strong and wide, but do not have the slope of the • Thoroughbred

mane is long, thick, • and often wavy

limbs have excellent joints and good bone •

feet are hard and well formed •

Environment Hot temperate	Origin 16th–17th century	Blood Warm

LUSITANO

The Lusitano is noted as a showy carriage horse as well
as a saddle horse of the highest quality, and was once the
mount of the Portuguese cavalry. It is the horse that is most
favoured by the Portuguese bullfighter and, in that role, is
schooled in the advanced movements of the *Haute Ecole*.
In more recent years, the Lusitano has become popular
outside the Iberian Peninsula and it has an enthusiastic
following in both Britain and the United States.
• **BREEDING** The breed is in effect the Portuguese
version of the Andalucian (see pp.166–167) and is claimed to
be indistinguishable from its neighbour, although it is
possible, in some cases, to discern slight differences in type.
• **CHARACTERISTICS** Although sometimes more "on
the leg" than the Andalucian, in the eyes of some observers,
the intelligent Lusitano is just as brave, quick, and superbly
balanced. The naturally elevated action is spectacular, and
the breed's agility is remarkable.

PORTUGAL

*full tail is well set into
a usually sloping quarter,
characterized by length
in the hindlegs* •

• *head is fine, with
the distinctive straight or
convex Spanish profile*

Colours All solid, esp. Grey	Uses Saddle, Harness

neck is short and
inclined to be thick •

withers are low,
rather than sharply
defined, but meld into
wide shoulders •

• powerful shoulders

short back and •
compact body, with
well-sprung ribs

limbs are generally •
long, with considerable
length in the cannons
below knee and hock

HEIGHT
Stands between 15 and 16hh.

INFLUENCES

BARB
Passed on fiery,
courageous spirit,
strength, stamina,
and great agility.

SORRAIA
The "primitive"
base stock, giving
hardiness and
endurance.

Environment Hot temperate	Origin 18th century	Blood Warm

ALTER-REAL

As its name suggests, the Alter-Real breed evolved as a horse fit to be the mount of royalty, presenting its rider in the heroic mould, and being ideally suited in spirit and action for classical school riding.

• **BREEDING** The breed was founded in 1748 by the ruling House of Braganza at Vila de Portel in Portugal's Alentejo province, but was moved to Alter in 1756. It started with some 300 of the finest Andalucian mares brought from the area around Jerez de la Frontera, Spain's most famous breeding centre. The stud flourished, furnishing horses for the Royal Manège at Lisbon, and the Alter breed became famous for the exhibitions staged there. In the early 19th century, however, much of the stock was lost or stolen when the stud was sacked by Napoleon's troops. In 1834, more disasters overtook Alter, culminating in the abolition of the Royal Stables. A reorganization was attempted under Queen Maria Pia in the late 19th century, and foreign blood was introduced – including English, Norman, Hanoverian, and, most particularly, Arab. These experiments were unsuccessful and the breed was almost ruined. It was saved by an import of Andalucians. However, the stud archives were largely destroyed after the advent of the Republic in 1910, and it was not until 1932 that constructive efforts were made by the Ministry of Economy to re-establish the breed.

• **CHARACTERISTICS** Despite the vicissitudes it has experienced, the modern Alter, virtually Andalucian again, survives as a highly courageous horse of distinct physical character with an extravagant, high, showy action, especially suited to the *Haute Ecole*.

PORTUGAL: ALTER

tail and mane are thick and luxuriant •

INFLUENCE

SPANISH Gave high courage and distinctive character.

Colours Bay, Brown, Grey	Uses Saddle

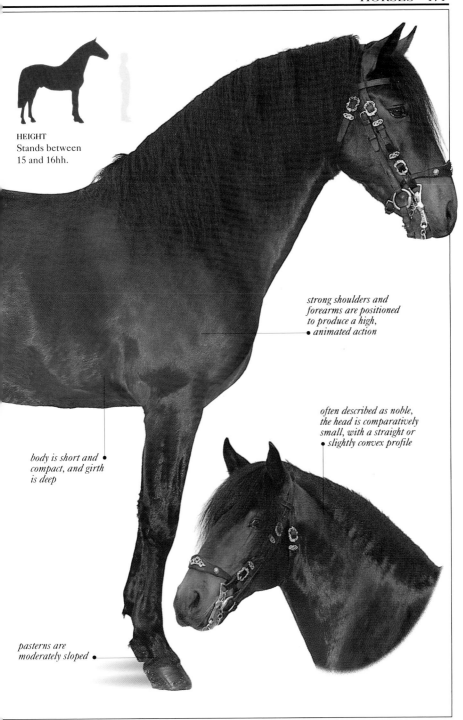

HEIGHT
Stands between
15 and 16hh.

strong shoulders and
forearms are positioned
to produce a high,
• animated action

often described as noble,
the head is comparatively
small, with a straight or
• slightly convex profile

body is short and •
compact, and girth
is deep

pasterns are
moderately sloped •

Environment Desert	Origin Prehistoric	Blood Hot

BARB

The Barb is second only to the Arab as one of the founding breeds of the world's horse population. Its derivative, the Spanish Horse, provided the basis for many of the foremost breeds of Europe and for most of those of the Americas. The Barb must also be recognized as having a part in the evolution of the Thoroughbred.

• **BREEDING** The breed comes from Morocco, in North Africa. It is postulated that it may have constituted a group of wild horses that escaped the effects of the Ice Age. If so, then it is a breed as old as, or older than, the Arab. At some time, the Barb must have acquired a percentage of Arab blood, but its conformation owes nothing to the Arab ideal; this points to the existence of a massively dominant gene. In recent years, there has been much refinement of the traditional Barb, which was the superlative mount of the Berber horsemen who played such a large part in the Muslim Conquest. Although there is no definitive answer to the vexed question of the Barb's origin, it is held that fundamental differences do exist between the Barb and the Arab.

• **CHARACTERISTICS** Not an impressive horse, the Barb has a sloping quarter, a low-set tail, and a plain head with a skull formation verging on that of the primitive horse types. The profile is straight and sometimes Roman-nosed. Nonetheless, the breed's endurance and stamina are unlimited, and indicative of primitive vigour. It is also exceptionally agile and can travel very fast over short distances.

quarters and hindlegs are far from perfect, but can carry the Barb very fast • over short distances

• limbs are not always well formed but are hard, never lymphatic, and free from disease

HEIGHT
Stands around 15.2hh.

MOROCCO

Colours All solid	Uses Saddle

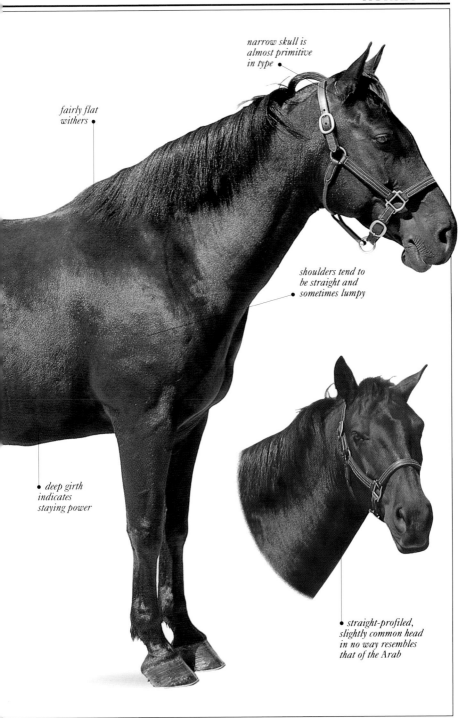

*narrow skull is
almost primitive
in type* •

*fairly flat
withers* •

*shoulders tend to
be straight and
• sometimes lumpy*

• *deep girth
indicates
staying power*

• *straight-profiled,
slightly common head
in no way resembles
that of the Arab*

Environment Desert	Origin Prehistoric	Blood Hot

ARAB

The Arab horse is considered to be the fountainhead of all the world's breeds and is acknowledged as the principal foundation of the Thoroughbred. It is of the purest descent and is the most ancient of all the equine races.

• **BREEDING** A race of horses of Arab type existed on the Arabian peninsula at least 2,000 years before the Christian era. This is indicated by the existence of art forms and the word-of-mouth evidence handed down by the Bedouin people, who were closely connected with the "desert horse". The prepotent Arab blood was spread throughout the known world by Muslim conquests initiated by the Prophet Mohammed in the 7th century. As a result, the Arab became the one essential factor in the development of the world's equines.

• **CHARACTERISTICS** The Arab horse is the most beautiful of all, at once unmistakable and unforgettable in appearance. The unique outline is governed by the proportions and the skeletal formation. Unlike other breeds, which have 18 ribs, 6 lumbar bones, and 18 tail vertebrae, the Arab has a 17–5–16 structure. This also accounts for the distinctively high tail carriage. The breed is unsurpassed in stamina; in movement it "floats", and, while it is fiery and courageous, it is innately gentle. The staying power, and the soundness of the breed in respect of wind and limb, make the Arab an obvious choice for the fast-growing discipline of long-distance, or endurance, riding. Although not nearly so fast as its derivative the Thoroughbred, flat-racing confined to Arabs and Anglo-Arabs is also carried on with enthusiasm in many parts of the world. Today, the Arab is bred extensively throughout the world, with the United States probably having the largest Arab horse population. All countries breeding Arabian horses have their own stud books which are approved, in the interests of harmonization, by the World Arab Horse Organization (WAHO).

MIDDLE EAST: ARABIAN PENINSULA

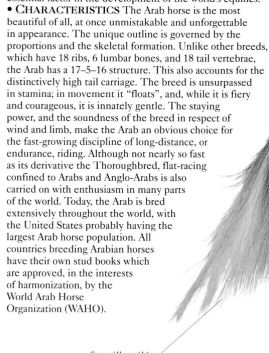

fine, silky tail is never trimmed •

hard, well-formed feet rarely suffer from disease •

Colours All solid	Uses Saddle

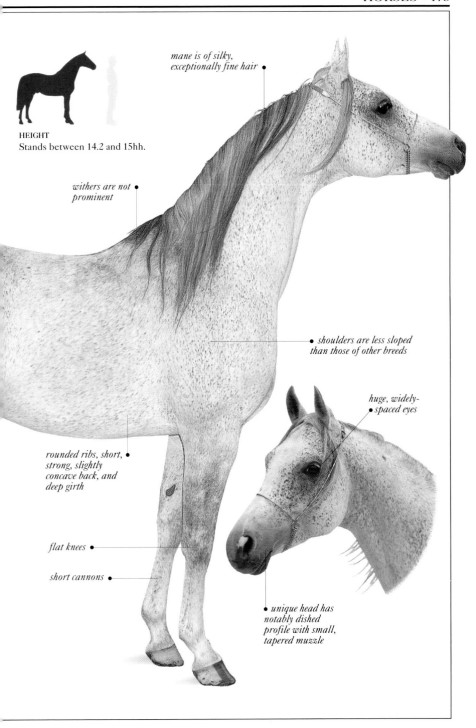

mane is of silky, exceptionally fine hair •

HEIGHT
Stands between 14.2 and 15hh.

withers are not prominent •

• *shoulders are less sloped than those of other breeds*

huge, widely- • *spaced eyes*

rounded ribs, short, strong, slightly concave back, and deep girth •

flat knees •

short cannons •

• *unique head has notably dished profile with small, tapered muzzle*

Environment Desert	Origin 3,000–2,000BC	Blood Hot

AKHAL-TEKE

The Akhal-Teke, the world's mystery horse, is the modern equivalent of the Horse Type 3 (see p.11). It epitomizes the thin-skinned, fine-coated, and heat-resistant desert horse, and there could be a relationship between the Akhal-Teke and the Arab *Munaghi* racing strain. There is evidence that it was in existence over 3,000 years ago in the area of present-day Turkmenistan.

• **BREEDING** The Akhal-Teke is bred around the oases of the Karakum Desert, the principal breeding centre being at Ashkhabad. It has contributed to many breeds but has been influenced by none. One unsuccessful attempt was made to outcross to the Thoroughbred. The Turkomans used the Akhal-Teke for racing, preparing it with great care. It was fed on alfalfa, pellets of mutton fat, eggs, barley, and fried dough cake, and was wrapped in felt as a protection against heat and cold.

• **CHARACTERISTICS** The Akhal-Teke is quite distinctive in appearance, although it hardly conforms to western ideals of conformation. The metallic, golden dun colouring is a particular feature. The Akhal-Teke is possessed of boundless stamina and endurance, horses of the breed performing unequalled feats over exceptional distances and in desert conditions. They were able to cover the 4,152km (2,580 miles) from Ashkhabad to Moscow in 84 days, on minimal rations of feed and water. Today, the Akhal-Teke races, is a long-distance performer, and competes in jumping and dressage.

NORTHERN EURASIA:
TURKMENISTAN

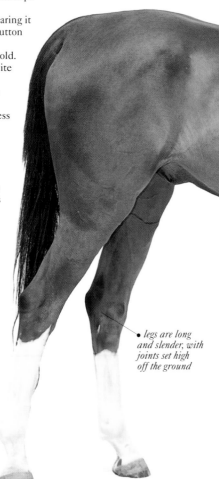

• *legs are long and slender, with joints set high off the ground*

HEIGHT
Stands around 15.2hh.

INFLUENCE

HORSE TYPE 3
Heat-resistant desert horse of great stamina and endurance.

Colours Metallic Chestnut	Uses Saddle

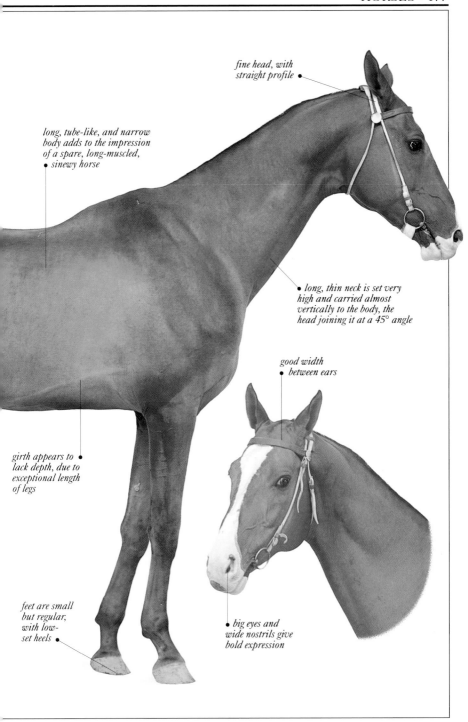

fine head, with
straight profile •

long, tube-like, and narrow
body adds to the impression
of a spare, long-muscled,
• sinewy horse

• long, thin neck is set very
high and carried almost
vertically to the body, the
head joining it at a 45° angle

good width
• between ears

girth appears to •
lack depth, due to
exceptional length
of legs

feet are small
but regular,
with low-
set heels •

• big eyes and
wide nostrils give
bold expression

Environment Temperate, Controlled	Origin 20th century	Blood Warm

BUDENNY

In the 1920s, the Soviet Union began an ambitious programme of selective breeding, designed to create new, improved breeds. The process involved experimental cross-breeding using the very varied native stock. The Budenny, now a kind of universal riding horse, is an example of the approach taken by the state studs.

• **BREEDING** Intended as a cavalry horse and named after Marshal Budenny, the breed, reared in the Rostov region, was based on Chernomor and Don mares crossed with Thoroughbred stallions. Kazakh and Kirghiz crosses were also introduced, but less successfully. Young stock were carefully reared and performance-tested. Three strains were established: Anglo-Don, Anglo-Don-Chernomor, and Anglo-Chernomor, which were less numerous. The mares were put to the selected Anglo-Don stallions, more Thoroughbred blood being introduced as it was thought necessary.

• **CHARACTERISTICS** The Budenny has a formidable record as an endurance horse, and has ability as a jumper and on the racecourse, where, like many Russian breeds, it is performance-tested. It is a lightly built, "breedy" horse of acceptable conformation, but inherits some of the failings of the base stock, particularly in the limbs and joints. Nonetheless, it is incredibly tough.

NORTHERN EURASIA:
RUSSIAN FEDERATION

hindlegs suffer from
• weak structure

• fine, somewhat oriental
head joins neck gracefully

Colours All solid, esp. Chestnut	Uses Saddle

neck is light and
straight, corresponding
with overall build •

short shoulders,
sometimes inclined
• to be upright

HEIGHT
Stands around 16hh.

limbs, not the •
best feature, reflect
quality of base stock

medium-sized
feet are quite
well formed •

INFLUENCES

DON
The base stock
which provided
the tough, hardy
character.

THOROUGHBRED
Contributed size,
better movement
and conformation,
and some quality.

Environment Mountain	Origin 16th century	Blood Warm

KABARDIN

The Kabardin is a mountain horse developed in the northern Caucasus. Like all mountain horses, it is sure-footed and agile, and it has an ability to find its way in mist and darkness.
• **BREEDING** The breed evolved in the 16th century as a result of crossing steppe horses with Persian, Turkmene, and Karabakh strains, and has since been improved by selective breeding at state studs. Kabardins, which are used to upgrade neighbouring stock, are performance-tested on the racetrack. Anglo-Kabardins, the result of crosses with the Thoroughbred, are bigger and faster, but retain much of the hereditary hardiness.
• **CHARACTERISTICS** The breed, in which some natural pacers are found, is noted for its endurance over long distances. Although primarily a saddle horse, the Kabardin is also used in harness.

INFLUENCES

ARAB
Upgrading effect gave spirit and greater physical soundness.

TURKMENE
Transmitted desert horse endurance and heat resistance.

KARABAKH
Gave greater speed and agility, and an even temperament.

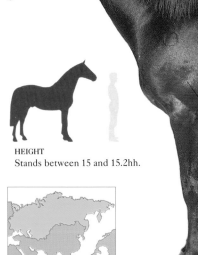

HEIGHT
Stands between 15 and 15.2hh.

NORTHERN EURASIA:
NORTHERN CAUCASUS

• *straight shoulders produce an elevated action*

hindlimbs are • sickle-shaped over hocks

Colours Bay, Black	Uses Saddle, Harness

Environment Mountain, Steppe	Origin 17th century	Blood Warm

KARABAKH

The metallic, dun-coloured Karabakh is a steppe-mountain horse. It is noted for its speed and ability in mounted games such as *chavgan* (a form of polo) and *surpamakh* (basketball), which are popular in the lands around the Caucasus mountains, and it is also used for a variety of general purposes.

• **BREEDING** Originally a native of the Karabakh mountain areas, the breed was crossed with Persian, Akhal-Teke, and Kabardin horses, and then increasingly with Arabs of the racing strains. It influenced the development of the Don horse in the 18th century. The Karabakh is performance-tested on the Baku racecourse in Azerbaijan.

• **CHARACTERISTICS** As well as being fast and agile, it is reputed to be very even-tempered, economical, easily managed, and courageous.

INFLUENCES

AKHAL-TEKE Contributed to stamina, speed, and excellent resistance to heat.

ARAB Added qualities of refinement, hardiness, and great endurance.

quarters are above average for a steppe breed •

top-line is similar to that of a light, elegant riding horse •

• *girth, like that of the Akhal-Teke, is not notably deep*

long, slender limbs •

good, hard feet •

HEIGHT
Stands around 14hh.

NORTHERN EURASIA:
AZERBAIJAN

Colours Metallic Chestnut, Dun	Uses Saddle

Environment Taiga	Origin 18th century	Blood Warm

ORLOV TROTTER

Before the Revolution, horse-breeding in Russia depended on the land-owning aristocracy. A notable breeder, Count Alexei Orlov, created the Orlov Trotter at his Khrenov Stud. The Orlov was intended to race, but was also bred as a carriage horse and as an improver of agricultural stock.

• **BREEDING** Orlov began his breeding programme in 1778. He used a white Arab, Smetanka, on a variety of mares. Polkan I, a direct descendant of Smetanka, and out of a Danish mare, was sire of the breed's foundation stallion, Bars I (1784). Bars I, out of a dun-coloured Dutch mare, was mated with Arab, Dutch, Danish, and English half-breds. The required type was obtained by in-breeding to the foundation horse. Systematic performance testing and racing were used to improve the breed. Orlovs were sometimes crossed with Standardbreds to produce Russian Trotters, which were faster but less useful.

• **CHARACTERISTICS** The Orlov is a tall, lightly built horse. It is powerfully muscled and has good general proportions.

NORTHERN EURASIA: MOSCOW, RUSSIAN FEDERATION

• *powerful, broad croup and loins*

INFLUENCES

NORFOLK TROTTER
Passed on strong constitution and trotting action.

ARAB
Used to refine the somewhat coarse, early agricultural stock.

DUTCH
Contributed its size, substance, and very even temperament.

THOROUGHBRED
Transmitted its physical abilities, improving the action and speed.

Colours Grey, Black, Bay	Uses Harness

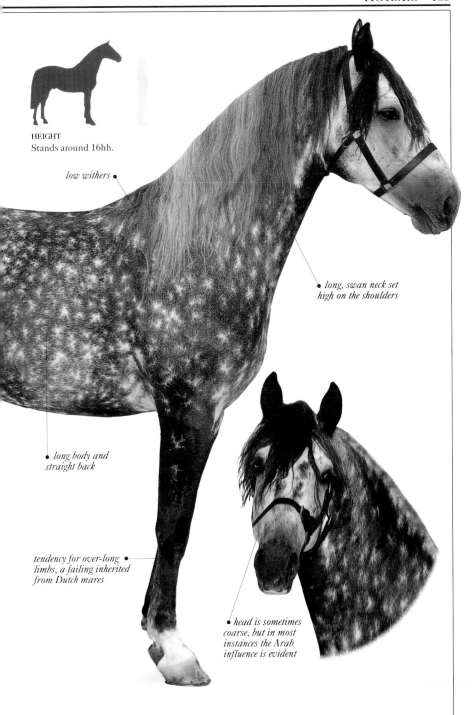

HEIGHT
Stands around 16hh.

low withers •

• *long, swan neck set high on the shoulders*

• *long body and straight back*

tendency for over-long • *limbs, a failing inherited from Dutch mares*

• *head is sometimes coarse, but in most instances the Arab influence is evident*

Environment Steppe	Origin 18th–19th century	Blood Warm

DON

Traditionally, the Don is associated with the Cossack cavalry. Today, it is raced mainly in long-distance events and is far superior to its predecessors. It was much used in the evolution of the Budenny (see pp.178–179).

• **BREEDING** The Don was founded on a mix of tough, steppe-bred Mongolian horses, and swift, heat-resistant Akhal-Tekes and Persian Arabs. Orlovs, Thoroughbreds, and high-class, part-bred Arabs were used to upgrade the breed in the early 19th century. Since the beginning of the 20th century, there has been little outside influence.

• **CHARACTERISTICS** The Don is a hardy horse, which is easily kept and capable of living on the frozen Don steppe. It is adaptable and good natured, but is physically unprepossessing. Although its many conformational deficiencies lead to a restricted, stilted action which is neither elegant nor comfortable, few horses can operate so effectively in conditions of extreme hardship.

NORTHERN EURASIA:
RUSSIAN FEDERATION

croup is rounded and quarters tend to slope away •

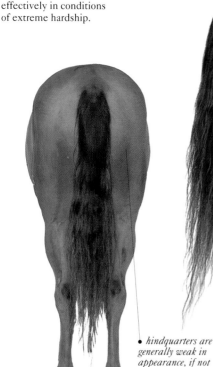

• *sickle hocks are often in evidence in hindlimbs*

• *hindquarters are generally weak in appearance, if not in reality*

Colours Chestnut, Brown	Uses Saddle, Harness

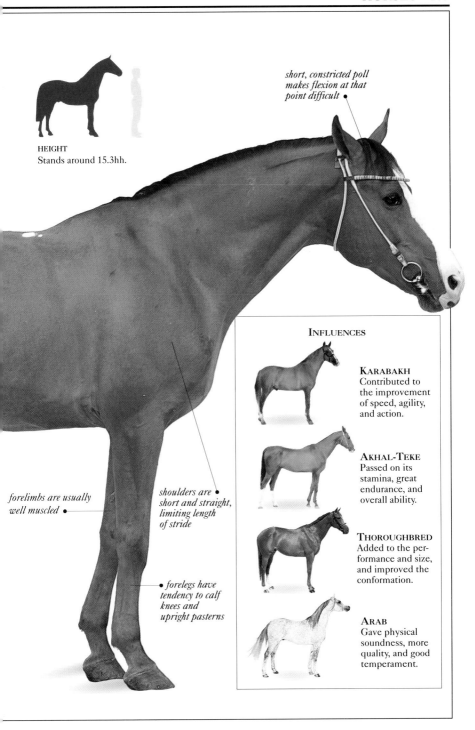

HEIGHT
Stands around 15.3hh.

short, constricted poll makes flexion at that point difficult •

INFLUENCES

KARABAKH
Contributed to the improvement of speed, agility, and action.

AKHAL-TEKE
Passed on its stamina, great endurance, and overall ability.

THOROUGHBRED
Added to the performance and size, and improved the conformation.

ARAB
Gave physical soundness, more quality, and good temperament.

• *shoulders are short and straight, limiting length of stride*

forelimbs are usually well muscled •

• *forelegs have tendency to calf knees and upright pasterns*

Environment Steppe, Taiga	Origin Prehistoric	Blood Warm

Przewalski's Horse

In general terms, it is possible to say that modern horse breeds derive from the four "primitive" equine strains that survived the Ice Age – the Tarpan, the Tundra Horse, the Forest Horse, and Przewalski's Horse. Of these, the forest and steppe Tarpan of eastern Europe, *Equus przewalski gmelini antonius*, survives only in a "replica" herd maintained at Popielno in Poland. The Tundra Horse of north-east Siberia, which has almost certainly not contributed to the domestic stock of horses, is extinct, and so too is the heavy, slow-moving horse of northern Europe, *Equus przewalski silvaticus*, the Forest or Diluvial Horse. Therefore, the sole survivor of these founding fathers is *Equus przewalski przewalski poliakov*, which is now known as Przewalski's Horse, or the Asian Wild Horse. Though extinct in the wild, it is preserved in zoos and some private stables.

MONGOLIA: TACHIN SCHAH MOUNTAINS

- **BREEDING** This primitive horse is named after the Polish colonel, N.M. Przewalski (1839–1888). He discovered a wild herd in Mongolia in 1881, in the area of the Tachin Schah Mountains (literally, the Mountains of the Yellow Horses), on the edge of the Gobi Desert.
- **CHARACTERISTICS** Przewalski's Horse is fierce and untamed, and has a unique, primitive vigour. It displays characteristics that are not found in the domestic horse – for instance, a chromosome count of 66 as opposed to 64 in the domestic animal. The mane is upright, the body colour is sand-dun with black legs, sometimes with zebra stripes, and there is a pronounced dorsal eel-stripe.

quarters slope away

lower half of tail carries coarse, black hair

HEIGHT
Stands between 12 and 14.2hh.

hooves are very hard, big, flat, and narrow

Colours Dun	Uses Feral

short, upright mane is typically primitive •

• profile is straight or convex

little or no • forelock

short • cannons

• head is long and heavy with small eyes set high, giving the impression of even greater length

Environment Tropical	Origin 13th–14th century	Blood Warm

KATHIAWARI

The Kathiawari can be looked upon as being indigenous to the Indian sub-continent. Its homeland is Kathiawari, the peninsula framed by the Gulfs of Kutch and Khamba on India's western coast. It is also found in Gujerat, in southern Rajasthan, and throughout Maharashta.

• **BREEDING** The origin of the distinctive Kathiawari breed lies with the Arab imports from the Gulf states to the province's principal port of Verval, in the days of the Mongol emperors, and then in later years to Bombay. These horses were crossed with native stock carrying much eastern blood – the Kabuli and Baluchi strains, for example. From that point, the horses were bred selectively by the princely houses. There are 28 distinct strains that are recognized.

• **CHARACTERISTICS** The tough and hardy Kathiawari is a narrow-built horse, like the Arab in general appearance. The best examples exhibit the characteristic high tail carriage. Many have a natural ability to pace, indicating an affinity with central Asian breeds. They are claimed to be intelligent, docile, and affectionate.

INDIA: KATHIAWARI
PROVINCE

• *quarters appear weak*

• *hindlegs seem to lack strength in comparison with European breeds*

• *very distinctive head, with exceptionally mobile ears which curve inwards until tips are touching*

Colours All, except Black	Uses Harness, Saddle

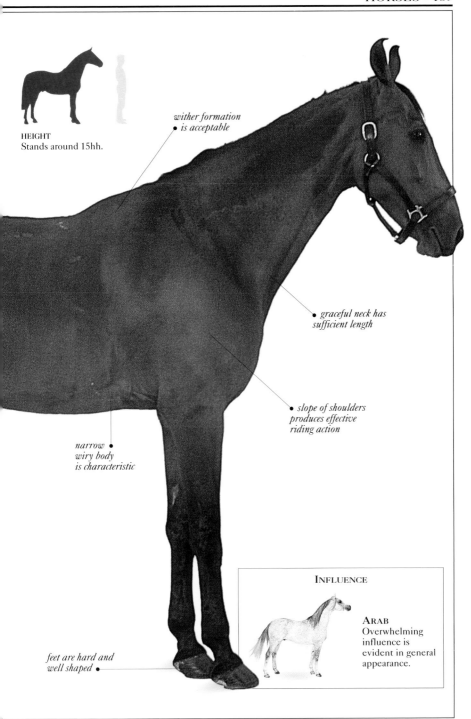

HEIGHT
Stands around 15hh.

*wither formation
is acceptable*

*graceful neck has
sufficient length*

*slope of shoulders
produces effective
riding action*

*narrow
wiry body
is characteristic*

*feet are hard and
well shaped*

INFLUENCE

ARAB
Overwhelming
influence is
evident in general
appearance.

Environment	Tropical	Origin	19th century	Blood	Warm

INDIANBRED

Military requirements in India still call for numbers of cavalry remounts, pack animals, and mules, and the Indianbred, developed specifically to fulfil the modern need for an all-round horse, continues to be produced at army studs and remount depots.

• **BREEDING** In the early days of the British Raj, Indian cavalry was mounted largely on horses that were predominantly Arab in origin, troopers under the prevailing system providing their own horses. In the early 1800s, the Kathiawari was in demand, as well as the Kabuli and Baluchi horses. Around the turn of the century, however, large numbers of Walers were imported from Australia, and these became the standard remount for Indian cavalry up to the time the regiments were mechanized. It is from the base provided by these elements, with substantial outcrosses to the Thoroughbred, that the modern Indianbred troop horse is bred for the mounted formations still in operation.

• **CHARACTERISTICS** The Indianbred horse is of the best trooper type, and is not dissimilar to a good stamp of middleweight hunter. It is proportionate and well made, with good limbs and feet. Outside of military duties, it is often a good, all-round performer in the competitive disciplines. The horses are noted for their equable temperament and soundness of constitution.

INDIA: NORTHERN AND CENTRAL

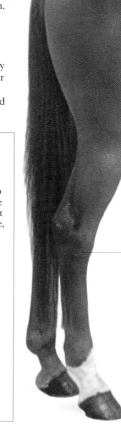

• *hindlegs are workmanlike and correct in their proportions*

INFLUENCES

THOROUGHBRED
Refining influence on conformation; it added to the scope, action, and spirit.

WALER
Gave versatility and substance; aided endurance and constitution.

ARAB
Endurance and temperament were paramount. Gave soundness.

Colours	All solid	Uses	Saddle

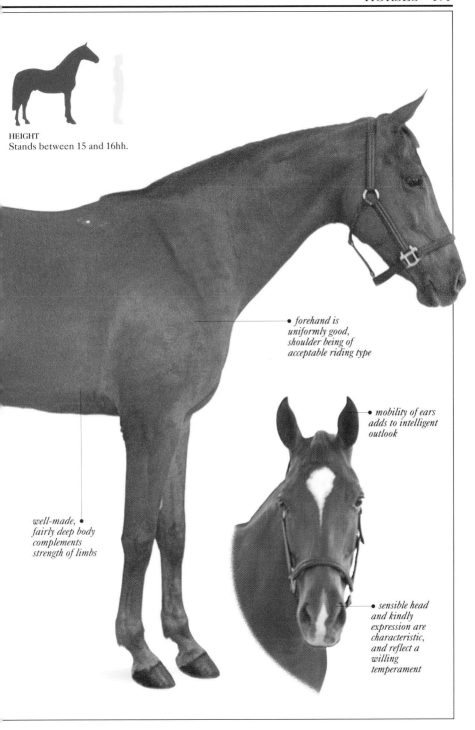

HEIGHT
Stands between 15 and 16hh.

• *forehand is uniformly good, shoulder being of acceptable riding type*

• *mobility of ears adds to intelligent outlook*

*well-made, •
fairly deep body complements strength of limbs*

• *sensible head and kindly expression are characteristic, and reflect a willing temperament*

Environment Temperate grassland	Origin 19th century	Blood Warm

AUSTRALIAN STOCK HORSE

Horses were first imported to Australia about 200 years ago. They came from South Africa and then increasingly from Europe, and were mainly Arab and Thoroughbred. The local stock, bred for work on the sheep and cattle stations, came to be known as Walers after the province in which they were principally bred, New South Wales.

• **BREEDING** During the First World War, and for some years afterwards, as long as there was a military requirement, the Waler was acknowledged as the world's finest cavalry horse. Thousands were employed in Allenby's campaign against the Turks in 1917–1918, and the Indian cavalry regiments were mounted on them before mechanization. From this base was developed what is now called the Australian Stock Horse. It is an Anglo-Arab type, inclining towards the Thoroughbred, and has been influenced by Percheron and pony blood, and also by Quarter Horse, a breed of increasing popularity in Australia.

• **CHARACTERISTICS** The modern Stock Horse is more Thoroughbred in appearance than the old Waler; it is a superb and very practical all-rounder, with great endurance and stamina. A hard, quality horse, it is exceptionally agile. It is up to weight, and has an easy disposition. As yet, there is an absence of fixed type and there are no specific standards of conformation.

AUSTRALIA: NEW
SOUTH WALES

• *strong quarters contribute to the agility for which the breed is renowned*

HEIGHT
Stands between 15 and 16hh.

hocks are strong, • the joints set low to the ground

Colours All solid, mainly Bay	Uses Saddle

strong, well-made
back, ideally suited
• to carry a saddle

head inclines towards the •
Thoroughbred but often
with a chunkiness suggestive
of the Quarter Horse

• deep chested, with
the good, sloped
shoulders of an all-
round riding horse

ood bone, short
annons, and hard feet
re characteristic •

INFLUENCES

WALER
Gave stamina,
versatility, and
an equable
temperament.

THOROUGHBRED
Added speed
and refinement;
improved the
action and scope.

Environment Cool temperate	Origin 19th century	Blood Warm

SADDLEBRED

The most famous and numerous of the American gaited breeds is the Saddlebred, formerly called the Kentucky Saddler. It originally evolved in the southern states as a practical all-rounder, but is now regarded as a brilliant, if artificial, show-ring horse, either under saddle or in harness.

• **BREEDING** The American Saddlebred was developed from the old Narragansett Pacer, workhorse of the Rhode Island plantations, and the Canadian Pacer – both naturally gaited breeds. The breed was refined and acquired its impressive, eye-catching appearance, speed, and brilliance of movement through the introduction of Morgan and Thoroughbred blood.

• **CHARACTERISTICS** An imposing horse of great presence and spirit, the Saddlebred performs the walk, trot, and canter with a high, elevated action (three-gaited). The additional paces, exhibited by a five-gaited horse, are the four-beat, prancing "slow gait" and the breath-taking, full-speed "rack". When its feet are trimmed normally, the Saddlebred can be used for pleasure and for trail-riding.

USA: KENTUCKY

quarters have a level croup, with the tail set high and nicked to emphasize carriage •

• *limbs are light and elegant*

INFLUENCES

THOROUGHBRED
Contributed quality, spirit, and further brilliance of movement.

NORFOLK ROADSTER
The source of trotting ability and outline.

NARRAGANSETT PACER
Contributed to the special gaits of the Saddlebred.

SPANISH
Transmitted hardiness, stamina, and spectacular gaits.

Colours All solid	Uses Saddle, Harness

HEIGHT
Stands between 15 and 16hh.

neck is set high into
shoulders, adding to
• elevated carriage

quality head is finely
drawn, with neat,
sharp ears, breadth
between the bold eyes,
a small muzzle, and
• wide, open nostrils

trunk is typical of the •
horse's elegant outline
and is wonderfully
sprung through the ribs

sloping pasterns
provide a comfortable,
springy ride •

feet are usually grown
long, especially in
front, and are shod
with heavy shoes •

Environment Cool temperate	Origin 18th century	Blood Warm

APPALOOSA

The spotted gene in horses is as old as the equine race, but the credit for the development of a distinctive spotted breed, the Appaloosa, has to be given to the Nez Percé Indians of North America. They lived in the north-east of Oregon, their lands including the valley of the Palouse River after which the horses were named.

USA: OREGON

• **BREEDING** The breed developed in the 18th century, and was founded on the Spanish stock brought to the Americas, which included a number of spotted strains. The Nez Percé, who were skilful horse breeders, practised strict selection policies. The result of their care was an unmistakable workhorse which was attractively coloured and essentially practical. In 1877, the tribe and its horses were almost exterminated as United States troops seized the tribal lands. However, the breed was revived in 1938 when the Appaloosa Horse Club was formed in Moscow, Idaho. Its registry is now the third largest in the world.

• **CHARACTERISTICS** The present-day Appaloosa is a stock and pleasure horse which is used increasingly for jumping and racing. It is noted for its endurance, stamina, and good temperament. There are five recognized Appaloosa coat patterns: blanket, marble, leopard, snowflake, and frost (see pp.22–23).

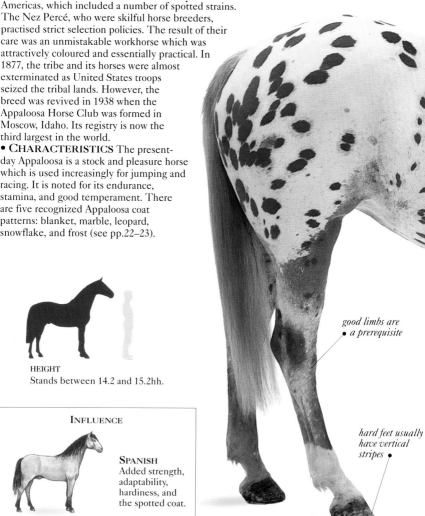

good limbs are a prerequisite

hard feet usually have vertical stripes

HEIGHT
Stands between 14.2 and 15.2hh.

INFLUENCE

SPANISH
Added strength, adaptability, hardiness, and the spotted coat.

Colours Spotted	Uses Saddle

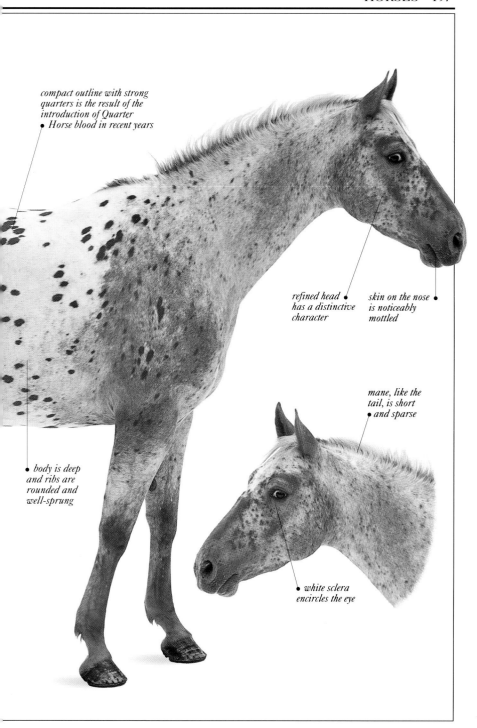

compact outline with strong
quarters is the result of the
introduction of Quarter
• Horse blood in recent years

refined head •
has a distinctive
character

skin on the nose •
is noticeably
mottled

mane, like the
tail, is short
• and sparse

• body is deep
and ribs are
rounded and
well-sprung

• white sclera
encircles the eye

Environment Cool temperate	Origin 19th century	Blood Warm

MISSOURI FOX TROTTER

The Missouri Fox Trotter is an American gaited breed, like
the Tennessee Walker and the Saddlebred. It was established
in the Ozark Mountains in Arkansas and Missouri, in about
1820, as a utility horse suited to the country and the needs of
the settlers. A stud book for the breed was opened in 1948.
The modern Fox Trotter is an all-round pleasure and show
horse. It is usually ridden in Western tack. The gaits evolved
naturally, and artificial aids are banned by the breed society.

USA: ARKANSAS AND MISSOURI

• **BREEDING** The early American settlers interbred
Morgans, Thoroughbreds, and horses of the initial Spanish-
Barb ancestry. They then introduced Saddlebred and
Tennessee Walking Horse blood to create a plain, compact
horse of easy temperament, which was distinguished by a
smooth, peculiarly broken gait which could be
maintained, over long distances and rough
ground, at a regular 8km/h (5mph).

• **CHARACTERISTICS** The most
notable characteristic is the comfortable,
sure-footed, sliding gait that produces
very little movement in the back.
The horse walks with a spirited
action in front while trotting with
the hindlegs. The hindfeet reach
well forward and touch down
with a sliding movement. Over
short distances, the famous
Fox Trot gait produces speeds
of 16km/h (10mph).

*although inclined to be
plain, the head is neat and
intelligent, without coarse
fleshiness, and has pointed
and mobile ears •*

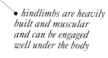

*• hindlimbs are heavily
built and muscular
and can be engaged
well under the body*

Colours All, primarily Chestnut	Uses Saddle

HEIGHT
Stands between 16 and 17hh.

*wide bridlepath is often
"hogged" at the top of
the neck* •

• *neck is proportionate to
the shoulders; its adequate
length contributes to a
fairly low action*

*body is wide and
deep chested, with
powerful shoulders* •

*breed is sure-footed
and noted for its
excellent feet* •

INFLUENCES

SADDLEBRED
Added freedom
and activity, and
complemented
the action.

SPANISH
Base for the gait;
contributed to
hardiness and
temperament.

MORGAN
Gave strength
of limb and
consolidated
the action.

Environment Temperate, Controlled	Origin 18th century	Blood Warm

MORGAN

The Morgan is unusual in that it descends from one prepotent stallion, Justin Morgan. It is an all-round pleasure horse, whether ridden Western or English style, and is increasingly a show horse, competing in Park classes either under saddle or in harness. Until mechanization, the Morgan was the chosen remount of the United States Army. A statue of Justin Morgan, at the Morgan Horse Farm at the University of Vermont, is a permanent memorial to one of the world's most extraordinary horses.

USA: MASSACHUSETTS AND VERMONT

• **BREEDING** The founder of the breed was born in either 1789 or 1793 at West Springfield, Massachusetts. In 1795, he was acquired by a Vermont school master, Justin Morgan, and was named after him. He was worked hard at the plough, at hauling timber, and clearing woodland. He was matched in severe weight-pulling contests and raced in harness and under saddle, but was never beaten. Also a most prolific and potent sire, all Morgans relate back to him, although his own breeding has never been established. It has been suggested that he was sired by an early Thoroughbred, True Briton. Another theory attributes the horse to a Friesian import, and the Welsh claim him as the progeny of a Welsh Cob – which is not impossible.

• **CHARACTERISTICS** The show Morgan is deliberately shod to produce an artificially elevated action. However, if the feet are trimmed normally, the horse moves freely at the basic gaits, without undue knee lift. The breed is hardy and possessed of great stamina and exceptional strength. More refined in appearance than the earlier and more chunky type, today's Morgan is spirited, but intelligent and easily managed.

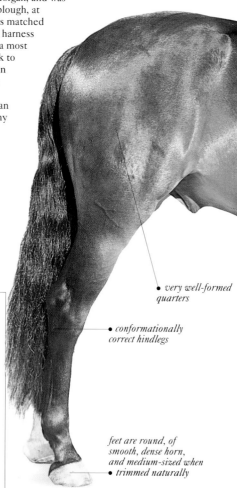

• *very well-formed quarters*

• *conformationally correct hindlegs*

feet are round, of smooth, dense horn, and medium-sized when • *trimmed naturally*

INFLUENCES

ARAB
The Arab was a possible, but unsubstantiated, influence.

THOROUGHBRED
Early Thorough-bred blood may have been an influence.

Colours All solid, except Grey	Uses Saddle, Harness

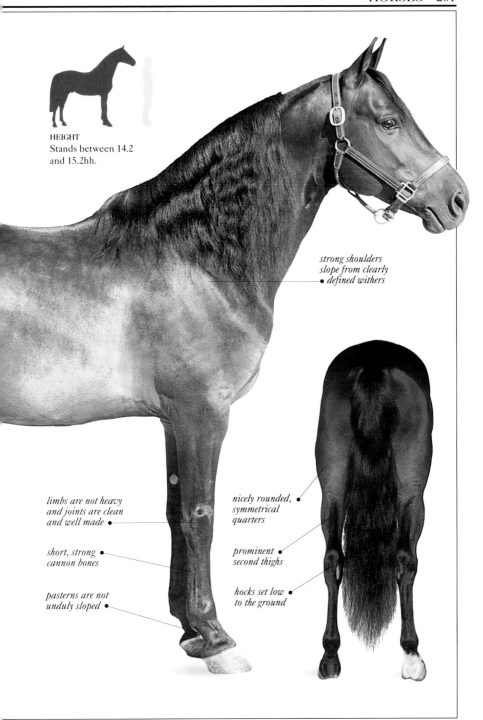

HEIGHT
Stands between 14.2 and 15.2hh.

strong shoulders slope from clearly defined withers

limbs are not heavy and joints are clean and well made

short, strong cannon bones

pasterns are not unduly sloped

nicely rounded, symmetrical quarters

prominent second thighs

hocks set low to the ground

Environment Desert, Savanna	Origin 16th–17th century	Blood Warm

MUSTANG

The name "mustang" is a corruption of the Spanish *mesteña*, meaning a group or herd of horses. At the beginning of the 20th century, there were about one million wild horses in the western United States. By 1970, the herds were drastically reduced as they were killed for pet food and meat for human consumption. They are now protected by law.

• **BREEDING** The Mustang herds originated in the horses that were brought to America by the Spanish in the 16th century. The Spanish established cattle ranches in Mexico, and horses that were turned loose or strayed eventually became feral, forming the nucleus of the herds that spread upwards into North America and the western plains.

• **CHARACTERISTICS** Mustangs are agile, hardy, and often very fast. Although they often degenerate into poor-quality scrub stock, they frequently retain the strength and some of the appearance of their Spanish forebears. Mustangs provided the base for stock like the legendary Chickasaw Indian Pony, which influenced the Quarter Horse.

INFLUENCE

SPANISH Responsible for wiry strength, speed, and hardy constitution.

head in this good specimen is essentially Spanish in character •

luxuriant mane and tail, and body colouring are typical of the Spanish horse •

• body is strong and broad but without prominence in withers

• hard and enduring limbs

feet do not need the • protection of shoes

HEIGHT
Stands between 13.2 and 15hh.

USA: WESTERN STATES

Colours All	Uses Feral

Environment Hot temperate	Origin 15th–16th century	Blood Warm

PALOMINO

The ancient golden palomino colouring occurs in a variety of horses and ponies as well as established breeds. The Palomino is, therefore, a "colour-type" and not a "breed" in the accepted sense. The Spanish brought palomino colouring to America, where it now occurs in the Quarter Horse and the Saddlebred. The name may derive from a Spanish don, Juan de Palomino, or a golden Spanish grape.

• **BREEDING** Although not strictly a breed, Palomino horses are bred extensively in the USA. The American Palomino Horse Association registers horses meeting specific standards and measuring between 14.1 and 16hh. For registration, one parent must be registered, and the other parent must be Quarter Horse, Arab, or Thoroughbred.

• **CHARACTERISTICS** These depend on the dominant genetic influence. The most favoured cross to produce palomino is chestnut with palomino, or chestnut with cream or albino.

INFLUENCE

SPANISH
Passed on many physical attributes, and also the distinctive colour.

USA

mane and tail are silvery white and should not contain more than 15 per cent dark hair

colour is that of a newly minted gold coin, or three shades lighter or darker

if white markings occur on legs, they must not extend above knees or hocks

HEIGHT
Any height is acceptable.

Colours Palomino	Uses Saddle

Environment Savanna	Origin 16th century	Blood Warm

PINTO, OR PAINT HORSE

In America, there are two breed societies for this horse – the Pinto Horse Association and the American Paint Horse Association, both with their headquarters in Fort Worth, Texas. The Pinto Horse Association registers any breed of horse that meets its colour requirement, dividing them into stock type, hunter, pleasure type, and saddle type. It has a similar classification for ponies. The American Paint Horse Association registers stock-type horses with blood lines from Paints, Quarter Horses, and Thoroughbreds.

USA

• **BREEDING** The Pinto is a descendant of the Spanish horses brought to America in the 16th century. Until the 18th and 19th centuries, a part-coloured strain was evident in Europe, in horses derived from Spanish blood. The name "Pinto" comes from the Spanish word *pintado*, meaning "painted", and in the vernacular of the western cowboy this became "paint". Part-coloured horses, or even spotted ones, were also called calicos.

• **CHARACTERISTICS** There are two types of colouring: ovaro and tobiano. Ovaro is a basic solid coat with large, irregular splashes of white over it. Tobiano is a white base coat with large, irregular patches of solid colour. It is difficult to accord the Pinto breed status, in the accepted meaning of the word, because of the lack of consistency in type and size.

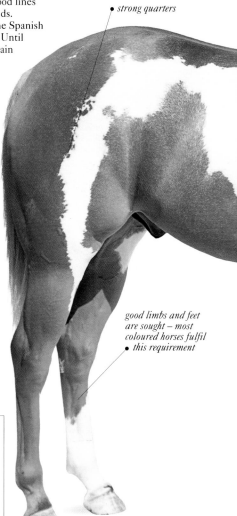

• *strong quarters*

good limbs and feet are sought – most coloured horses fulfil
• *this requirement*

HEIGHT
Stands between 15 and 16hh.

INFLUENCE

SPANISH
Gave physical attributes as well as the coloured coat patterns.

Colours Part	Uses Saddle

inclining towards a stock-
horse type, the build of this
• Pinto is powerful

forehand of this specimen is
• of exemplary riding type

this type of •
colouring is
called "ovaro"

sensible, quality •
head of this particular
Pinto reflects underlying
Thoroughbred influence

Environment Cool temperate	Origin 18th–19th century	Blood Warm

QUARTER HORSE

The Quarter Horse, the first all-American breed, is claimed to be "the most popular horse in the world". Over 3 million are registered with the American Quarter Horse Association.

• **BREEDING** Its foundation was English horses, imported into Virginia in about 1611, and Spanish stock, brought to America in the previous century. It was used for every sort of work: farming, hauling, working cattle, in harness, and under saddle. The English settlers raced them over stretches of about a quarter of a mile, hence the name Quarter Horse, and the horse's ability to sprint flat-out over this distance. In the West, the Quarter Horse was the supreme cattle pony, working cattle with an uncanny instinct.

• **CHARACTERISTICS** The old Quarter Horse was noted for massive quarters which facilitated its sprinting ability from a standing start. The recent use of more Thoroughbred blood, with the aim of increasing racing speed, has tended to reduce this notable characteristic.

USA

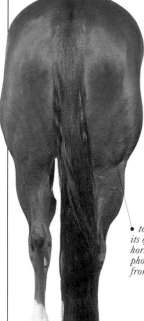

• *hips are wide and limbs are heavily muscled in thighs and gaskins*

• *to accentuate its quarters, the horse is often photographed from behind*

Colours All solid	Uses Saddle

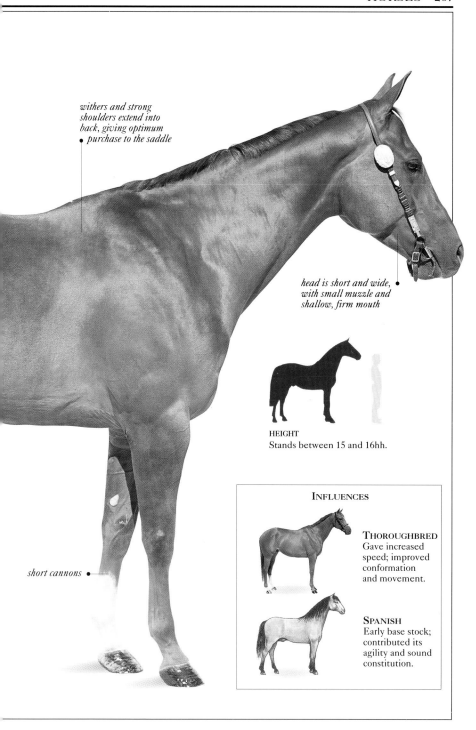

withers and strong
shoulders extend into
back, giving optimum
• purchase to the saddle

head is short and wide, •
with small muzzle and
shallow, firm mouth

HEIGHT
Stands between 15 and 16hh.

short cannons •

INFLUENCES

THOROUGHBRED
Gave increased
speed; improved
conformation
and movement.

SPANISH
Early base stock;
contributed its
agility and sound
constitution.

Environment Cool temperate	Origin 18th–19th century	Blood Warm

TENNESSEE WALKING HORSE

"If you ride one today, you'll own one tomorrow" says the Tennessee Walking Horse Breeders' and Exhibitors' Association. The modern Walker is one of the unique group of American gaited horses developed in the 19th century. Originally ridden by the plantation owner, today's Walker is a popular family horse.

• **BREEDING** The Walker derives from the old Narragansett Pacer and evolved as a mix of Standardbred, Morgan, Thoroughbred, and American Saddlebred. The foundation sire is the Standardbred trotter, Black Allan, whose peculiar walk was inherited by his progeny.

• **CHARACTERISTICS** The Walker has three "bounce-free" gaits: a flat walk; a running walk, which has four beats and in which the head nods in time and the teeth click; and a high, smooth, rocking-chair canter. The breed is said to be the most naturally good-tempered of all equines.

INFLUENCES

NARRAGANSETT PACER
Provided the original, natural pacing gait.

THOROUGHBRED
Introduced additional refinement; improved conformation.

STANDARDBRED
Gave the peculiar walk through the foundation sire, Black Allan.

short-coupled body with barrel having square appearance

HEIGHT
Stands between 15 and 16hh.

USA: TENNESSEE

Colours All solid	Uses Saddle

Environment Cool temperate	Origin 19th century	Blood Warm

STANDARDBRED

In many countries harness racing is more popular than flat racing. In America, it has a following of over 30 million people. The Standardbred is the supreme harness racer. It can cover 1.6km (1 mile) in 1 minute 55 seconds. The breed got its name in 1879, when a speed standard was set for entry into the register.

• **BREEDING** The Standardbred was based on the English Thoroughbred, Messenger, a horse with strong Norfolk Trotter connections, who was imported in 1788. The foundation sire was Messenger's descendant, Hambletonian 10, foaled in 1849. Between 1851 and 1875, this horse sired 1,335 offspring. Hambletonian's peculiar and high-crouped conformation contributed to his success as a sire of harness racers.

• **CHARACTERISTICS** Standardbreds either trot conventionally or pace, employing the lateral, swaying gait. Pacers are faster and less likely to break the gait, and are preferred in America. In Europe, trotters are more numerous. Both have iron-hard legs and good feet.

INFLUENCES

THOROUGHBRED
Added speed, and improved straightness of action and conformation.

NARRAGANSETT PACER
Provided the basis for a natural pacing gait.

MORGAN
Transmitted robust constitution, endurance, and stamina.

croup is usually higher than withers – giving enormous propulsive thrust to quarters

HEIGHT
Stands around 15.2hh.

USA: EASTERN SEABOARD

Colours Bay, Brown, Chestnut	Uses Harness

Environment Cool temperate	Origin 19th century	Blood Warm

COLORADO RANGER

Besides the Appaloosa, another American spotted breed of
interest is the Colorado Ranger, or Rangerbred. This has
records dating from 1878 and incorporates some illustrious
bloodlines. It is less well-known than the Appaloosa
because, up to 1968, membership of the Colorado Ranger
Horse Association, Inc. was limited to 50 persons.

• **BREEDING** The Colorado Ranger was founded on two
horses presented to General Ulysses Grant by Sultan Abdul
Hamid II of Turkey in 1878. They were the pure-bred grey
Arab called Leopard, and a Barb stallion called Linden
Tree. Since then, outcrosses have been made to
Thoroughbreds and Quarter Horses.

• **CHARACTERISTICS** The lines established by the
Colorado breeders produced excellent working horses
of a particular refinement. Most Rangers have a
patterned coat, but it is their pedigree that is the
prime requirement for registration.

USA: COLORADO

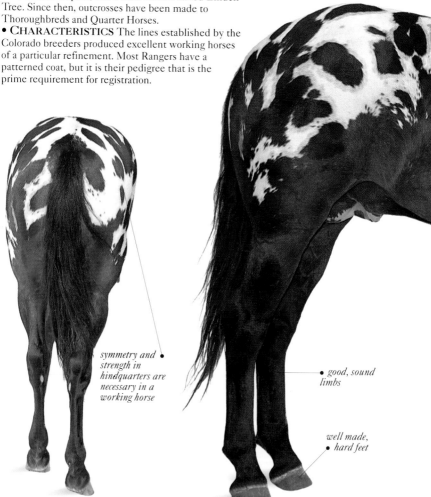

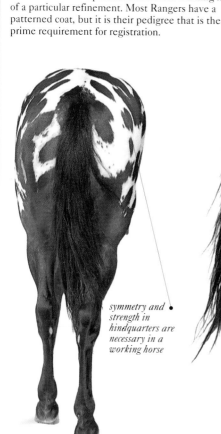

symmetry and
strength in
hindquarters are
necessary in a
working horse

• good, sound
limbs

well made,
• hard feet

Colours Spotted	Uses Saddle

HEIGHT
Stands around 15.2hh.

*head has pleasing
proportions and an
intelligent outlook*

*body is compact
and deep, but not
heavy – evidence of
Arab/Barb ancestry*

INFLUENCES

ARAB
Contributed to
the symmetry of
form; transmitted
prepotency.

BARB
Complemented
the Arab qualities
and added
increased agility.

SPANISH
This sound and
hardy breed
provided the
base stock.

Environment Savanna	Origin 16th century	Blood Warm

CRIOLLO

Although the Criollo is the native horse of
Argentina, it appears in slightly different forms
and under a variety of names all over the South
American continent. For instance, in Brazil, it
is the *Crioulo Brazileiro*. In Argentina, the
Criollo is the indispensable mount of the
gaucho, the cowboy of the pampas, and has
played an important part in the evolution of
the famous Argentinian polo pony.
• **BREEDING** The Criollo originated in the
Spanish stock brought to South America from
the 16th century. These horses carried much
enduring Barb blood. The first significant
imports were made in 1535 by Don Pedro
Mendoza, the founder of Buenos Aires. Later,
when the city had been sacked by the Indians,
these horses ran wild over large areas of the
country and bred freely.
• **CHARACTERISTICS** The Criollo is
probably the toughest, soundest horse in the
world, a tribute to its Spanish ancestry. It is
capable of living in climatic extremes on
minimal feed, has incredible powers of
endurance, and is noted for its longevity.

INFLUENCE

SPANISH
Contributed to
phenomenal
toughness and
endurance.

*medium-sized head is
sometimes convex in
profile, denoting
Spanish origin* •

body is short and •
*deep, with well-
sprung ribs*

HEIGHT
Stands between 14
and 15hh.

ARGENTINA

Colours Predominantly Dun	Uses Saddle

Environment Savanna	Origin 16th century	Blood Warm

PASO

The Peruvian Paso, or stepping horse, shares a common ancestry with the Criollo. It is distinguished by its unique lateral gait and a particular conformation, confirmed by selective breeding over three centuries or more.

• **BREEDING** Breeding is directed at perfecting the natural gait – the paso. The action involves a vigorous, round movement of the forelegs, supported by powerful use of the hindlegs, the quarters being held low. This can be kept up for long periods over rough country.

• **CHARACTERISTICS** The breed is very tough. The hindlegs and hind pasterns are long, and the joints are unusually flexible overall. These factors contribute to the comfort of the paso gait.

INFLUENCE

SPANISH
Early Spanish gaited strains were responsible for paso action.

PERU

HEIGHT
Stands between 14 and 15hh.

• *chest is broad and deep, and musculature is very well developed*

great depth in body, allowing room for unusually large lungs

Colours All solid	Uses Saddle

HEAVY HORSES

Environment Taiga	Origin 19th century	Blood Cold

NORTH SWEDISH HORSE

The attractive North Swedish Horse is a close relation of
Norway's Døle Gudbrandsdal, and at one time was much
influenced by that breed. It is a small, compact, and very
active draught horse much used in forestry, at which it
excels, and in agriculture. The lighter Døle crosses (which
share the stud book) are specialist harness racers.

• **BREEDING** The principal stud is at Wangen. From
early this century, stringent performance testing has been
in force. The horses are subject to log-hauling tests, and
their pulling power is measured against an ergometer.
Mature animals undergo further draught tests, and
all stock have feet and limbs checked radiologically.

• **CHARACTERISTICS** The horses are noted for
their good temperament, freedom of action, courage,
and strength. The breed is exceptionally long-lived
and appears immune to most common diseases.

SWEDEN: NORTH

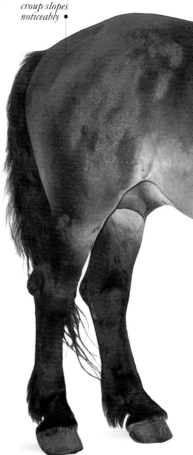

*croup slopes
noticeably* •

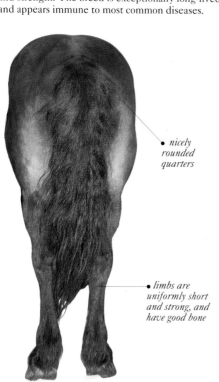

• *nicely
rounded
quarters*

• *limbs are
uniformly short
and strong, and
have good bone*

Colours All solid	Uses Light Draught

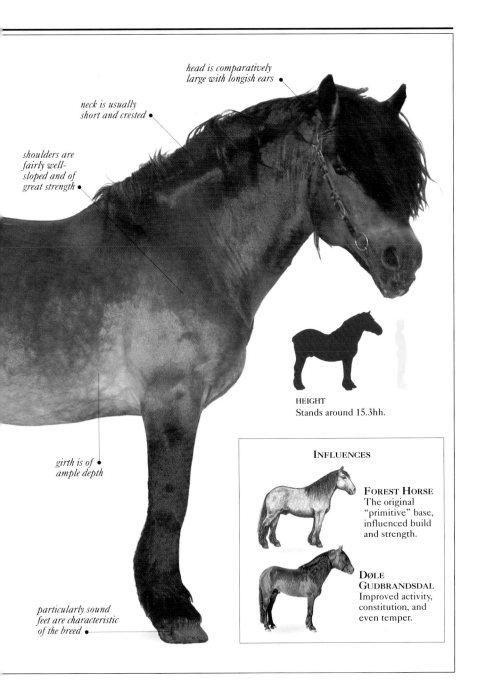

head is comparatively large with longish ears •

neck is usually short and crested •

shoulders are fairly well-sloped and of great strength •

girth is of ample depth •

particularly sound feet are characteristic of the breed •

HEIGHT
Stands around 15.3hh.

INFLUENCES

FOREST HORSE
The original "primitive" base, influenced build and strength.

DØLE GUDBRANDSDAL
Improved activity, constitution, and even temper.

Environment Temperate, Controlled	Origin 12th century	Blood Cold

JUTLAND

The Jutland, Denmark's own breed of heavy horse, has been bred on the Jutland Peninsula since the Middle Ages and before. It was used for agriculture and all types of draught but today, when its numbers have declined, it is most often seen hauling brewers' drays on city streets.

• **BREEDING** Like other heavy horse breeds, the Jutland is derived from the coldblood Forest Horse of prehistory. By the 12th century, it had been developed as a sturdy war-horse, up to weight, enduring, and economical to keep. In the 19th century, the modern Jutland began to take shape. This was as a result of outcrosses to the Cleveland Bay and the Yorkshire Coach Horse; however, the overwhelming influence is that of the Suffolk Punch, which it resembles so closely, through Oppenheim LXII, imported in 1860. The most important bloodline is that of his descendant, Oldrup Munkedal. The Jutland is largely responsible for the neighbouring Schleswig horse, and crosses were still being made well into the 20th century.

• **CHARACTERISTICS** The Jutland is a medium-sized draught horse with a quick, free action. Like that of the Suffolk Punch, the coat is almost always chestnut with a flaxen mane and tail, and the breed's connection with the Suffolk is evident in the compact, round body, the deep girth, and the massive quarters. In one respect, it differs entirely from the Suffolk Punch, for the Jutland's legs carry a heavy feather that is not found in the former. The breed has a reputation for being docile, kindly, and a tireless, willing worker.

DENMARK: JUTLAND
PENINSULA

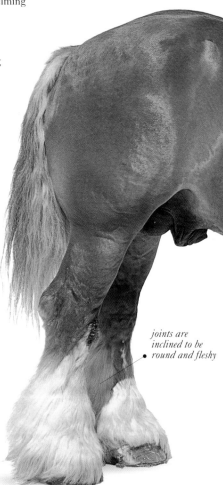

joints are inclined to be round and fleshy •

HEIGHT
Stands between 15 and 16hh.

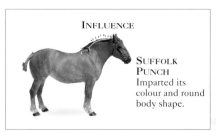

INFLUENCE

SUFFOLK PUNCH Imparted its colour and round body shape.

Colours Chestnut, Roan	Uses Draught

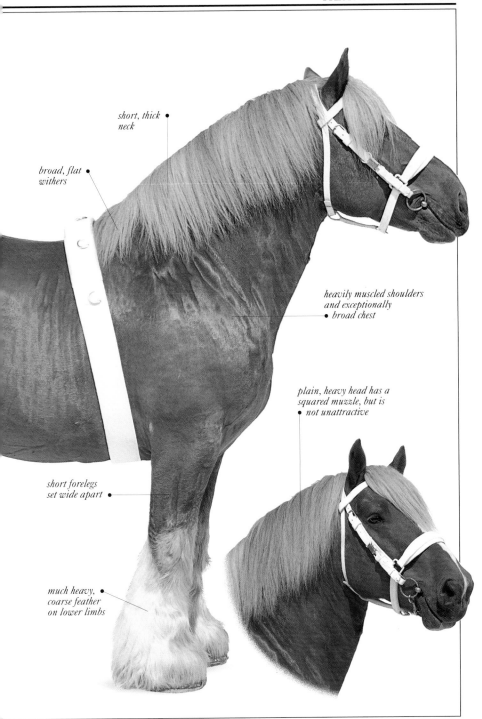

short, thick
neck

broad, flat
withers

heavily muscled shoulders
and exceptionally
broad chest

plain, heavy head has a
squared muzzle, but is
not unattractive

short forelegs
set wide apart

much heavy,
coarse feather
on lower limbs

Environment Cool temperate	Origin 1st–2nd century AD	Blood Cold

BRABANT

The Brabant, also known as the Belgian Heavy Draught or *race de trait Belge*, takes its name from one of the breed's principal breeding areas. Although no longer well-known outside its native country, it is one of the most important heavy horse breeds, and has a strong following in the USA.

• **BREEDING** The breed is very old and is thought to descend directly from the Forest or Diluvial horse (*Equus przewalski silvaticus*). Horses like this were known to the Romans, and from the 11th to the 16th centuries, heavy warhorses were produced in Brabant and Flanders. Flanders horses had a profound influence in Europe. For example, in Britain, they were a foundation for Shires and Clydesdales, and may have contributed to the Suffolk Punch. Belgian breeders used established bloodlines to produce a horse that was suited to their climate, types of soil, and economic and social conditions. They resisted the inclusion of foreign blood, practised a policy of stringent selection, and inbred where it was necessary to preserve exceptional qualities.

• **CHARACTERISTICS** The three principal lines, established in the 19th century, are: *Gros de la Dendre*, founded by Orange 1 and noted for massive bay horses; *Gris du Hainaut*, founded by the stallion Bayard, which has grey, dun, and the distinctive red-roan colouring; the third, founded on Jean 1, is the *Colosses de la Mehaique*, which has exceptionally good limbs and tremendous strength in the back and loins.

BELGIUM: BRABANT AND FLANDERS

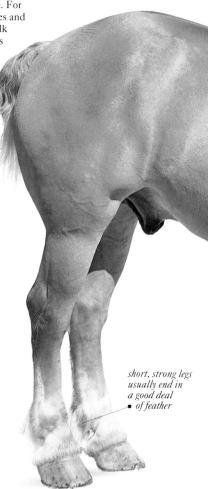

short, strong legs usually end in a good deal • of feather

HEIGHT
Stands between 16.2 and 17hh.

INFLUENCE

FLANDERS HORSE
Gave strength, size, weight, and coat colourings.

Colours Roan, Chestnut	Uses Heavy Draught

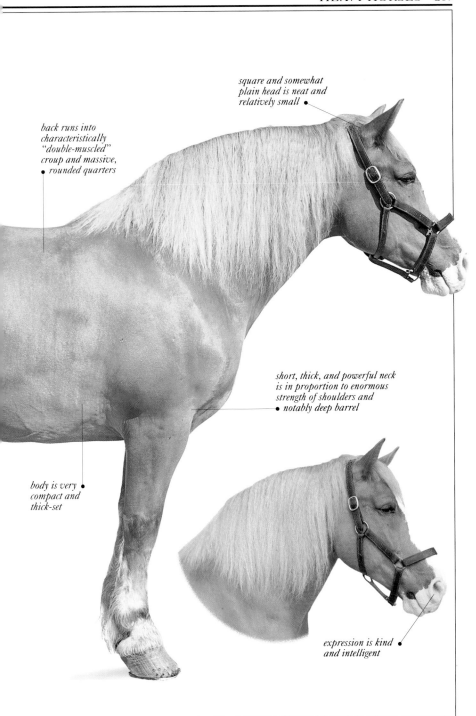

square and somewhat
plain head is neat and
relatively small •

back runs into
characteristically
"double-muscled"
croup and massive,
• rounded quarters

short, thick, and powerful neck
is in proportion to enormous
strength of shoulders and
• notably deep barrel

body is very •
compact and
thick-set

expression is kind •
and intelligent

Environment Cool temperate	Origin 16th century	Blood Cold

NORIKER

The Noriker is one of Europe's ancient coldblood breeds. It derives its name from the state of Noricum, a vassal province of the Roman Empire, corresponding to present-day Austria. Noricum was adjacent to the lands of the horse-raising Venetii, which were to become the home of the Haflinger, and there is, therefore, a natural connection between the two breeds. The modern Noriker is still exceptionally popular in Austria and is the established all-purpose workhorse of the central Alps region. Now a breed of fixed and clearly recognizable type, the Noriker is subject to strictly enforced breed standards and there is a rigorous system of inspection and performance testing.

• **BREEDING** The early ancestors of the breed developed by the Romans were heavy warhorses, which could also be used in draught and under pack. The Noriker was recognized as a breed from about 1565, when it was taken under the wing of the monasteries and the Salzburg Stud Book, initiated by the Prince-Archbishop of Salzburg. Heavy Burgundian horses were used to increase the size of the stock but more important was the introduction of the all-pervasive Spanish blood. Spotted horses, Pinzgauer-Noriker, appeared and these still occur. The Spanish legacy is still evident in a number of other distinctive coat patterns.

• **CHARACTERISTICS** This is a hard, powerful, medium-sized workhorse. The conformational standards stipulate 22–24cm (8½–9½in) of bone, short limbs of exceptional strength, and a girth measurement of not less than 60 per cent of the height at the withers. The breed is hardy, inherently sound, economical, and easily managed.

AUSTRIA AND THE CENTRAL ALPS

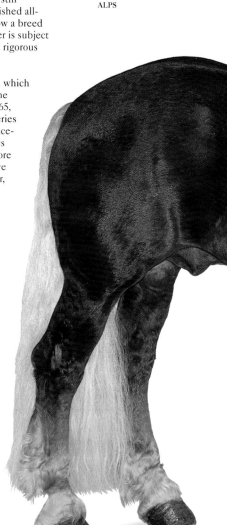

INFLUENCES

SPANISH Contributed to refinement and to freedom of action.

FOREST HORSE Primitive base stock gave increased size.

Colours Brown, Black, Chestnut	Uses Light Draught

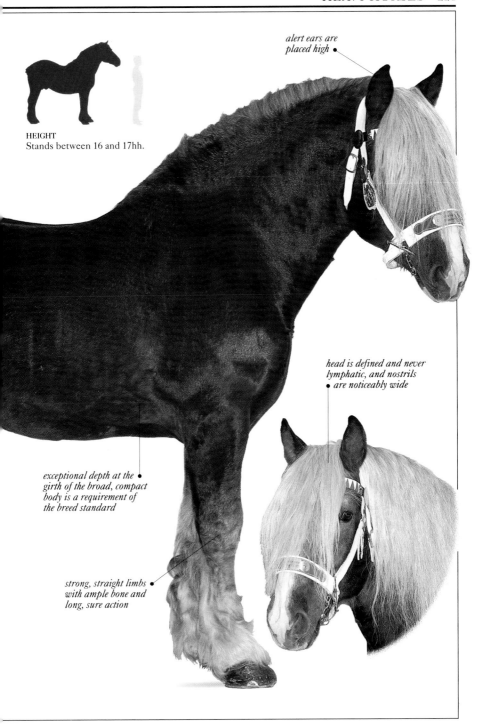

alert ears are
placed high •

HEIGHT
Stands between 16 and 17hh.

head is defined and never
lymphatic, and nostrils
• are noticeably wide

exceptional depth at the •
girth of the broad, compact
body is a requirement of
the breed standard

strong, straight limbs •
with ample bone and
long, sure action

Environment Cool temperate	Origin Pre-Christian	Blood Cold

ARDENNAIS

The heavily boned, snub-nosed heavy horses of
the Ardennes region of France and Belgium are
among the oldest in the world. They were
developed during the 19th century to fulfil a
variety of requirements, and two types evolved
– the lively, light draught type and the slower
but very powerful heavy type, which was the
workhorse of northern France.

• **BREEDING** The Ardennes horses developed
into specific types by various outcrosses. Arab,
Thoroughbred, Percheron, and Boulonnais
produced the now rare, light, Postier-type; the
bigger Ardennes du Nord was derived from
outcrosses to the Brabant, as was the larger and
very powerful Burgundy horse, the Auxois.

• **CHARACTERISTICS** This docile and
easily handled breed is naturally hardy due to
its harsh environment. Although still used in
agriculture, it is also
bred for meat.

INFLUENCE

FOREST HORSE
The source of
the size, weight,
and docile
temperament.

HEIGHT
Stands around 15.3hh.

*compact body, with very
short back and exceptional
breadth over loins •*

*straight-profiled head •
has low forehead and
prominent eye-sockets*

*legs are massive and
covered with heavy,
coarse feathering •*

FRANCE: ARDENNES, AND
BELGIUM: SOUTH-EAST

Colours Roan	Uses Heavy Draught

Environment Cool temperate	Origin 1st–2nd century AD	Blood Cold

BOULONNAIS

The pronounced oriental influence in the Boulonnais breed has produced a draught horse of singular beauty and refinement.

• **BREEDING** The Boulonnais is a native of north-west France, where there was a special breed of heavy horses in pre-Christian times. Eastern horses were first introduced by the Romans in the first century AD. In the 14th century, the Boulonnais was used as a warhorse, so heavier stallions were used to increase its size. From then, Spanish stock was also used.

• **CHARACTERISTICS** In the 17th century, two types emerged: the small, fast *mareyeur*, for delivering fish from Boulogne; and the heavy, agricultural horse, which is still bred.

INFLUENCES

SPANISH
Gave soundness of limb, better constitution, and increased activity.

ARAB
Transmitted its refinement and spirit; greatly improved action.

FOREST HORSE
Supplied the basis for the considerable size and substance.

refined, graceful head is evidence of oriental influence

HEIGHT
Stands between 15.3 and 16.3hh.

FRANCE: BOULOGNE

• prominently veined skin

muscular limbs have short, thick • cannons

Colours Grey	Uses Heavy Draught

Environment Cool temperate	Origin Middle Ages	Blood Cold

BRETON

The Breton is the indigenous horse of north-west France. It is based on the primitive horse of the Black Mountains. At one time, there were four distinct types, one of which was a riding horse. Two types are now recognized: the massive draught and the lighter Breton Postier.
• **BREEDING** The heavy draught Breton was developed from outcrosses to the Ardennais, Boulonnais, and Percheron. The smaller Postier carries Boulonnais and Percheron blood and also some Norfolk Roadster. Both types share one stud book. They are selectively bred and performance-tested in harness.
• **CHARACTERISTICS** The heavy draught, an early maturing horse, is in demand for meat. The Postier, a clean-legged horse, like a lightweight Suffolk Punch, displays energy and freedom at the trot. Once used as an artillery horse, it is ideal for light agricultural draught and is used to improve less developed stock.

FRANCE: BLACK MOUNTAINS

tail is customarily docked, like that of • the Norman Cob

feet are hard, well-shaped, and not too • large

INFLUENCES

BOULONNAIS
Transmitted refinement and greater freedom of action.

ARDENNAIS
Was used to increase the size, substance, and weight.

PERCHERON
Complemented the Boulonnais' qualities, giving great strength.

NORFOLK ROADSTER
Gave robust constitution and trotting ability.

Colours Roan, Chestnut	Uses Heavy Draught, Light Draught

HEIGHT
Stands between 15.3
and 16.3hh.

*neck corresponds to
overall outline and
is short, thick, and
• arched*

*• small,
mobile ears*

*• head is square
and straight-
profiled*

*quarters are broad •
and square with
pronounced muscles,
the movement behind
being particularly
straight and free*

*legs are short
and strong,
with little
feathering •*

Environment Cool temperate	Origin 18th century	Blood Cold

PERCHERON

The attractive Percheron, an elegant horse owing much to
Arab blood, is one of the most popular heavy breeds. One
authority described it as "an Arab influenced by the climate
and the agricultural work for which it has been used for
centuries". The Percheron, much appreciated because of
its lack of feathering, a frequent cause of skin problems,
was exported extensively to Canada and the USA.

FRANCE: NORMANDY

• **BREEDING** The Percheron originated in the limestone
region of La Perche, Normandy. Its ancestors may have
carried the knights of Charles Martel, who broke the Muslim
invasion of Europe at Poitiers in AD732. It is claimed that,
from then, oriental blood was available to French breeders.
More eastern blood was used after the 11th century,
and Arab sires were used at Le Pin from 1760. The
most influential Percheron lines are dominated
by Arab outcrosses, particularly that of the
stallion, Jean le Blanc, foaled in 1830. Despite
this, the breed has lost none of its size and
power. The world's biggest horse was the
Percheron Dr Le Gear. He stood at 21hh
and weighed 1,372kg (3,024lb).

• **CHARACTERISTICS** The Percheron has
filled many roles: warhorse, coach-horse, farm-
horse, and has even been used under saddle. The
breed is hardy, versatile, and very even tempered.
Like the Boulonnais, the action is long, low, and
free, and distinguishes it from other heavy breeds.

*limbs are short
and massive, and
are not heavily
• feathered*

*fine head has long •
ears, large eyes, and
a broad forehead*

Colours Grey, Black	Uses Heavy Draught

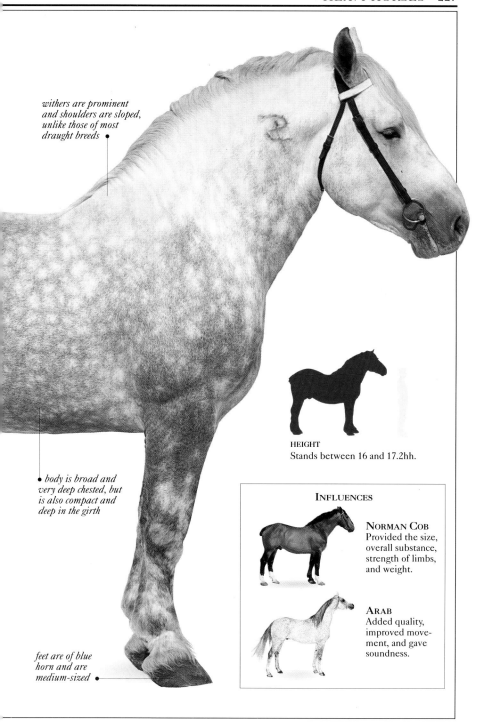

withers are prominent
and shoulders are sloped,
unlike those of most
draught breeds •

• body is broad and
very deep chested, but
is also compact and
deep in the girth

feet are of blue
horn and are
medium-sized •

HEIGHT
Stands between 16 and 17.2hh.

INFLUENCES

NORMAN COB
Provided the size,
overall substance,
strength of limbs,
and weight.

ARAB
Added quality,
improved move-
ment, and gave
soundness.

Environment Cool temperate	Origin 19th–20th century	Blood Cold

NORMAN COB

The enduring, ever popular Norman Cob is still produced at the centuries-old studs of Le Pin and Sainte Lô in Normandy. It is less well-known than the prestigious French Trotters, Percherons, Thoroughbreds, Boulonnais, and Anglo-Normans resident at both centres.

- **BREEDING** At the end of the 19th century, a distinction was made between cavalry remounts and heavier, light-draught type horses. The tails of the light-draught type were docked according to the custom and the horses were called cobs, after their British counterparts. These horses were documented and performance-tested but were never entered in a stud book, although many stallions were kept at both studs.
- **CHARACTERISTICS** Norman Cobs are still used for agricultural work, especially in the La Manche region, with which they are closely associated. They are heavier than previously, but retain their energetic pace at the trot.

FRANCE: LA MANCHE, NORMANDY

• *quarters are muscular and powerful but not as massive as those of the heavy breeds*

little or no • feathering

Colours Chestnut, Bay	Uses Light Draught

strong, crested neck
and sensible head are
characteristic

back is short

good shoulders allow
great freedom at trot –
the working pace

body is compact
and stocky, like that
of the English Cob

limbs are short and
have good bone
measurement

HEIGHT
Stands between 15.3 and 16.3hh.

INFLUENCE

**NORMAN
DRAUGHT**
Provided base of
size, strength,
and weight.

Environment Cool temperate	Origin 18th century	Blood Cold

CLYDESDALE

The Clydesdale Horse Society was formed in Britain in 1877 and in the following year the American Clydesdale Society was founded. Within a short time, the breed was firmly established in both the USA and Canada, and overseas sales became a notable feature in Clydesdale breeding. Clydesdales were also exported in considerable numbers to Germany, Russia, Japan, South Africa, Australia, and New Zealand.

• **BREEDING** The breed originated in the Clyde Valley, Lanarkshire. In the 18th century, the Duke of Hamilton and John Paterson of Lochlyoch imported Flemish stallions. The object was to increase the size of the small native draught horse. Shire blood was also used to such an extent that it could be claimed that Shire and Clydesdale were two branches of a single breed. Nonetheless, by the 19th century, breeders had produced an entirely distinctive breed of draught horse.

• **CHARACTERISTICS** Of lighter build than the Shire, the Clydesdale is noted for its very active paces. Although bred for agricultural work, this versatile breed is particularly suited to heavy urban draught.

UK: LANARKSHIRE, SCOTLAND

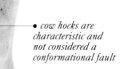

• *cow hocks are characteristic and not considered a conformational fault*

• *head is finer than most draught breeds, with a straight, rather than convex, profile*

feathering is heavy, but not coarse •

Colours Bay, Roan with White	Uses Heavy Draught

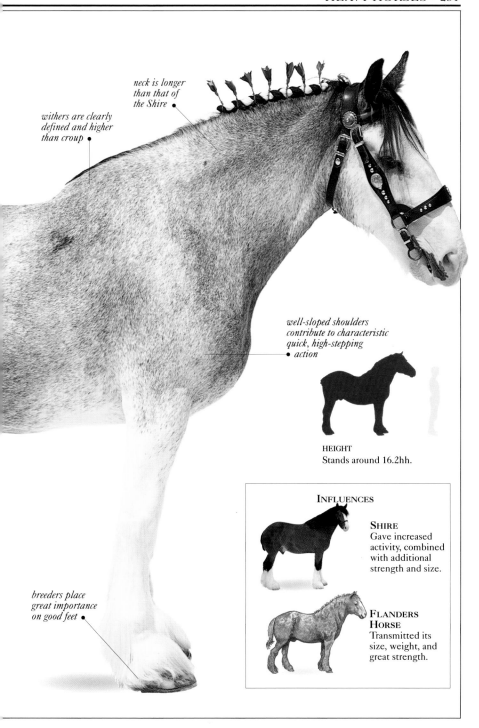

neck is longer
than that of
the Shire •

withers are clearly
defined and higher
than croup •

well-sloped shoulders
contribute to characteristic
quick, high-stepping
• action

HEIGHT
Stands around 16.2hh.

INFLUENCES

SHIRE
Gave increased
activity, combined
with additional
strength and size.

FLANDERS
HORSE
Transmitted its
size, weight, and
great strength.

breeders place
great importance
on good feet •

Environment Cool temperate	Origin 18th century	Blood Cold

SUFFOLK PUNCH

The Suffolk Punch is entirely distinctive due to its "chesnut" colouring (the Suffolk Horse Society always employs that peculiar spelling) and its general appearance. "Punch" is often defined as a short-legged, barrel-bodied English horse – "a short, fat fellow", an apt description of this breed. This East Anglian horse is the oldest and purest of the British heavy breeds. All Suffolks trace their descent from one stallion, Thomas Crisp's Horse of Ufford (Orford), foaled in 1768.

UK: SUFFOLK, ENGLAND

• **BREEDING** It is very likely that the early Suffolks were influenced by the Norfolk Roadsters, developed in East Anglia from the 16th century on. It is also probable that the active-trotting Flanders mares, which were also mainly chestnut, played a part in the breed's evolution.

• **CHARACTERISTICS** The Suffolk is an all-round farm horse. Its legs have no feathering, making it suitable for work on heavy clay lands. It is also an immensely powerful draught horse that was once in great demand in the cities and towns. The breed is long-lived, early-maturing, and economical to keep – needing less feed than other horses of similar size and type. The action at the trot is especially energetic.

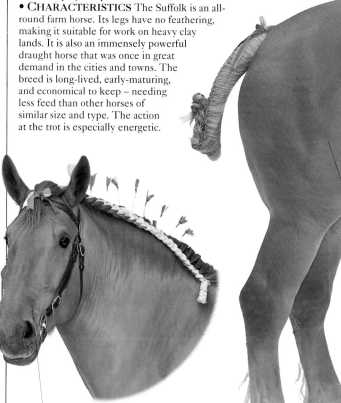

• *quarters are massive and rounded and complement the breed's endearing "roly-poly" character*

• *feet are small for a draught horse, but are hard and sound*

• *relatively large head has a broad forehead and a straight or slightly convex profile*

Colours Chestnut	Uses Heavy Draught

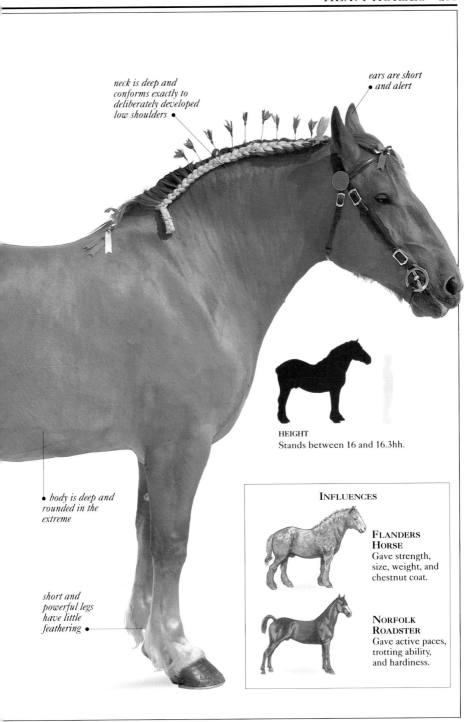

neck is deep and conforms exactly to deliberately developed low shoulders

ears are short and alert

body is deep and rounded in the extreme

short and powerful legs have little feathering

HEIGHT
Stands between 16 and 16.3hh.

INFLUENCES

FLANDERS HORSE
Gave strength, size, weight, and chestnut coat.

NORFOLK ROADSTER
Gave active paces, trotting ability, and hardiness.

Environment Cool temperate	Origin 19th century	Blood Cold

SHIRE

The Shire is considered to be the supreme draught horse. It is remarkably popular in Britain and, if anything, its numbers are on the increase. The name Shire derives from the Midland shires of Lincoln, Leicester, Stafford, and Derby.

• **BREEDING** The breed descends from England's Great Horse of the Middle Ages, which was subsequently known as the English, or Old English, Black. During the 16th and 17th centuries, the native stock was much influenced by Flanders horses. These had been imported by Dutch contractors who were draining the English fenlands. The active black Friesian was another element. The Shire's foundation stallion was the Packington Blind Horse. He stood at Ashby-de-la-Zouche between 1755 and 1770 and appears in the first stud book, published in 1878. In 1884, the Shire Horse Society replaced the English Cart Horse Society and the name "Shire" came into being.

• **CHARACTERISTICS** The Shire is noted for its great strength and is probably the heaviest of the draught breeds. Its weight, when full grown, may be 1,016–1,219kg (2,240–2,688lb). Despite its size and strength, the Shire is essentially gentle and easily managed.

UK: MIDLANDS, ENGLAND

bone measurement is 28–30cm
• (11–12in)

HEIGHT
Stands between 16.2 and 17.2hh.

INFLUENCES

FRIESIAN
Improved the breed's carriage, and added to its freedom of action.

FLANDERS HORSE
Provided the great strength, size, and weight.

Colours Black, Bay, Grey	Uses Heavy Draught

relatively
long neck •

overall structure is one of
strength, with width across
the body and short,
• thick musculature

shoulders are
wide and deep to
• accommodate a collar

the girth of a full- •
grown Shire may be
1.8–2.4m (6–8ft)

lower limbs are
heavily feathered with
fine, silky hair •

• head is broad between
large and kindly eyes, and
nose is Roman (convex)

Environment Temperate, Controlled	Origin 18th–19th century	Blood Cold

ITALIAN HEAVY DRAUGHT

The Italian Heavy Draught, often termed the Italian
Agricultural Horse, was the most popular heavy horse in
Italy. It was bred extensively in northern and central
Italy, particularly around Venice. Today, the horse is
required as much for meat as for work, and its
numbers are decreasing.

ITALY: NORTHERN AND
CENTRAL

• **BREEDING** Before the establishment of a national
heavy draught breed, Italy relied on imports of Brabant
horses from Belgium. These animals were crossed with
local mares. As the results were not entirely suitable,
further outcrosses were made to the Boulonnais and
Percheron. Finally, this much improved stock was
outcrossed to the clean-legged, fast-trotting Breton
Postier, itself influenced by the Norfolk Trotter.
The resultant stock was quick-moving and of
smaller proportions, and was ideal for light
draught and farm work. The relatively swift
trotting action gave rise to the Italian breed
title, *Tiro Pesante Rapido*.

• **CHARACTERISTICS** The overall
conformation reflects the strong influence of
the Breton. There is also a suggestion of the
lighter Avelignese, which may have been
involved in the base stock. The Italian Heavy
Draught is generally a compact, symmetrical
animal with a surprisingly fine head. Some
coarseness is apparent in the limbs, round
joints, and boxy feet. It is kind and willing,
and it has an energetic action.

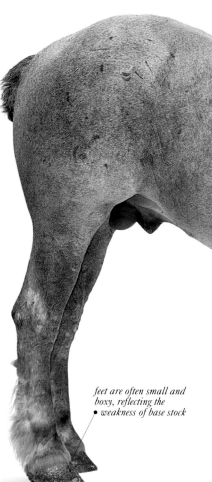

HEIGHT
Stands between 15 and 16hh.

*feet are often small and
boxy, reflecting the
• weakness of base stock*

INFLUENCE

BRETON
Active movement
was derived
from this fast-
trotting breed.

Colours Chestnut, Roan	Uses Draught

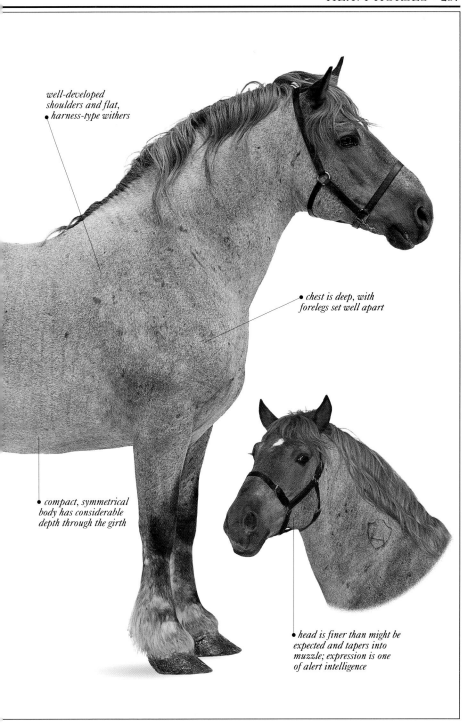

well-developed
shoulders and flat,
• harness-type withers

• chest is deep, with
forelegs set well apart

• compact, symmetrical
body has considerable
depth through the girth

• head is finer than might be
expected and tapers into
muzzle; expression is one
of alert intelligence

TYPES

Environment Temperate, Controlled	Origin 18th–19th century	Blood Warm

HUNTER

The hunter is a type that is peculiar to Britain and Ireland. It is not a breed, because it lacks fixed common characteristics and may vary according to the requirements of the country in which it is ridden. In strongly-fenced, grass country, for instance, a near-Thoroughbred horse is required. In countries where speed is not of the essence, a sensible half-bred horse, with staying power and the ability to jump, is more suitable.

UK AND IRELAND

• **BREEDING** The best hunters are those bred in Britain and Ireland, where hunting has been a part of rural life for centuries. Often, both Irish and English hunters are based on a cross between the Irish Draught and the Thoroughbred. Many good horses also carry pony blood, some may be Cleveland Bay crosses, and others have heavy horse blood in their ancestry. Whatever the mix, the best hunters will always carry a good proportion of Thoroughbred blood to give speed, courage, and athletic ability.
• **CHARACTERISTICS** A hunter must be sound, well-proportioned, and have all the conformational attributes of a good riding horse. He needs to be well-balanced, fast enough, and sufficiently bold to tackle every sort of obstacle in all riding conditions. He should be temperate, have good manners, and a robust constitution.

• *limbs built for strength and speed*

feet must be exemplary •

INFLUENCES

THOROUGHBRED
Provided the essential scope and boldness in the hunter.

IRISH DRAUGHT
Supplied bone, substance, and a sensible outlook.

CLEVELAND BAY
Imparted bone, size, and the jumping ability.

Colours All, including part	Uses Saddle

HEIGHT
Stands between
16 and 16.2hh.

• *this hunter has a great "front" beyond the saddle and corresponding length over the neck's top-line*

• *compact body with well-sprung ribs and ample depth through girth*

• *the best hunters show quality in their heads, with an honest, workman-like outlook*

Environment Temperate, Controlled	Origin 18th–19th century	Blood Warm, Hot

HACK

The modern hack, a British phenomenon, is essentially a show horse of supreme elegance, full of presence, beautifully balanced in its paces, and with perfect manners.

• **BREEDING** The majority of show hacks are Thoroughbred, although some may be part-bred or Anglo-Arabs. In the past, a distinction was made between the "covert" hack, which conveyed the rider to the hunt meet, and the more refined "park" hack, which fashionable socialites rode in places like London's Rotten Row. Modern show hacks are the equivalent of the latter, while "riding horses" take the place of the covert hacks and have their own classes.

• **CHARACTERISTICS** A hack has to be a model of good conformation. Although light and graceful, it must be neither ponyish, nor a "blood weed", and it is expected to have 20cm (8in) of bone below the knee.

INFLUENCES

THOROUGHBRED Gave elegance, balance, good conformation, and movement.

ANGLO-ARAB Provided similar elegance with a more equable temperament.

classic shoulders of the • quality riding horse

notably straight hindlimbs, with long musculature and prominent second thigh •

HEIGHT
Stands between 14.2 and 15.3hh.

limbs are light and graceful, but there must be ample bone • below the knee

UK: ENGLAND

Colours All solid	Uses Saddle

Environment Temperate, Controlled	Origin 20th century	Blood Warm

RIDING PONY

The riding pony is the juvenile equivalent of the show hack, but, while having the proportions of the Thoroughbred, it retains the essential pony look and character. In Britain, show-ring riding ponies are exhibited in three divisions: up to 12.2hh, up to 13.2hh, and up to 14.2hh.

• **BREEDING** The riding pony has evolved in Britain over the last half-century as a result of a skilful amalgam of bloods. It represents a remarkable accomplishment in the history of horse breeding. The base stock was largely Welsh ponies (Sections A and B), or ponies with Welsh and possibly some Arab blood. These were crossed with small Thoroughbred sires of polo type, and at least one notable strain descends from an Arab, the stallion, Naseel.

• **CHARACTERISTICS** The action is free, long, and low like the Thoroughbred. Ideally, it retains some of the substance of its native forebear and a lot of its good sense.

INFLUENCES

THOROUGHBRED
Gave long, low action; provided extra brilliance and quality.

WELSH A
Gave essential pony character and added to the substance.

ARAB
Added to soundness of limb and manageable temperament.

HEIGHT
Stands between 12 and 14.2hh.

overall outline and proportion is a scaled-down version of the hack

UK: ENGLAND

Colours All solid	Uses Saddle

Environment Temperate, Controlled	Origin 18th–19th century	Blood Warm

COB

The cob is one of the most appealing horses. Although it is immediately recognizable, it is not a breed, for there is no set pattern to its production. In Britain, the cob is still an all-round horse and will often, in the old Roadster tradition, go as well in harness as under saddle.

• **BREEDING** Some very good cobs are bred in Ireland from Irish Draught crosses, and some are pure Irish Draught. Welsh Cobs are another source, and there are cobs that have been bred from heavy horse breeds crossed with small Thoroughbreds, or from Cleveland Bays. On the whole, the breeding of cobs is likely to be accidental rather than deliberate.

• **CHARACTERISTICS** Cobs (those standing up to 15.1hh) are exhibited in British show classes with their manes hogged, and are expected to walk, trot, canter, and gallop. The traditional practice of hogging sets off the strong, short neck and gives the horse a jaunty, sporting look. Otherwise, the cob is thick-set, with powerful quarters and short, strong limbs. It is a structure that is predisposed to the carrying of weight rather than to speed, although cobs are still expected to gallop and jump. Above all, a cob, while being a "character", must also have the best of manners. He is considered to be a "gentleman's gentleman", and is expected to behave as such.

IRELAND, AND UK: ENGLAND

• *limbs have plenty of bone*

INFLUENCES

IRISH DRAUGHT
Base stock gave bone, strength, substance, and good sense.

THOROUGHBRED
A touch of the Thoroughbred gave a refining and riding quality.

WELSH COB
Gave power, excellent limbs and feet, and some character.

Colours All, including part	Uses Saddle, Harness

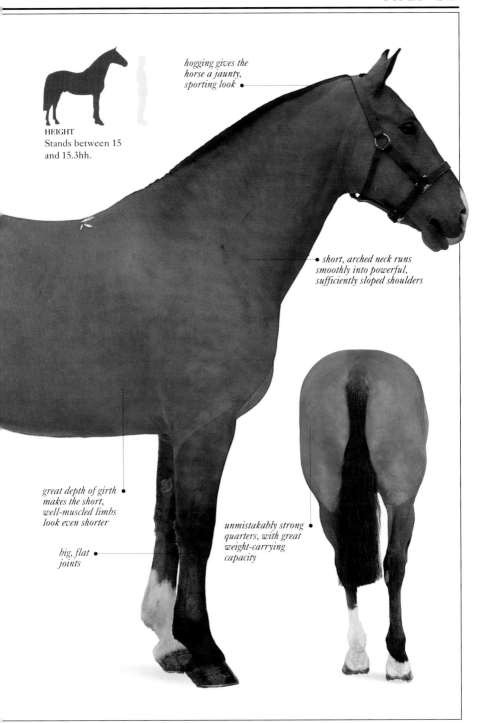

HEIGHT
Stands between 15
and 15.3hh.

*hogging gives the
horse a jaunty,
sporting look* •

• *short, arched neck runs
smoothly into powerful,
sufficiently sloped shoulders*

great depth of girth •
*makes the short,
well-muscled limbs
look even shorter*

unmistakably strong •
*quarters, with great
weight-carrying
capacity*

big, flat •
joints

| Environment Temperate, Controlled | Origin 19th–20th century | Blood Warm, Hot |

POLO PONY

Although the polo pony is not a breed (nor a pony
any more), it is a specifically developed type and is
recognizable by its outline and general appearance.
Originally, height limits were imposed under the rules
of the game of polo, but these were abolished after the
First World War and now the height of the average
polo pony is about 15.1hh.

ARGENTINA

• **BREEDING** The ancient game of polo originated in
Persia as long ago as 525BC, and was introduced to
Europe and the Americas by the British, who had
learned the game in India. British-bred ponies were
based on native pony mares crossed with small
Thoroughbreds, but today's pony is likely to have
strong Argentine connections. The Argentinians
dominate the game and have the facilities
to produce quality ponies in quantity. They
imported Thoroughbreds and crossed
them with the tough, part-bred Criollo
stock, putting the progeny back to the
Thoroughbred to increase speed. In recent
years, American Quarter Horses have also
become an element in polo pony breeding.

• **CHARACTERISTICS** The polo pony is
distinctly Thoroughbred in appearance. It
has to be fast, courageous, balanced, and
very agile. A long, low stride is not a
necessary attribute, as it is easier to hit
the ball from a shorter-striding pony.

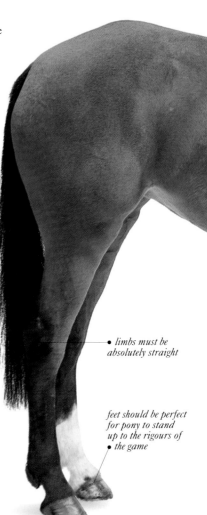

• *limbs must be
absolutely straight*

*feet should be perfect
for pony to stand
up to the rigours of
• the game*

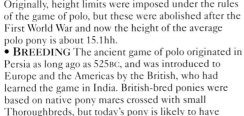

*head is wiry and •
clean, without
fleshiness*

| Colours All, including part | Uses Saddle |

HEIGHT
Stands around 15.1hh.

mane is always
hogged, to avoid
interference
with the stick •

• typically lean,
graceful neck and very
prominent withers

short cannons
and good bone
are characteristic •

INFLUENCES

THOROUGHBRED
Imparted its
speed, quick
responses, agility,
and courage.

**QUARTER
HORSE**
Gave speed, intell-
igence, agility, and
responsiveness.

CRIOLLO
The wiry base
stock was tough,
sound, hardy,
and sagacious.

HORSE CREDITS

We are indebted to the many owners and breeders who allowed their horses to be photographed for this book; without their cooperation, it could not have been produced. The horses are listed in page order, accompanied by the name of the breed, the name of the horse, and the name and brief address of the owner.

PONIES

- **48** *Icelandic Horse*: Leiknir, Kentucky Horse Park, USA
- **50** *Fjord Pony*: Maple Klaus, John Goddard Fenwick and Lyn Moran, Ausdan Stud, UK
- **52** *Gotland*: Ripadals Benni 398, Carina Andersson, Sweden
- **54** *Huçul*: Lubas, Janusz Utrata, Poland
- **56** *Konik*: Hewal, S J Skoki, Poland
- **58** *Haflinger*: Nomad, Miss Helen Blair, Silvretta Haflinger Stud, UK
- **60** *Ariègeois*: Radium, Haras National de Tarbes, France
- **62** *Landais*: Hippolyte, Haras National de Pau, France
- **63** *Pottock*: Thouarec III, Haras National de Pau, France
- **64** *Shetland*: Chatsworth Belle, Mrs Hampton, Briar Stud, UK
- **66** *Highland*: Nashend Sabine, Mr and Mrs Clive Smith, Nashend Stud, UK
- **68** *Dales*: Warrenlane Duke, Mr Dickinson, Millbeck Pony Stud, UK
- **69** *Fell*: Waverhead William, Mr and Mrs Errington, UK
- **70** *Hackney Pony*: Hurstwood Consort, Mr and Mrs Hayden, Hurstwood Stud, UK
- **72** *Exmoor*: Murrayton Delphinus, June Freeman, Murrayton Stud, UK
- **73** *Dartmoor*: Allendale Vampire, Miss M Houlden, Haven Stud, UK
- **74** *New Forest Pony*: Bowerwood Aquila, Mrs Ray Turner, Bowerwood Stud, UK
- **76** *Connemara*: Garryhack Tooreen, Mrs Beckett, Shipton Connemara Pony Stud, UK
- **78** *Welsh Mountain Pony*: Bengad Dark Mullein, Mrs C Bowyer, Symondsbury Stud, UK
- **79** *Welsh Pony*: Twyford Signal, Mr and Mrs L E Bigley, Llanarth Stud, UK
- **80** *Welsh Pony of Cob Type*: Llygedyn Solo, Kitty Williams, Glebedale Stud, UK
- **82** *Bardigiano*: Pippo, Istituto Incremento Ippico di Crema, Italy
- **84** *Sorraia*: Giro, Portuguese National Stud (EFPAA), Portugal
- **86** *Skyrian Horse*: Mitsibonas, Dinos Maroudis, Greece
- **87** *Pindos Pony*: Maro, Penny Turner, Greece
- **88** *Caspian*: Hopstone Shabdiz, Mrs Scott, Henden Caspian Stud, UK

- **90** *Bashkir*: Mel's Lucky Boy, Dan Stewart Family, Kentucky Horse Park, USA
- **92** *Australian Pony*: Australian Pony Promotion Group, Pitchwood Stud, Australia
- **94** *American Shetland*: Little Trouble, Marvin McCabe, Kentucky Horse Park, USA
- **96** *Rocky Mountain Pony*: Mocha Monday, Rea Swan, Kentucky Horse Park, USA
- **98** *Chincoteague*: Clover, Kenneth Burton, USA
- **99** *Sable Island Pony*: (State of) Nova Scotia, Canada
- **100** *Galiceno*: Java Gold, Billy Jack Jiles, Texas, USA
- **102** *Falabella*: Pegasus of Kilverstone, Lady Fisher, Kilverstone Wildlife Park, UK

HORSES

- **104** *Døle Gudbrandsdal*: Pajagutt, Gunnar Skjervheim, Norway
- **106** *Finnish Horse*: Oikka, Hevostalouden Tutkimusasema, Finland
- **108** *Swedish Warmblood*: Asterix 694, Swedish National Stud, Sweden
- **110** *Frederiksborg*: Zarif Langløkkegard, Harry Nielsen, Denmark
- **112** *Knabstrup*: Føniks, Poul Elmerkjær, Denmark
- **114** *Danish Warmblood*: Rambo, Jorgen Olsen, Denmark
- **116** *Friesian*: Sjouke, Sonia Gray, Tattondale Carriages, UK
- **118** *Gelderlander*: Spooks, Peter Munt, Ascot Driving Stables, UK
- **120** *Groningen*: Elza, Mr J Dank, Netherlands
- **122** *Dutch Warmblood*: Edison, Mrs Dejonge, UK
- **124** *Belgian Warmblood*: Didi, Mr A. Schwartz, Belgium
- **126** *Trakehner*: Nemo, Ileen Poole, Canada
- **128** *Wielkopolski*: Snapjack, Mrs S Bates, UK
- **130** *Bavarian Warmblood*: Donator, Mr John Hindle, UK
- **131** *Hanoverian*: Défilante, Barry Mawdsley, European Horse Enterprises, UK
- **132** *Holstein*: Lenard, Sue Watson, Trenawin Stud, UK
- **134** *Oldenburg*: Renoir, Louise Tomkins, UK
- **136** *Württemberg*: Tees Hanaeur, Mrs Tees, UK
- **138** *Rhinelander*: Arabella, Mrs Lucinda Marchessini, UK
- **140** *Nonius*: Pampas & **141** *Furioso*: Furioso IV: both owned by A G Kishumseigi, Hungary
- **142** *Shagya Arab*: Artaxerxes, Jeanette Bauch and Jens Brinksten, Denmark
- **144** *Lipizzaner*: Siglavy Szella, J G Fenwick and L Moran, Ausdan Stud, UK

• **146** *Selle Français*: Prince D'elle, Haras National de Saint Lô, France
• **147** *French Trotter*: Pur Historien, Haras National de Compiègne, France
• **148** *Camargue*: Redounet, Mr Contreras, France
• **150** *Anglo-Arab*: Restif, Haras National de Compiègne, France
• **152** *Thoroughbred*: Amoco Park, Spruce Meadows, Canada
• **154** *Hackney Horse*: Whiteavon Step High, David Vyse, UK
• **156** *Cleveland Bay*: Oaten Mainbrace, Mr and Mrs Dimock, UK
• **157** *Irish Draught*: Miss Mill, Mr R J Lampard, UK
• **158** *Welsh Cob*: Treflys Jacko, Mr and Mrs L E Bigley, Llanarth Stud, UK
• **160** *Salerno*: Jeraz, Sig. Giorgio Caponitti, Italy
• **162** *Sardinian*: O'Hara, Sig. P Adriano, Italy
• **164** *Maremmana*: Barone, Mr Attilio Tavazzani, Centro Ippico De Castelverde, Italy
• **165** *Murgese*: Obscuro, Istituto Incremento Ippico di Crema, Italy
• **166** *Andalucian*: Campanero XXIV, Nigel Oliver, Singleborough Stud, UK
• **168** *Lusitano*: Montemere-O-Nova (Romano), Nan Thurman, Turville Valley Stud, UK
• **170** *Alter-Real*: Castro, Portuguese National Stud (EFPAA), Portugal
• **172** *Barb*: Taw's Little Buck, Kentucky Horse Park, USA
• **174** *Arab*: Altruista, Pat and Joanna Maxwell, Lodge Farm Arabian Stud, UK
• **176** *Akhal-Teke*: Fafakir-Bola, Moscow Agricultural Academy, Russia
• **178** *Budenny*: Barin, Moscow Agricultural Academy, Russia
• **180** *Kabardin*: Daufuz, Korache Stud, Russia
• **181** *Karabakh*: Moscow Race Track, Russia
• **182** *Orlov Trotter*: Moscow Hippodrome, Russia
• **184** *Don*: Bageg, Moscow Agricultural Academy, Russia
• **186** *Przewalski's Horse*: Marwell Zoological Park, UK
• **188** *Kathiawari*: refer to publisher
• **190** *Indianbred*: refer to publisher
• **192** *Australian Stock Horse*: Scrumlo Victory, Mrs R Waller, Ophir Stud, Australia
• **194** *Saddlebred*: Dr Technical, Adrian Neufeld, Canada
• **196** *Appaloosa*: Golden Nugget, Sally Chaplin, UK
• **198** *Missouri Fox Trotter*: Easy Street, Ruth Massey, Kentucky Horse Park, USA
• **200** *Morgan*: Fox Creek's Dynasty, Darwin Olsen, Kentucky Horse `Park, USA
• **202** *Mustang*: Patrick, Kentucky Horse Park, USA
• **203** *Palomino*: Golden Wildfire, Monica Comm, Canada

• **204** *Pinto*: Hit Man, Boyd Cantrell, Kentucky Horse Park, USA
• **206** *Quarter Horse*: Mi Starpasser (Dexter), Pat Buckler, Canada
• **208** *Tennessee Walking Horse*: Midnight Toddy, Grethe Broholm, Canada
• **209** *Standardbred*: Rambling Willie, Farrington Stables and the Estate of Paul Siebert, Kentucky Horse Park, USA
• **210** *Colorado Ranger*: Skippers Valentine, T J Crouch, Texas, USA
• **212** *Criollo*: Azulecha, Clare Tomlinson, UK
• **213** *Paso*: Medianoche, D McIntosh, Canada

HEAVY HORSES
• **214** *North Swedish Horse*: Ysterman, Ingvar Andersson, Sweden
• **216** *Jutland*: Tempo, Jørgen Neilsen, Denmark
• **218** *Brabant*: Roy, Kentucky Horse Park, USA
• **220** *Noriker*: Dinolino, Mr J Waldhem, Germany
• **222** *Ardennais*: Ramses du Vallon, Haras National de Pau, France
• **223** *Boulonnais*: Urus, Haras National de Compiègne, France
• **224** *Breton*: Ulysses, Haras National de Tarbes, France
• **226** *Percheron*: Tango & **228** *Norman Cob*: Ibis: owned by Haras National de Saint Lô, France
• **230** *Clydesdale*: Blue Print, Mervyn and Pauline Ramage, Mount Farm Clydesdale Horses, UK
• **232** *Suffolk Punch*: Laurel Keepsake II, P Adams and Sons, UK
• **234** *Shire*: Duke, Jim Lockwood, Courage Shire Horse Centre, UK
• **236** *Italian Heavy Draught*: Nobile, Istituto Incremento di Crema, Italy

TYPES
• **238** *Hunter*: Hobo; **240** *Hack*: Rye Tangle; **241** *Riding Pony*: Brutt; **242** *Cob*: Super Ted: all owned by Robert Oliver, UK
• **244** *Polo Pony*: refer to publisher

GLOSSARY

ALTHOUGH TECHNICAL EXPRESSIONS have been avoided wherever possible, a limited use of them is unavoidable in a book of this nature. Many of the terms listed below are unique to horses and the equestrian world. Words that appear in bold type are explained elsewhere in the glossary, and you may also find it helpful to look at the annotated illustrations on pp.18–19 in order to clarify some of the terms relating to horse anatomy.

• **ABOVE THE BIT**
When the horse carries its mouth above the level of the rider's hand, reducing the rider's control.

• **ABOVE THE GROUND**
Haute Ecole movements performed with either the forelegs or all four feet off the ground.

• **ACTION**
Movement of the skeletal frame in respect of locomotion.

• **AIRS**
Movements associated with classical or advanced equitation. (e.g. airs **above the ground**).

• **AGED**
Horse seven or more years old.

• **AGEING**
Process of estimating a horse's age by the appearance of the teeth.

• **AIDS**
Signals made by the rider or driver to communicate his wishes to the horse. "Natural" riding aids are the legs, hands, body weight, and voice. "Artificial" aids are the whip and spur.

• **AMBLE**
Slower form of the lateral pacing gait (see also **Pacer**).

• **ARTICULATION**
Where two or more bones meet to form a joint.

• **BACK AT THE KNEE**
Conformational fault in which forelegs are curved back below the knee. (Also called "Calf-knee" or "Buck-knee".)

• **BACK (TO BACK)**
First mounting of an unbroken horse (e.g. "this horse is ready to be backed").

• **BARREL**
Body between forearms and loins.

• **BARS (OF THE MOUTH)**
Area between the molars and incisors of the lower jaw on which the bit rests.

• **BLEMISH**
Permanent mark left by either an injury or disease.

• **BLOOD HORSE**
Thoroughbred horse.

• **BLOOD STOCK**
Thoroughbred horses bred to race.

• **BLOOD WEED**
Lightly-built Thoroughbred horse that is of poor quality, lacking bone and substance.

• **BLUE FEET**
Dense, blue-black colouring of the horn.

• **BONE**
Measurement taken around the leg immediately below the knee or hock. Bone measurement determines ability to carry weight.

• **BOOK, THE**
See **General Stud Book**.

• **BOSOMY**
Over-wide and heavy chest.

• **BOTH LEGS FROM THE SAME HOLE**
Forelegs placed too close together because of an unduly narrow chest.

• **BOW-HOCKS**
Outward turned hock joints (opposite of **cow hocks**).

• **BOXY FOOT**
Narrow, upright foot with small **frog** and a closed heel. (Also called "club", "donkey", or "mule foot".)

• **BREAKING**
Early schooling or education of the horse for the various purposes for which it may be required.

• **BREED**
Equine group that has been bred selectively for consistent characteristics over an extended period. The pedigrees of a breed are entered in a **stud book**.

• **BROKEN COLOURED**
Term applied to coats of two colours (e.g. skewbald, piebald). Generally refers to donkeys.

• **BROOD MARE**
Mare used for breeding.

• **BRUSHING**
Action of the hoof or shoe striking the opposite fetlock. Usually a conformational fault.

• **BUCK**
To leap in the air with the back arched, the horse coming down on stiff forelegs with lowered head.

• **BUNG TAIL**
Docked tail.

• **BY**
Used in conjunction with the sire, i.e. *by* so and so. (See also **Out of**.)

• **CANNON BONE**
Bone of foreleg between knee and fetlock. Also called "shin bone".

• **CARRIAGE HORSE**
Relatively light, elegant horse for private or hackney carriage use.

• **CART HORSE**
Heavy, **coldblood** draught horse.

• **CARTY**
Description of a horse of common appearance.

• **CAVALRY REMOUNT**
Horse used for service in an army unit. (Also called a "trooper".)

• **CAYUSE**
Tough American Indian pony descending from Spanish stock.

• **CHARGER**
Mount of military officers.

• **CHESTNUT (OR CASTOR)**
Small, horny excrescences on the inside of all four legs; or a coat colour.

• **CHIN GROOVE**
Declivity above the lower lip in which the curb chain of the bit lies. (Also called "curb groove".)

• **CLEAN BRED**
Horse of any breed of pure pedigree blood.

• **CLEAN-LEGGED**
Without feather on the lower limbs.

• **CLOSE-COUPLED**
Short connections between component parts, with no slackness in the loins.

• **COACH HORSE**
Powerful, strongly built horse capable of drawing a heavy coach.

• **COARSE IN THE JOWL**
Notable fleshiness round the jowl, restricting the **flexion** of the head.

• COFFIN HEAD
Plain, ugly face with no prominence of the jowl.

• COLDBLOOD
Generic name for heavy, European horse breeds descended from the prehistoric Forest Horse.

• COLT
Uncastrated male horse under four years old. Male foals are denoted as "colt foals".

• COMMON
Horse of coarse appearance, usually the progeny of coldblood or non-pedigree parents.

• COMMON BONE
Bone of inferior quality; it is coarse-grained, lacking density, and with a large, central core.

• COMMON-BRED
Horse bred from mixed, non-pedigree parents.

• CONFORMATION
Manner in which the horse is "put together", with particular regard to its proportions.

• COW HOCKS
Hocks that turn inwards like those of a cow; the opposite to **bow-hocks**.

• CROSS-BREEDING
Mating of pure-bred individuals of different breeds.

• CURB
Thickening of the tendon or ligament below the point of the hock as a result of strain. "Curby hocks" are those affected by curbs, or those so shaped as to be predisposed to the formation of curbs.

• DAISY-CUTTING
Descriptive of low action at walk or trot, as characterized by Thoroughbreds and Arabs.

• DAM
Horse's female parent.

• DEEP GOING
Wet or soft ground, made heavy by rain, into which the feet sink.

• DEPTH OF GIRTH
Measurement from wither to elbow. "Good depth of girth" describes a generous measurement between the two points.

• DIPPED BACK
Descriptive of an unusually dipped back between withers and croup.

• DISHED FACE
Concave head profile, as exemplified by the Arab.

• DISHING
Action of the foreleg when the toe is thrown outward in a circular movement. Considered to be a faulty action.

• DOCK
Part of the tail on which the hair grows; also the hairless underside.

• DOCKING
Amputation of the tail for the sake of appearance. Illegal in Britain.

• DOUBLE MUSCLING
Pronounced muscling at the croup found in some heavy horse breeds.

• DROOPING QUARTERS
Hindquarters with a pronounced fall away behind the croup.

• ELK LIP
Wide, overhanging upper lip.

• ENTIRE
Uncastrated male horse – a stallion.

• ERGOT
Horny growth on the back of the fetlock joint.

• ESCUTCHEON
Division of the hair below the point of the hips extending downwards on the flanks.

• EWE NECK
Concavity of neck along its upper edge, with consequent protrusion of muscle on the underside.

• EXTRAVAGANT ACTION
High knee and hock action, as in Hackney and Saddlebred breeds.

• FALSE RIBS
Ten (asternal) ribs to the rear of the eight "true" (sternal) ribs.

• FEATHER
Long hair on the lower limbs and fetlocks; abundant on heavy horses.

• FILLY
Female horse under four years old.

• FIVE-GAITED
American term for the Saddlebred horse, which is shown at the **slow gait** and **rack** as well as walk, trot, and canter.

• FLEXION
A horse flexes when it yields the lower jaw to the bit, with the head bent at the poll. Also describes the full bending of the hock joints.

• FOAL
Colt, **gelding**, or **filly** up to the age of 12 months.

• FOREHAND
Horse's head, neck, shoulder, withers, and forelegs.

• FORELOCK
Extension of the mane lying between ears and over forehead.

• FROG
Rubbery, triangular pad of horn in the sole of the foot, which acts as a shock absorber.

• FULL MOUTH
At six years, a horse with permanent teeth has a "full mouth".

• GAITED HORSE
American term for horse schooled to artificial as well as natural gaits.

• GALVAYNE'S MARK
Groove appearing on the corner incisor at ten years. It runs down the tooth reaching the bottom at about 20 years. Named after the 19th-century horse-tamer Sydney Galvayne.

• GASKIN
"Second thigh", extending from above the hock towards the stifle.

• GELDING
Castrated male horse.

• GENERAL STUD BOOK
Stud book in which are entered all Thoroughbred mares and their progeny foaled in the UK and the Republic of Ireland. Also known as "G.S.B." and "the Book".

• GIRTH
Circumference of the body measured from behind the withers around the barrel.

• GOING
Term indicating the nature of the ground, e.g. good, deep, rough.

• GOOD FRONT
Horse carrying its saddle behind a long, sloped shoulder and generous length of neck.

• GOOSE-RUMP
Pronounced muscular development at the croup, from whence the quarters run down to the tail. Also called the "jumper's bump".

• GREASE
Disease of the lower legs characterized by swelling, foul discharge, and irritation. Heavy horses with abundant feather are particularly vulnerable.

• HACK
Recognized type of light riding horse; or "to hack" – to go for a ride.

• "HAIRIES"
Originally a friendly name for heavy breeds, but now frequently applied to British mountain and moorland ponies.

• HALTER-CLASS
American term for classes of horses shown **in-hand**.

• HAND
Unit of measurement to describe horse's height (medieval origin). One hand equals 10cm (4in).

- **HARD HORSE**
Tough, enduring horse not suscep-
tible to unsoundness or injury.
- **HARNESS**
Collective term for the equipment
of a driven horse. Not applicable to
the riding horse.
- **HARNESS HORSE**
Horse used in **harness**, having
"harness"-type **conformation**
(i.e. straighter shoulders, etc.),
and, consequently, an elevated
"harness action".
- *HAUTE ECOLE*
Classical art of advanced
horsemanship.
- **HEAVY HORSE**
Any large draught horse.
- **HEAVY TOP**
Heavy body carried on dis-
proportionately light limbs.
- **HERRING-GUTTED**
Horse with a flat-sided, mean body
running sharply upwards from
girth to stifle.
- **HINDQUARTERS**
Body from the rear of the flank to
the beginning of the tail, and down
to the top of the **gaskin**.
- **HOCKS WELL LET DOWN**
Indicates short **cannon bones**,
considered a structure of great
strength. Long cannons are seen as
a conformational weakness.
- **HOGGED MANE**
When the mane has been removed
by clipping. (Termed "roached" in
America.)
- **HOLLOW BACK**
See **Dipped Back**.
- **HOT**
If a horse becomes unduly excited
is said to be "hot" or to "hot up".
- **HOT BLOOD**
Term describing Arabs, Barbs, and
Thoroughbreds.
- **HYBRID**
Cross between a horse on one side
and an ass, zebra, or other similar
species, on the other.
- **INBREEDING**
Mating of brother–sister,
sire–daughter, son–**dam**, to fix
or accentuate a particular
characteristic.
- **IN FRONT OF THE BIT**
When a horse pulls or hangs
heavily on the hands with its
head outstretched.
- **IN-HAND**
Not ridden, as in show classes
where horses are paraded in
halters.

- **JIBBAH**
Peculiar bulged formation of the
forehead of the Arab horse.
- **JOG-TROT**
Short-paced trot.
- **LEAN HEAD**
Fine, very lightly skinned head,
with muscles, veins, and bony
protuberances showing clearly.
Often described as a "dry" head
in Arabs.
- **LIGHT HORSE**
Horse, other than a heavy horse or
a pony, that is suitable for riding.
- **LIGHT OF BONE**
Insufficient bone below the knee
to support weight of horse and
rider without strain – and therefore
a serious fault.
- **LINE BREEDING**
Mating of individuals with a
common ancestor some genera-
tions removed, with the purpose of
accentuating particular features.
- **LOADED SHOULDER**
Excessive muscle formation lying
over and inhibiting the shoulder
region.
- **LOINS**
Area either side of the spinal
vertebrae lying immediately
behind the saddle.
- **LOPE**
Slow Western canter performed
with natural head carriage.
- **LOP EARS**
Ears that flop downwards or are
carried horizontally to either side.
There is no effect upon perfor-
mance or well-being.
- **MARE**
Female horse of four years old
and upwards.
- **MEALY NOSE**
Oatmeal-coloured muzzle, as in
the Exmoor pony.
- **MITBAH**
Angle at which the neck of the
Arab horse enters the head. This
gives the arched set to the neck
and enables near all-round
movement of the neck.
- **NARROW BEHIND**
Deficiency in musculature of croup
and thigh, giving a narrow appear-
ance when viewed from behind.
- **NATIVE PONIES**
Another name for the British
indigenous mountain and moor-
land breeds.
- **NICK**
Division and re-setting of the
muscles under the tail to give an

artificially high carriage; or a
mating likely to produce the
desired offspring – "a good nick".
- **ON THE BIT**
A horse is said to be "on the bit"
when he carries the head in a near-
vertical plane, the mouth a little
below the rider's hand.
- **ON THE LEG**
Describes a horse that is dis-
proportionately long in the leg. It
is a condition that is usually
associated with inadequate depth
in the body
- **ORIENTAL HORSE**
Term loosely applied to horses of
Eastern origin, either Arab or Barb,
in use during the formative years
of the English Thoroughbred.
- **OUTCROSS**
Mating of unrelated horses;
introduction of outside blood to
the breed.
- **OUT OF**
Used in conjunction with the
mare, e.g. so-and-so *out of*
so-and-so.
- **OVER AT THE KNEE**
Forward curve of the knees over
the cannon, which may be the
result of wear.
- **OVERBENT**
When the horse carries its mouth
close to the chest to evade control.
The horse is "behind the bit".
- **OVERSHOT MOUTH**
See **Parrot mouth**.
- **PACER**
Horse employing a lateral action at
trot rather than the conventional
diagonal movement, i.e. near fore
and near hind together, followed
by the offside pair.
- **PALFREY**
Medieval light saddle horse that
could amble.
- **PARIETAL BONES**
Bones on the top of the skull.
- **PARROT MOUTH**
Malformation in which the incisors
of the upper jaw overhang those of
the lower jaw.
- **PEDIGREE**
Details of ancestry recorded in a
stud book.
- **PENDULOUS LIP**
Flabby underlip hanging loose.
Sometimes found in cart breeds
and old **common-bred** horses.
- **PIGEON TOES**
Conformational fault in which the
feet are turned inwards. (Also
known as "pin-toes".)

• **PIG-EYE**
Small eye giving a mean and
unintelligent expression.
• **PLAITING**
Faulty and dangerous **action** in
which the feet cross over each
other in movement.
• **POINTS**
External features of the horse,
comprising its **conformation**; or a
term relative to colour, e.g. "bay
with black points", meaning bay
with black lower limbs, mane,
and tail.
• **QUALITY**
Element of refinement in breeds
and types, usually due to Arab or
Thoroughbred influence.
• **QUARTERS**
See **Hindquarters**.
• **RACEHORSE**
Horse bred for racing – usually
refers to a Thoroughbred, but
other breeds are also raced.
• **RACK**
Fifth gait of the American Saddle-
bred – a fast, four-beat gait
unrelated to pacing (see **Pacer**).
• **RAGGED HIPS**
Prominent hip bones lacking flesh
and muscle.
• **RAM HEAD**
Convex profile like that of the
Barb. Similar to **Roman nose**.
• **RANGY**
Description of a horse having size
and scope of movement.
• **REMOUNT**
See **Cavalry remount**.
• **RHUM PONY**
Ancient strain of Highland pony.
• **RIBBED UP (WELL)**
Describes a short, deep body that
is rounded, with well-sprung ribs.
• **RIDING HORSE**
Horse suitable for riding, having
the **conformation** associated with
comfortable riding **action** (as
opposed to draught or carriage).
• **RISING**
Term used in ageing. A horse
approaching five years is said to be
"rising five".
• **ROACH BACK**
Convex curvature of the spine
between wither and loin. Opposite
to **dipped back**.
• **ROADSTER**
Trotting saddle-horse, ancestor of
the modern Hackney, e.g. the
Norfolk Roadster. In America, a
light harness horse, usually
the Standardbred.

• **ROMAN NOSE**
Convex profile as found in the
Shire and other heavy breeds.
• **SADDLE HORSE**
Riding horse; or a wooden trestle
stand on which to put saddles.
• **SADDLE MARKS**
White hair in the saddle area
probably caused by galls.
• **SCLERA**
White outer membrane of the
eyeball. Characteristic of the
Appaloosa.
• **SECOND THIGH**
See **Gaskin**.
• **SET TAIL**
Tail broken or **nicked** and set to
give artificially high carriage.
• **SHANNON BONE**
Hind **cannon bone**.
• **SHORT-COUPLED**
See **Close-coupled**.
• **SHORT OF A RIB**
Conformational fault arising from
slack loins, in which there is a
marked space between the last rib
and the hip. Occurs in overly long-
backed horses.
• **SICKLE HOCKS**
Conformational fault in which,
seen from the side, the hocks are
angled too much at the joint,
resulting in weak hindlegs.
• **SLAB-SIDED**
Horse with flat ribs.
• **SLACK IN THE LOINS**
Condition in which loins are weak
– the last rib is short, with notice-
able space between it and the hip.
• **SLIPHEAD**
Head strap and cheekpiece
supporting the bradoon of a
double bridle.
• **SLOW GAIT**
Slow, high-stepping, four-beat gait
employed by Saddlebred horses.
• **SOUND HORSE**
Horse possessing a good frame,
bodily health, and free from
blemishes, defects, and "all
impediments to sight and action".
• **SPLIT UP BEHIND**
Conformational fault caused by
weakness of **gaskins**. Seen from
behind, the thighs divide too high,
just beneath the dock.
• **STALLION**
Uncastrated male horse four or
more years old.
• **STAMP OF HORSE**
Type or pattern of horse.
• **STANDING OVER**
See **Over at the knee**.

• **STUD BOOK**
A book kept by a breed society in
which the pedigrees of stock
eligible for entry are recorded.
• **SUBSTANCE**
Physical quality of the body in
terms of its build and general
musculature.
• **TACK**
Stable word for riding and driving
equipment.
• **THROAT LATCH**
Leather strap, part of the
headpiece, that passes around the
horse's throat.
• **TIED IN BELOW THE
KNEE**
Condition in which the length
below the knee is substantially less
than that above the fetlock; or a
conformational fault in which a
horse is necessarily **light of bone**.
• **TOP-LINE**
Line of the back from the withers
to the end of the croup.
• **TYPE**
Horse that fulfils a particular
purpose, like a cob, hunter, or
hack, but does not necessarily
belong to a specific breed.
• **UNDERSHOT**
Deformity in which the lower jaw
projects beyond the upper.
• **UP TO WEIGHT**
A term describing a horse that, due
to its substance, bone, size, and
overall **conformation**, can carry a
substantial weight.
• **WARMBLOOD**
In general terms, half- or part-bred
horses, the result of Thoroughbred
or Arab crosses with other blood or
bloods. See also **Coldblood**.
• **WEED**
Horse of poor, mean **conformation** carrying little flesh and often
long-legged. Generally of
Thoroughbred type.
• **WEIGHT CARRIER**
Horse capable of carrying 95kg
(15 stone). Also called a
"heavyweight" horse.
• **WELL-SPRUNG RIBS**
Long, rounded ribs giving ample
room for lung expansion and being
well-suited to a saddle.
• **WHIP**
Driver of a carriage.
• **WOLF TEETH**
Rudimentary teeth occurring in
front of the upper and lower molars
on each side of the jaw. More
usually found in upper jaw.

INDEX

ACKNOWLEDGMENTS

THIS BOOK could not have been completed without the help, material and otherwise, of several persons and institutions. The author and publisher are greatly indebted to the following: the Arab Horse Society for the use of their stud book (p.8); Mr Walton, The Mossiman Collection of Carriages (pp.36–39); Shires Equestrian Products, Worcester, for the use of the Western saddle and bridle, and bits (pp.32–33); Mr Compton of Calcutts for the use of the general-purpose saddle and snaffle bridle (pp.32–33); the Australian Pony Promotion Group; Dee Bennett of the Pitchwood Stud; Mrs Catselis of the Greek Tourist Board; Mrs Mandilara of the Municipality of Skyros for organizing photography of the Skyros Pony (p.86); Penny Turner of the Philippian Riding School, Thessalonika, for organizing photography of the Pindos Pony (p.87); and Mr Ersoy of the Turkish Embassy, London, for arranging photography at the Gemlick Institute, Turkey.

Dorling Kindersley would like to thank: Judith Payne for authenticating the book; Caroline Church for the endpapers; Janos Marffy for airbrush work on pp.20–21; Bill Payne for retouching on pp.92–93, 98–99; Roy Hutchins, Linden Artists, for all horse illustrations, except for pp.14–15 by Eric Rowe, Linden Artists. We are also indebted to Deborah Myatt for line drawings on pp.10–11, 18–19, 21–23; Sharon Lunn for horse and man images used throughout the book; Alastair Wardle for the maps; Susan Thompson for proofreading; Michael Allaby for compiling the index; Alison Edmonds, Jonathan Metcalf, and Tony Mudd for editorial assistance..

PICTURE CREDITS
b=bottom, t=top, c=centre, l=left, r=right
All specially comissioned photographs are by Bob Langrish, except for:
Jimmy Barucha and Ronnie Sopher pp.188–191
Mrs Robyn Bashford pp.91–92
Andy Crawford p.8 tr
Steve Gorton, all on pp.20–21, except foal by Jane Burton, p.20 lc
Hawkesbury Photographics p.192

Steven Oliver pp.196–7
Tim Ridley p.35 c, p.36 tl, p.37 tr, pp.38–39 (all)
Karl Shone p.11 tl, cr
Jerry Young p.11 tr, cl; p.28 cb; p.29 tr, br; p.52 tr; p.31 tr, cb; p.37 cb

The publishers would like to thank the following photographers and organizations for their permission to reproduce the following photographs: Bruce Coleman Picture Library pp.28–29 tr, 30–31 bl (Hans Reinhard), 30-31 cl; The Dean and Chapter of Westminster for the transparency of Henry V's saddle, p.32

Picture research: Julia Pashley